THEY STAND BESIDE US

The lives of the Old Colcestrians
who died in the Second World War

"Soldiers must die, but by their death they nourish
the nation which gave them birth."

— *Winston S Churchill, 1943*

The photograph on the front cover of this book shows CRGS students standing beside the stained-glass window recording the names of the war dead in the school's Second World War Memorial Library. It was taken at the time of the window's unveiling and dedication on Sunday 24th February 1952. See page 313 for an account of the Memorial Library.

The poem "To CRGS" on the back cover was written by Flight Lieutenant Benjamin Robinson DFC RAF, a pupil at CRGS from 1925 to 1930. He was killed in action over Germany on 17th June 1944. The poem was published in *The Colcestrian* magazine while he was in the Sixth Form. See page 245 for an account of Benjamin Robinson's life.

The illustration on the back cover is by local publisher and newspaper editor, Sir William Gurney Benham; this is an early version of the school crest - used during Percy Shaw Jeffrey's time as Headmaster in the early 1900s – which gradually became the one we are familiar with today. Thrice Mayor of Colchester, he was an old boy of the school, and became the first President of the Old Colcestrian Society in 1901.

Published by Colchester Royal Grammar School and the Old Colcestrian Society
Publishing partner: Paragon Publishing, Rothersthorpe
First published: 2020

ISBN 978-1-78222-794-6

Book design, layout and production management by Into Print
www.intoprint.net
01604 832149

THEY STAND BESIDE US

The title of this book is from the poem below by pupil JK Sansom (CRGS 1939-1947) Upper 4th/Year 10, published in *The Colcestrian* July 1943. Sansom went on to win the Hewitt Scholarship to Corpus Christi College, Cambridge to read Modern Languages.

To Fall Asleep...

Be not sorrowful, when Death doth take away
The dear ones we have cherished from our birth,
And parts us from the ones we love the most,
For Death is but a gate into Eternity,
A portal leading to the realms of light,
Where those same dear ones play on harps of gold.

Be not sorrowful! They have escaped the suffering,
Hardships, labours, tears of this our world
Made vile by the ungodliness and avarice of Man.
Now they sing the praises of their King
In most wonderful polyphony, and bow
To Him who died that we should die no more.

Be not sorrowful! For they are always near,
They would not wish for mourning, sad and dull,
For where they dwell the daylight is serene.
We do not see them as they were; but in our hearts
Their memories live on, and ne'er will die.
They stand beside us, and encourage us to be
More pure in spirit than they themselves had been.

Be not sorrowful! For Death is but a sleep
From which we wake into a world blessed
With eternal light.

Dedicated to the memory of
the Old Colcestrians
who died in the Second World War

In Piam Memoriam Huius Scholae Alumnorum Qui Terra Mari Caelo
Obierunt   MCMXXXIX – MCMXLV   Absentes Adsunt   Mortui Vivunt

'In faithful memory of the students of this school who died on land, sea
and air, 1939-1945. Though absent, they are here; though dead, they
live.'

CRGS Second World War memorial window

CONTRIBUTORS

Neil Brinded taught at CRGS for 37 years, including 24 years as Head of Classics, before retiring in 2018. He has been married to Laurie Holmes since 2007 after meeting on their respective school trips to Sorrento, Italy, in 2005.

Michael Green OC (1965-1972) is an information technology consultant who specialises in wireless network design. Married, with a son and a daughter, his interests include genealogy and 20th century military history.

Neil and Michael researched and wrote all the biographies included in this book.

Laurie Holmes was born in Canada and was a high-school English teacher in Toronto before becoming the CRGS Archives Librarian in 2007.

Col. Richard Kemp CBE OC attended CRGS from 1970-1977. He served for 30 years in the Royal Anglian Regiment, successor to many of the regiments in which our war dead fought. He completed operational tours of duty in Northern Ireland, Iraq, Afghanistan, the Balkans and elsewhere. He is currently Chairman of the Old Colcestrian Society, CRGS's alumni association. He is the author of *Attack State Red,* an account of combat in Afghanistan, and writes for *The Times* and other national newspapers.

Peter Rowbottom is a former local History teacher who regularly visits both First and Second World War battlefields. He is a member of the Independent Board for the Military Correction Training Centre (MCTC) in Colchester. Peter's other interests include military memorabilia and DIY.

Paul Ma OC (2004-2009) was pleased to co-edit this book with Laurie Holmes. He has worked in the fields of information technology, bioinformatics and data science, with stints in the UK, Canada, Russia and China. In 2014 he took a year off to assist Laurie Holmes in co-editing the book *The Colcestrian: Colchester Royal Grammar School and the Great War.*

CONTENTS

ACKNOWLEDGEMENTS

This book acknowledges the debt to the former staff and students of Colchester Royal Grammar School, whose sacrifices helped make Allied victory possible. It is these ordinary men, doing the extraordinary things documented in this book, whom we should never forget.

In putting together the various chapters of this book, the publication of which marks the end of many years of research, reflection and remembrance at Colchester Royal Grammar School, we are indebted to the many people who have contributed in numerous ways to this project. In particular, Colonel Richard Kemp, Chair of the Old Colcestrian Society, has given invaluable support and guidance which has maintained the momentum of various other World War projects. These include the creation of the CRGS Garden of Remembrance and planting of poppies therein, visits to the graves and memorials of those former staff and students who died in both World Wars and the dedication of a plaque in St George's Church in Ypres.

Through the generosity of the Old Colcestrian Society we have now published the last of the three books on the school and the members of its community who gave their lives in both World Wars.

Our sincere appreciation goes to CRGS archives volunteer, Nicole Wright, for her thoughtful and timely responses to our many requests for research from the digitised version of *The Colcestrian* school magazines, from where many of the photographs in this book are taken. Her dedication to the various archives' projects has been invaluable.

Nicole's son, Jack, now an OC and reading International Relations at King's College, London, has over the years been a stalwart support to the Archives. His 2018 video for The Great War was a great success and he has recently created another video that will also be used at Remembrance services in the future. Jack could be counted on to assist in various other capacities as required, whether at the laying of the wreaths at our war memorials or planting poppies in memory of the fallen.

BAB 'Dick' Barton, Past-President of the Old Colcestrian Society, has long been a stalwart supporter of the school. One of the many donations he has made to the library and to the archives is a leather-bound book - embossed with a school crest in gold - which had been previously awarded on Prize Day to James Douglas Sargeant as a young pupil. We are grateful for this memento and intend to put it on permanent display in the library, joining a similar book (donated by Nicole Wright) which was won by a former pupil who died during the First World War.

Our sincere thanks go to all those family members who provided stories, photographs and other materials for the book. We are especially indebted to the families and friends of HJ Broom, RC Chopping, IM Carter, K Coney, E Dalgleish, EJ Dunton, AG Flory, RS Frost, D Glasse, AV Gowers, EC Gilders, CP Hickey, JW Leach, P Pawsey, ER Pearson, BH Ramsay, FE Richardson, BR Robinson, PC Sayce, PEG Sayer, J Scales, EA Stone, GF Studley, EJ Tracey, OM Wightman, HV Winch and BE Wright. Valuable material was also obtained from *The Colcestrian* magazine and the CRGS Archives. The photo of RV Whitehead is from unithistories.com and courtesy of Mr Mick Prendergast.

We are grateful to Andrew J Begent of the Chelmsford War Memorial website, as well as military historian and author Philip Mills. Useful information was also derived from aircrewremembered.com and WW2 People's War, an online archive of wartime memories contributed by members of the public and gathered by the BBC. The archive can be found at bbc.co.uk/ww2people's war.

We should also like to thank all those who visited the graves and memorials of our former students: Michael Green OC, Colonel Richard Kemp OC, Peter Rowbottom, Jack Wright OC, Stuart Smith OC, Andrew MacKinley OC, Jerry and Alex Hadcock OC, and Dr Simon Dowling, Head of English. The photographs of the graves of Herbert Broom and George Nott were taken by Simon Dowling, and those of the memorials to Jack Bendall, Leslie Goldspink and Henry Parsloe in Malta are by Peter Rowbottom and his son, Jack Wright. Michael Green and his wife were responsible for almost all the other grave visits and photographs thereof, for which we are most grateful.

Last but not least, we are appreciative of Paul Woodward for his beautiful artwork, both in this book and on the cover of our previous book on The Great War, *None Have Done Better.* (For more of Paul's artwork, please visit https://www.etsy.com/ca/shop/PaulWoodwardArt)

WAR-TIME A.B.C.

A is for air raid which all of us dread ;
B is for bomb : if one hits you you're dead ;
C is for candle when switches don't work ;
D is for duty we never must shirk.
E is for engine, the aeroplane's heart ;
F is for fighters who all do their part ;
G is for gunners who try not to miss ;
H is for horror, we're sure to feel this ;
I is for iron with which you make guns ;
J is for Jerry, nickname for the Huns ;
K is for knockout we hope they'll get soon ;
L is for lunch we have about noon ;
M is for munitions so important in war ;
N is for Navy that still guards our shore ;
O is for obstacle o'er which we must get ;
P is for paratroops who haven't come yet ;
Q is for quantity and quality, too ;
R is for raiders, we hope they'll be few ;
S is for siren when danger is near ;
T is for trouble that's coming, we fear ;
U is for U-boats that everyone hates ;
V is for vessels that England awaits ;
W's for wardens who patrol round the street ;
X is for exercise, good for your feet
Y for the yearning we all have for peace,
Z is zip-fastener which brings quick release.

J. K. Sansom, 2a.

Poem by JK Sansom, June 1941

FOREWORD

Col. Richard Kemp CBE
Chairman of the Old Colcestrian Society

'They stand beside us, and encourage us.' These inspirational words from fifteen-year-old CRGS schoolboy JK Sansom were written about the dead in 1943 — at the height of the Second World War. Sansom started at Colchester Royal Grammar School the year war broke out in 1939 and remained there until after it had ended in 1945. Death was more familiar than it should have been to young Sansom and his fellow pupils who lived through a time when their home town was bombed from the air with explosives and incendiaries; when many of them lost brothers, sisters, fathers and mothers; and when the names of those who had worn the purple blazer, killed in battle, were read out in assembly.

This book brings together the life and death stories of the 73 former pupils and staff of CRGS who were killed fighting for their country in the Second World War. They fought and died with the Royal Navy, Army, Royal Air Force, Merchant Navy and the Australian Imperial Force in places as far afield as North Africa, the Middle East, Holland, Italy, Greece, France, Belgium, Germany, Malta, Burma, India, Singapore, the Mediterranean Sea and the Pacific and Atlantic Oceans.

Although the last of these brave men died 75 years ago, they stand beside us still. Our very way of life today, our freedom, our prosperity, were paid for with their blood, with the blood of the even more numerous wounded and with the sacrifices of those who fought but were mercifully unscathed. Imagine how we might be living today if they had not gone forward into the fight and the greatest tyranny ever to darken this planet had been allowed to prevail over us. Despite the leadership of the generals and ministers, the industry of the massed working men and women, the ingenuity of the scientists and the indispensable labours of all who supported the war effort and kept the country running, if these brave men — from infantryman to admiral — had not put their lives directly on the line, we could not have overcome.

They do indeed encourage us and inspire us as JK Sansom wrote. Take for example 26-year-old former CRGS pupil Captain David Glasse. He was commanding a platoon of The Royal Norfolk Regiment at Kohima in north eastern India. Kohima was one of the greatest and most costly battles of the Second World War, a turning point in the campaign against Imperial Japan and sometimes referred to as the 'Stalingrad of the East'.

At a critical point in the battle, on 4th May 1944, Glasse was ordered to make an immediate improvised attack into the teeth of enemy fire to seize a vital Japanese machine gun post. There was no time to arrange artillery support to suppress the enemy. As he rallied his men, Glasse handed his watch to a fellow officer with the words: 'Take that and write to Louise, won't you, and see that she gets it'. The officer said: 'We're going to see you again shortly, David!' He replied: 'I doubt it! I doubt it!'. Glasse and his men captured the position and he was killed doing so. He knew he would die. Yet still he went.

It was not that he was unafraid. How could he be? Courage is not an absence of fear, it is the moral strength to overcome that fear. At Kohima David Glasse displayed undiluted courage and dedication to duty. Today he stands beside us.

On the centenary of the end of the First World War, CRGS and the Old Colcestrian Society published a book commemorating former pupils and teachers killed in that horrific bloodbath. Its title, 'None Have Done Better', comes from the words of Percy Shaw Jeffrey, Headmaster at the start of the conflict, who said of CRGS's war record: 'Many schools may have done as well but none have done better'. That sentiment was equally true of the school, its pupils and staff during the Second World War.

We can read about the impact on CRGS of the war years and the contribution that it made in Neil Brinded's excellent chapter that follows, including the story of the school's Scout Troop that found itself in France as the French Army mobilised for war. And the wider context of Colchester in the war is set out in Peter Rowbottom's fascinating account. Few other towns in this country can have endured more or endowed so much to the war effort on land, at sea and in the air, through 'blood, toil, tears and sweat', in the words of Winston Churchill in 1940.

The CRGS death toll of 73 in the Second World War was very similar to that in the First, despite the fact that, nationally, fewer than half as many military deaths were sustained in the Second. We don't measure contribution to the country's struggles by death toll but this figure does provide a stark indication of the immense commitment of the school between 1939 and 1945 and the war's impact on its register and on those left behind.

'Be not sorrowful!' JK Sansom exhorts us four times in his fine 1943 poem. We might well grieve that so many young lives were cut short so soon. But although many of us wore the same school uniforms, sat in the same classrooms, raced across the same sports fields, and can proudly associate ourselves with them, we did not know them and cannot mourn them. We can admire them and be grateful to them. We can put ourselves into the boots of David Glasse at Kohima and recognise how much we owe him and the 72 others like him that laid down their lives for us.

And we can remember all of them. I believe we have a duty to do so. As the shadows lengthen for them there is a growing danger that individually they will be forgotten, even among their own descendants. This book means that need not happen. It is thanks to the remarkable dedication of Laurie Holmes and Neil Brinded, both Old Colcestrians, who conceived of this work, as well as its companion volume about the First World War, and dedicated so much energy to bringing it to fruition. It is also due to the efforts of Michael Green OC, who researched and wrote the lives of many of our war dead, and to the others who contributed so much, including Paul Ma OC whose ingenuity is responsible for the design and layout of this book, and the talented Paul Woodward whose colourful pictures so beautifully supplement the contemporary illustrations re-published here from war-time editions of *The Colcestrian* magazine. *They Stand Beside Us* could not have been completed without the devotion and energy of Nicole Wright, mother of Jack (OC 2010-2017) and stalwart supporter of the school, who gave so generously of her time in meticulous research and proof-reading.

By taking the time to read about our Great Fallen in the pages that follow, and by passing this volume on to our own descendants to do the same, we will honour them and, to borrow another line from JK Sansom's evocative poem, we will ensure that 'Their memories live on and ne'er will die'.

Paul Woodward

INTRODUCTION
THE OC WHO WON THE SECOND WORLD WAR

Col. Richard Kemp CBE

In the 2017 film *Dunkirk*, Tommy, a young soldier played by Fionn Whitehead, reads the last words of Churchill's 'We shall fight on the beaches' speech, evoking what has become known as the 'Dunkirk' spirit of embattled British soldiers, sailors, airmen and civilians pulling together in the face of the mind-numbing peril which the film so powerfully conveys.

The man behind the creation of this spirit was a former pupil of Colchester Royal Grammar School – one of 73 OCs who gave their lives in WW2. His only appearance in the film is a single mention of his name, yet his achievement pervades its every moment.

Admiral Ramsay

Vice Admiral Bertram Ramsay masterminded the Dunkirk evacuation and by doing so won the Second World War. Why?

Churchill said to the Commons on 4th June 1940, the day Dunkirk ended: 'We must be very careful not to assign to this deliverance the attributes of a victory. Wars are not won by evacuations.' But the evacuation of the British Army from Dunkirk- against all odds- was the turning point that paved the way to Allied victory over Nazi Germany five years later.

With the British Expeditionary Force routed through France and Belgium by the scything German blitzkrieg, General Brooke, commander of II Corps - which included 2nd Battalion, The Essex Regiment- lamented: 'Nothing but a miracle can save the BEF now'. Ramsay delivered it.

At a meeting in his underground headquarters beneath Dover Castle, Ramsay and Churchill envisaged the rescue of 30,000 men from the beaches. Within a week, Ramsay launched 'Operation Dynamo' and nine days later had brought more than ten times that number back across the Channel, while under attack from all sides.

Ramsay rescued 338,226 battle-hardened soldiers who could be put to immediate use defending Britain. Their return made the threatened German invasion less likely. Of even greater strategic significance, Dunkirk boosted the nation's morale, giving hope after a long succession of military and political

Ramsay with Churchill at Dover

disasters. It steeled the country for the Battle of Britain, unleashed by the Luftwaffe the following month, and shaped the character and resilience of our nation for the rest of the war.

Dunkirk kept Britain in the war, enabling all that followed and culminating in the Allied invasion of Europe in 1944. Without Dunkirk 400,000 British soldiers - five times as many as our entire regular army today - would have been killed or in prison camps in Germany. Churchill might then have found spurring the British people on to eventual victory an impossible task. That is assuming he had survived as Prime Minister.

Without the iron discipline and stoicism of the troops on the beach, the fighting spirit and heroic sacrifice of the rear-guard, the skill and courage of the RAF, the bravery and fighting prowess of the Royal Navy and the selfless patriotism of hundreds of civilian mariners, fishermen and yachtsmen, Dunkirk could not have succeeded.

Men from Colchester and Essex took part in each of these great endeavours, achieved, in Churchill's words, 'by valour, by perseverance, by perfect discipline, by faultless service, by resource, by skill, by unconquerable fidelity'.

Among them were former pupils of CRGS, including VA White, serving with the Royal Artillery, who was wounded at Dunkirk. Some of these Old Colcestrians may have been saved by the 57-foot motor yacht *Riis 1*, whose home port is West Mersea. Then named *White Heather*, she steamed to Dunkirk on 1ˢᵗ June, ferried troops from the beach to bigger ships offshore under enemy fire and then made three crossings, carrying soldiers to England in waters infested by U-boats and mines and exposed to air attack.

Riis 1, formerly White Heather

This entire colossal effort would have achieved little without Admiral Ramsay's guiding hand. What made him the man for the job? Long experience at sea, including fighting commands in the First World War, plus a genius for planning and improvisation. But above all he was a moderniser and pioneer of delegated, decentralised and flexible command. It is unlikely that any practitioner of the more orthodox methods could have achieved Ramsay's miracle.

For Ramsay there was no let-up after Dunkirk. He organised the sea passage of two new British divisions into France and their subsequent withdrawal, and drew up plans to defeat 'Operation Sealion', the German seaborne invasion of southern England, while the Battle of Britain raged overhead. Churchill knew exactly what he had achieved at Dunkirk and increasingly sought Ramsay's counsel. In 1942 Ramsay planned the amphibious landings in North Africa and in 1943 commanded naval forces for the invasion of Sicily.

By now promoted to full Admiral, he was Eisenhower's naval commander for D-Day, directing a fleet of almost 7,000 vessels and landing a million soldiers over the coast of France, a feat described as 'a never surpassed masterpiece of planning'. The war had come full circle, and Ramsay with it.

Ramsay was a driven man and a hard taskmaster, but first-hand accounts show the affection his staff had for him. A 'Ramsay Wren' during Dunkirk and D-Day wrote: 'The Admiral's attitude to his junior staff was always impeccable. … We were a truly happy ship.' In proper CRGS style, as D-Day approached he found time to play cricket with his headquarters staff.

Admiral Ramsay directs the D-Day fleet

Like the other CRGS students whose lives are described in this book, Ramsay did not live to see the Allied victory he had helped bring about. Heading from Paris to Brussels for a meeting with Montgomery, his Lockheed Hudson crashed during take-off on 2nd January 1945. One of the most senior officers to be killed in the war, he is buried at St Germain-en-Laye in France.

In tribute to Admiral Sir Bertram Ramsay, knighted for his command at Dunkirk, the British writer AP Herbert, himself a naval officer in the First World War, wrote these lines after his death:

> I ploughed a passage through the foam,
> Dunkirk and Deal — Dieppe and Dover,
> I brought the flower of Britain home
> And took the fruit of freedom over.

A version of this introduction was published in the Essex County Standard *in August 2017.*

Paul Woodward

TIMELINE OF EVENTS

1939   Hitler invades Poland on 1st September. Britain and France declare war on Germany two days later.

1940   Rationing starts in the UK.

German 'Blitzkrieg' overwhelms Belgium, Holland and France.

Churchill becomes Prime Minister of Great Britain.

The British Expeditionary Force is evacuated from Dunkirk.

British victory in the Battle of Britain forces Hitler to postpone invasion plans.

1941   Germany invades Russia ('Operation Barbarossa').

The Blitz continues against Britain's cities.

The Allies take Tobruk in North Africa and resist German attacks there.

Japan attacks Pearl Harbor and the USA enters the war.

1942   Germany suffers setbacks at Stalingrad in Russia and El Alamein in North Africa.

Singapore falls to the Japanese in February - around 25,000 prisoners taken.

US naval victory at the Battle of Midway - a turning point in the Pacific War.

Mass murder of Jewish people at Auschwitz begins.

1943 German surrender at Stalingrad.

Allied victory in North Africa enables the invasion of Italy to be launched.

Italy surrenders, but Germany takes over the fight there.

British and Indian forces fight the Japanese in Burma.

1944 Allies land in Italy at Anzio and bomb the monastery at Monte Cassino.

Soviet offensive gathers pace in Eastern Europe.

4th June: Rome liberated.

D-Day 6th June: Allied invasion of France.

Paris liberated in August.

1945 Auschwitz liberated by Soviet troops.

Allied forces advance into Germany from the west.

The Russians reach Berlin: Hitler commits suicide and Germany surrenders (7th May).

Truman becomes US President on Roosevelt's death, and Attlee replaces Churchill.

Atomic bombs dropped on Hiroshima & Nagasaki: Japan surrenders on 14th August.

COLCHESTER ROYAL GRAMMAR SCHOOL DURING THE SECOND WORLD WAR

Neil Brinded

On Monday 21st August 1939, a party of thirteen CRGS scouts and staff left England for a two-week trip to Switzerland. After three days travelling, the group set up camp, as planned, near the village of Martigny, south of Geneva. However, tensions in Europe were rising and, having already experienced a gas drill while staying the night at the Monastery of Saint Maurice, near Lausanne, it was decided to return across the border to France and begin their hiking from there. This they did, but next day, after covering some distance through the mountains, the group heard the news that Germany had made a non-aggression treaty with Soviet Russia - the infamous Molotov-Ribbentrop Pact - which was to pave the way for the German invasion of Poland. Immediately they decided to consult the British Consul in a nearby village. The advice was to leave the country as soon as possible, since French mobilisation was now imminent and, once it began, there would be little transport available for civilians.

RJ Fullerton, a student on the trip who went to the Consulate along with Scoutmaster, Mr Double, recalls running the three kilometres up and down hills back to the camp. The group then had 32 minutes to pack up all their tents, equipment and belongings, and catch the only train that day back over the mountains to Martigny. Running all the way to the station, they made it just in time. At Martigny they caught another train, non-stop to Dieppe. This was packed with people lying asleep in the corridors. Five of the scouts slept standing up in the toilet and the group had no food except for raw eggs which the older boys cracked and swallowed whole. From Dieppe they took the boat - again packed - back to England, arriving in Colchester, safe and sound, on Saturday 26th August.

This was the first effect on CRGS of the turmoil in Europe and, just eight days later on 3rd September 1939, following Hitler's invasion of Poland, Britain and France declared war on Germany. The immediate result of this was a delay to the start of the new school year through fear of bombing raids. When these failed to materialise, term finally began, though with some new procedures. An air-raid shelter was set up in the garden of Gurney Benham House and frequent practices were now held. A school stretcher-bearer squad was formed by teachers Messrs. Saunders (Deputy-Head) and Lamb. It was to report for duty whenever an air-raid warning was given, for the purpose of unloading the ambulances and the buses which would be bringing the expected large numbers of civilian casualties to the nearby Essex County Hospital. However, the first term of the war saw just one air-raid warning during school hours, so the squad saw little real activity. Another immediate change as a consequence of war was that Speech Day was now moved from the Corn Exchange in the High Street to the School Hall.

A far more significant effect on CRGS during the autumn term of 1939 was the arrival, on 17th November 1939, of students from the Sir George Monoux Grammar School in Walthamstow. Following the outbreak of war, schools in areas regarded as being at risk from air-raids were evacuated to supposedly safer areas. The Sir George Monoux School had already been evacuated to Ampthill in Bedfordshire, but in November 1939 Colchester was deemed more suitable: the school could be set up there as a single unit in one place and students could even return home to Walthamstow by train at weekends. The two schools shared the main CRGS buildings with a half-day timetable for each, and 12 Lexden Road became 'Monoux House' - a place for the storage of books, a Staff and Prefects' Room, and another room used for classes and recreation. Among the many 'Monovian' students who were taught at CRGS during this period were future jazz musician and composer, Sir John Dankworth, and Essex and England cricketer, administrator and selector, Doug Insole. Probably of greater import to the school was that in 1948, following the retirement of AW Fletcher, the Headmaster of Monoux, Mr Jack Elam, became the next Headmaster of CRGS. Presumably, CRGS had made a favourable impression on him during the Monoux School's exile there!

Sir George Monoux Grammar School

The beginning of 1940 saw six inches of frozen snow on the ground in Colchester and the worst winter for 50 years. A merchant seaman and OC, Leslie Frost from Brightlingsea, came into the school to give the boys an account of his imprisonment on a German ship the *Altmark*. This had taken place after his own ship, the *Huntsman*, had, along with several other vessels, been captured in the South Atlantic by the *Graf Spee*, then sunk. Eventually a British destroyer, HMS *Cossack*, had rescued the 300 prisoners as they were being transported through supposedly neutral Norwegian waters. This resulted in much morale-boosting publicity when the men were brought back to land in Scotland. Leslie Frost himself received a civic welcome on his return to Brightlingsea and became a local celebrity for a while. Unfortunately, he was to be among those OCs who were killed in action later on in the war.

The Monoux School's presence at CRGS lasted until 2nd June, 1940 when they moved again, this time to Herefordshire. However, far from resuming a normal routine, it was now the turn of CRGS to face evacuation. After the summer holidays, on 17th September, and following official pressure due to the perceived threat of invasion, the school was moved to the Midlands. The largest number of students went to Kettering

(49 boys and three masters), but boys also went to Stoke-on-Trent, Burton-on-Trent and Rushden. Those who went to Kettering attended the Grammar School there from 1.30pm to 5.30pm every day, and doubtless there were similar arrangements in the other towns. Mornings were spent on visits to factories and places of local interest, farm work, walks and cycle trips. One of the masters who accompanied the boys to Kettering was English teacher RN (Ralph) Currey, himself a poet who would become acclaimed for his WW2 verse. Here is part of his poem on the journey.

RN Currey

Evacuation by RN Currey

> The boys laughed and ate, and played like puppies
> There was no holding them – but soon they started
> The never-ending question: 'How many stations?'
>
> How many stations? We went half way round
> England to half-traverse it: the boys groaned
> At each digression, cheered to pass a truck-load
> Of shot-down German planes, and ate, and wrestled,
> Read bloods, slept against each other's shoulders,
> Asking repeatedly: How many stations?'
> How many miles?
> How many miles to Babylon, porter, porter?
> How many stations more to Xanadu?
> ......
> Next day, after the serpent had been searched
> For lice and infectious diseases, we waited
> For billets to be found; by supper-time
> The last boy of our batch was fitted in
> A dozen being taken in a bus
> From road to road, and hawked from door to door.

CRGS was, therefore, temporarily closed. However, by December 1940, with the threat of invasion receding, almost all the evacuees had returned, and, in January 1941, the school was open again. PR Wormell, OC President 1970-71, began his career at CRGS at that time. He recalls the Headmaster, AW Fletcher, telling his parents that there were no longer any full-school assemblies because of the danger of having too many boys under one roof at any one time. He notes an influx of women teachers, as nine of the CRGS male staff had by now joined up. These were Messrs. Casey, Holden, Brown, Cunningham, Dixon, Ford, Gubb, Ormandy and Stuart; by the end of 1941 two more, Messrs. Currey and Denne had joined them. He also recalls the first war casualty to be seen at the school, a new Geography teacher called Mr Burke who had returned from the North Africa campaign in 1943 to teach at CRGS – minus a leg!

By now a national 'Dig for Victory' campaign was underway to encourage people to grow vegetables. The part of the main close where the Technology building now stands was given over to vegetable plots which were supervised by Mr Mabbs - a teacher especially tough on boys who 'wasted' food at lunchtimes (lunch was then eaten in what is now the library): 'Woe betide any boy who passed down his plate if it contained any vestige of food upon it' writes PR Wormell. 'Mabbo', he says, would then launch a tirade against all boys, not just the miscreant, 'his voice rising to an imitation of Hitler as he ranted on'!

Part of the playing-field was also used for vegetable-growing, limiting the amount of sport the boys played. In general, sport was restricted and reserved for those who were good enough to play in House matches or other team events, which were themselves few and far between. In 1941 the cricket 1st XI played just five matches, the 2nd XI three and a 'Junior XI' another three. PR Wormell remembers playing rugby and cricket only once during his five years at the school during the war, although he recalls that athletic sports and cross-country running were still done by all.

From 1941, *The Colcestrian* Magazine appeared just twice a year (in June/July and December) instead of termly. This was due to a sharp increase in the cost of paper for printing, which also limited the content of the magazine, with articles and accounts of school activities much reduced in length. The print-size also became smaller.

5

The regular school clubs and societies continued for the time being - debating, chess, stamps, music and science were all represented, along with a new Historical Research and Archaeological Society, which aimed to continue the archaeological explorations of the 1930s, both at the school and in Colchester itself. These had uncovered, among other things, a Romano-British temple at the school field. There was also a new Allotments Society, under the direction of the aforementioned Mr Mabbs. However, by December 1944 *The Colcestrian* states that the Science Society was the only one which continued to flourish. School concerts appear to have suffered a similar fate. In 1940 the school production of AP Herbert's 'Two Gentlemen of Soho' was accompanied by a performance of 'Lawyer Quince' by the Colchester Operatic Society. This ran for five evenings. The music for the latter was written by CRGS Head of Music Mr WH Swinburne – the composition being part of the Doctorate in Music which he was awarded from London University in 1942. However, as the war went on, it seems that school concerts ceased. The Scout Troop and the Cadet Corps did, for obvious reasons, continue to flourish throughout the war, and the cricket school was converted back to its original use as a rifle-range. *The Colcestrian* now regularly included a long list of boys engaged in different forms of National Service – most often as messengers, but also as members of fire parties, telephonists and Home Guard cadets. Some sixth-formers also formed a squad of stretcher-bearers, responsible for removing casualties from ambulances during air-raids, thus becoming the subject of another poem by RN Currey:

Among Strangers by RN Currey
  .....
  We lifted him down from the top rack of the ambulance
  At eleven o'clock at night in pouring rain;
  Rain on our hands, torch shining under the hood,
  We eased the stretcher out so as not to catch the blankets,
  And carried him in to the white electric light:
  .....

Perhaps influenced by the work of RN Currey, the war saw a marked increase in the amount of original poetry and prose by students which was published in *The Colcestrian*. The December 1941 edition of the magazine refers to 'the unprecedented quantity of verse which has been submitted', stating (correctly) that 'the standard has been remarkably high'. Much, though by no means all, of it was based on war-time experiences. Here is a poem published in December 1942:

On a Picture of St Paul's Cathedral taken during the Blitz on London by R Rashbrook

> It stands serene, like some great marble rock,
>   Above the gloomy rolling smoke of war,
> Unmoved by gun-fire or the blinding shock
>   Of bombs that shake the city to the core.
> The raging fires out-line it, starkly white
>   Against the sullen blackness of the sky,
> Seeming a symbol of the truth and right
>   That we uphold, and for whose sake defy
> Those evil powers, those spoilers in the night.
>
> But we can hope that from this funeral pyre
>   Of our great city, there will soon arise,
> Like a new Phoenix from the ash and fire,
>   A city, which, before our wondering eyes,
> Will grow in splendour through the coming years:
>   A city, where free men can walk in peace,
> And go unharmed, devoid of any fears,
>   Where thoughts of truth and love shall never cease.

As its title acknowledges, Rashbrook's poem was inspired by the famous wartime photograph of St Paul's in the Blitz. This was an image first evoked - two years before it became a reality - by another OC, (John) Edgell Rickword MC, in a poem entitled 'To the Wife of any Non-Interventionist Statesman'. Written in 1938 following a visit to Spain during the civil war, it had been the most successful political poem of the pre-war period. In it, Rickword conveys the horror of aerial bombardment, prophesies that British cities will suffer a similar fate to Guernica, and argues that responsibility lies with the appeasement policies of leading British Conservative politicians. Here are just two of its verses:

> On Barcelona slums he rains
> German bombs from Fiat planes.
> Five hundred dead at ten a second
> is the world record so far reckoned;
> a hundred children in one street,
> their little hands and guts and feet
> like offal round a butcher's stall,
> scattered where they'd been playing ball.
>
> Euzkadi's mines supply the ore
> to feed the Nazi dogs of war:
> Guernika's thermite rain transpires
> in doom on Oxford's dreaming spires:
> in Hitler's frantic mental haze
> already Hull and Cardiff blaze,
> and Paul's grey dome rocks to the blast
> of air-torpedoes screaming past.

In 1943 the school learned of the death of the only CRGS teacher to be killed in action, Mr Herbert Dixon, an RAF pilot, who had taught Geography and been Scoutmaster of the CRGS troop. In 1944, Modern Languages teacher, Dr George Purkis, lost his son, Michael, who had been a pupil at the school and was killed in Burma.

From now until the end of the war, the pages of *The Colcestrian* are increasingly dominated by the OCs' section. Many letters from those in the services were sent to former Headmaster, Harry Cape, and 'Mr Cape's Postbag' became a regular wartime feature. More poignant, of course, are the obituaries of the OCs killed in action and notices of those missing or held as prisoners of war. There are also letters sent directly to the magazine from OCs stationed in a variety of locations all over the world. These include first-hand accounts of the D-Day landings and other military operations.

There was one final effect of the war years on CRGS. The 1944 Education Act (the 'Butler' Act) aimed to introduce, for the first time in Britain, a system of free secondary education for all, comprising Grammar and Secondary Modern Schools (and, in theory, Technical Schools too). Prior to this, CRGS had been an Independent School, though one with a strong connection to Essex County Council, who provided some scholarships. While most Independent Schools decided to retain their independent status after the war, CRGS - to its credit - chose otherwise. From 1947, when the 1944 Act was implemented, CRGS became fully integrated into the state system as a county Grammar School for boys. As such, it was no longer allowed to charge fees. Thus in 1947 the Pre (Preparatory School) had to be closed, and the school now took its entire first-form (Year 7) entry solely on the basis of students' performances in the 11+ exam, rather than on the ability of parents to pay for a place.

Although there have been some changes over the years in the operation of this system, it still remains the pathway by which most students come to the school. After the war it guaranteed pupil numbers of 650+ and underpinned the further expansion of the 1990s/2000s. It has also formed the basis of the school's success as a high-performing academic institution, helping enhance its reputation and popularity over many generations.

COLCHESTER IN THE SECOND WORLD WAR

Peter Rowbottom

Just before midnight on the evening of April 30th 1940 a lone but damaged German Heinkel 111 bomber was heard circling above the rooftops of Clacton. Moments later it crashed with a deafening ferocity in Victoria Road killing a Mr and Mrs Gill and seriously injuring their son. Four German airmen were also killed and later buried with military honours. In the blast (heard in Colchester) and inferno that followed some 156 people were injured and about 50 other homes destroyed. It transpired that the bomber was actually laying magnetic mines off the coast and had probably been hit by anti-aircraft guns along the Thames Estuary. A further unexploded mine was recovered intact the next day once workmen were informed that their tools were resting on it!

These were the first civilian deaths on British soil and attracted the attention of news and film crews. The so called 'phoney war' was over. In just a few days' time, first Belgium and then France would fall. The people of Colchester and surrounding areas like Clacton were at war. Over the next five years they would see many more air raids. Indeed over 1,000 air raid warnings would be recorded. In Colchester, over 1,800 bombs would fall – that figure almost doubling if Lexden and Winstree are included. 54 people would lose their lives (6.4% of the Essex total) and over 100 would be injured, with over 50 houses totally destroyed and 1,750 badly damaged.[1]

The town would see a huge influx of soldiers from across the Empire (this was a garrison town after all) and an exodus of its young due to the countrywide evacuation of children. Local farms would be taken over in the drive to increase food production, aided by a new female land army. Aerodromes such as Boxted, Birch, Earls Colne and Wormingford would host the US 8th Airforce fleets of B-26 and B-17 Bombers and later P-51

---

[1] Benham 1945 Essex at War p87

Mustangs.[2] They would take part in attacks at Arnhem and, later and more successfully, on D-Day. Colchester companies such as the engineering firm Paxman would mass produce tank and submarine parts; Mason's would produce photographic paper used in reconnaissance photographs and shipyards at Wivenhoe, Rowhedge and Brightlingsea would build and repair a variety of coasters, minesweepers and motor torpedo boats. In secret they would also produce parts for the floating Mulberry harbour used as a pontoon-style causeway off the Normandy beaches after D-Day. Civil defence organisations such as the ARP were set up. The town was mobilised for war just as it had been back in 1914.

Colchester, of course, was vulnerable to attack for three reasons. The first was its significance as a garrison town, allied to its engineering prowess. Second was its geography: it was on the outward and return legs for German bombers on their way to bomb London. Keen to make escape if bombs had not been dropped, these were often jettisoned in the fields, and sometimes the villages surrounding Colchester, much to the chagrin of Elmstead, Marks Tey, Copford and Chappel. A third reason, also geographical, was that being on the east coast, the town was always a possible target for invasion. Indeed, invasion fears dominated the thoughts of many in 1940 and 1941. Even in 1942 the Eastern Regional Commissioner was quoted as stating: 'Invasion is improbable at the moment', before going on to say: 'it might well take place in the early spring and if it does not take place then, that creates no probability that it will not take place later.'[3]

Buoyed by this 'probability', Colchester was part of a planned 'stop line' to hold back German invaders by all means possible. One Government leaflet enthusiastically bore the title "Beating the Invader" and reassured its readers that "The Home Guard will immediately come to grips with the invaders, and there is little doubt will soon destroy them. If you see an enemy tank or a few enemy soldiers, what you have seen may be a party of stragglers who can easily be rounded up." Modern day readers may scoff at this having seen far too many repeats of "Dad's Army"

---

[2] Smith 1996 Essex Airfields in the Second World war p5
[3] Quoted in Benham 1945 Essex at War p42

but it shows the Government's efforts to calm a nervous population. Secretly, small bands of civilian men were recruited all over the country, Colchester included, to disrupt and dislocate any German occupation.

Over 120 defensive positions surrounded the town, making use of natural features like the River Colne and the Iron Age Lexden Dyke. Some pillboxes and remains of gun emplacements can still be seen today. The town was also defended by the placement of Ack-Ack (AA/anti-aircraft) batteries and coastal guns at locations such as West Mersea as part of a general east coast warning system.[4] A less well known, though interesting, feature was the installation of a bombing decoy at West Mersea - kerosene (aviation fuel) could be pumped onto a set of dummy buildings and lit to draw night time bombers away from Harwich and Colchester. A similar fire decoy was established at Great Bromley which was also part of the 'Chain Home' radar system. Curiously though, and unlike Chelmsford, Colchester received no barrage balloon protection. Colchester itself was in a ten-mile coastal 'prohibited area' with restricted access.

Despite the presence, or indeed absence, of some defensive measures, Colchester endured several attacks from the air, but only four were really serious in terms of lives lost or damage done. The first was on 3rd October 1940 when the Scarletts Road area was hit by bombs from a single plane. Eric Rudsdale, castle curator and keeper of a journal throughout the war, records how he, as a special constable, held back traffic and heard that three girls working at a nearby laundry in Old Heath Road had been killed. A house in Scarletts Road was destroyed, and although a man survived, his wife, child and sister were buried in the rubble. As Rudsdale drily noted, 'It seems incredible that at one o'clock this man had a wife and family and a home. At five past he had nothing.'[5]

The inter war prophecy that the 'bomber would always get through' was grimly experienced on 11th August 1942 when the largest loss of life in a single incident in Colchester befell Severalls Hospital, which was used as a mental home. There were 38 deaths among 63 casualties, including members of the nursing staff. Of the four bombs dropped, three

[4] https://colchesterheritage.co.uk/world-war-two accessed May 2020
[5] Pearson 2010 EJ Rudsdale's Journals of Wartime Colchester p45

exploded onto the hospital. A fourth did not explode though narrowly missed the nurses' home. This was a stark warning about the suddenness of death from the air and must have been the focus of discussion in the town. Indeed, in the following weeks several other attacks were recorded, giving the town a 'distaste for Dorniers.'[6] Although some houses, roofs and factories (including the Arclight Works) were hit, no serious damage was done and no deaths recorded. Some stories are recounted of parts of houses being demolished by bombs or incendiaries, yet the occupants surviving in the half not touched.[7]

Direct hit on Colchester Works.   The engineering shop at E. N. Mason and Sons' Arclight Works, Colchester, as it appeared after bombing on October 19, 1942.

This was not the case just a month later, on September 28th, when another Dornier Do 217 dropped four 250 kg bombs from a low height at 11am. Clearly our air defence was awake but not alert. Worse, the area hit was residential and smashed houses into a smouldering pile of rubble, cement, fractured pipes and body parts. Eight people were killed in the

---

[6] Benham 1945 Essex at War p47
[7] Benham 1945 Essex at War p46

debris strewn over Essex, Chapel and South Streets with Wellington and Butt Roads also affected. William Price, who attended St John's Green school at the time, witnessed 'a black shape' dropping from under a German plane. Teachers who also witnessed this, ushered the children into the school. The bomb 'bounced along the houses destroying the whole row on one side of the street before going off and destroying more houses at the end of the street. At that time, we did not know how lucky we had been.'[8] A dazed man was asked where his wife and daughter were: 'They're in there,' came the reply. Happily, they were rescued, though the ticking of what turned out to be a grandfather clock did hold up recovery teams for a while. The landlord of the New Inn, Mr Joe Girling, displayed spirit when he invited rescue teams and surviving relatives to have a drink at what remained of his glass-strewn bar. Apparently, he displayed the same fortitude and benevolence when a pub he later managed, the Queens Head, was also hit and partially destroyed, allowing him to sell 'real draught beer.' It is curious that the Germans, a

Chapel Street following the bombing

---

[8] William Price
https://www.bbc.co.uk/history/ww2peopleswar/stories/77/a2065227 accessed May 2020

nation of beer lovers, should inflict such damage on public houses! Today, a stone monument erected in 2017 to commemorate the event is situated on Southway, adjoining Chapel Street.

One positive result of the raid was that at long last, and at the insistence of the Mayor, early air raid warnings would be sent directly to Colchester Police, who would sound the alarm. Previously, alarms or warnings given by the local Royal Observer Corps would be sent as a 'crash' alert to local factories and schools, then on to Eastern Command at Cambridge and only finally back to Colchester. During this time bombs had often fallen and people killed, as in the Old Heath Road bombings in 1940. This brought much complaint from residents in town and countryside alike. As one resident noted: 'Only in England could such an insane system be worked.'[9] Notices were later posted across the town advising people to take cover as soon as the alarm was heard.

Despite there being scores of other incidents, including the strafing of the town centre by lone aircraft and the derailment of a train with the death of its driver, the last major attack of consequence was in February 1944 when Essex Street and the St Botolph's area was severely damaged by sticks of incendiary bombs or 'IBs' as they were abbreviated in bomb census reports. This time many commercial properties were decimated. Hollington's clothing factory and Griffin's removal company in Mersea Road were destroyed. The Britannia Works part of the engineering complex of Paxman was severely damaged and a host of smaller shops in the area. As Rudsdale noted: 'After hundreds of explosives have been dropped on the town with very little effect, one 'plane drops sufficient firebombs to destroy two factories, a furniture store, part of an engineering works and about 30 shops and other premises.'[10] The blaze could apparently be seen from Bury St Edmunds and almost two million gallons of water were used to extinguish the flames. US military police, with revolvers, prevented civilians from getting too close.[11] Amazingly only one casualty was recorded - hit by an incendiary whilst in bed.

---

[9] Pearson 2010 EJ Rudsdale's Journals of Wartime Colchester p108
[10] Pearson 2010 EJ Rudsdale's Journals of Wartime Colchester p162
[11] Ibid p162

One possible explanation for the relatively small number of major incidents is that Colchester, despite its garrison and industries, was really a lesser, secondary target after London and the other big cities such as Liverpool, Belfast and Glasgow. Serious factory damage only occurred once in Colchester when the St Botolph's area was hit in 1944. Even when a series of towns with historical monuments was bombed in what became known as the Baedeker raids[12] of March/April 1942, Colchester still

Debris on the site of Blomfield's shop.

Osborne Street—St. Botolph's Street Corner.

---

[12] So called after the name of a German tourist-style guide that gave map guides to historic British towns.

escaped being targeted though many thought it would be likely. Norwich did not escape and suffered much damage.

The truth is that Germany did not have the resources to attack all economic sites at will. After the postponement of 'Operation Sea Lion' in September 1940, Germany's air strategy was influenced more by trying to maintain a blockade to demoralise the population, as they themselves had experienced in World War One.[13] A second feature was to attack aircraft and aero-engine production, especially since the Battle of Britain had demonstrated that British fighter production exceeded that of Germany.[14] For these reasons Colchester escaped intense bombing (despite the presence of American air bases after 1942) and more often than not it was a lone opportunist or occasionally a small group of planes that fired cannons or dropped HE (high explosives) in or around the town.

But what was life like for those on the ground? One of the first real wake-up events was when Colchester saw its first evacuees, some 12,000, enter the town and surrounding areas from London in September 1939. A local journalist recorded with some alacrity: 'boys and girls with no vestige of house training, whose boundaries of behaviour at least revealed to the complacent outside world the true state of affairs in the city slums.'[15]

Colchester had its own call for evacuation of the town in September 1940, amidst invasion fears and just as the London Blitz was getting underway. As the number of enemy aircraft dramatically increased over the town, so did the air raid warnings and the tension that went with them. Around 13,000 old and infirm, but mainly children and babies with their mothers, left for towns in the Midlands. One of them was Harry Carlo, an Old Colcestrian, who recalls assembling at the Wilson Marriage school with his mother, complete with gas mask. Harry ended up in Wellingborough, billeted with an elderly couple and taught the essential

---

[13] Exeter University History research centre: The bombing of Britain pdf p 4 accessed May 2020

[14] Vajda F and Dancey P: 1998, German Aircraft Industry and Production 1933-45, p58

[15] Benham 1945 Essex at War p18

skill of knitting at his new school. Many, like Harry, would later return. A further evacuation notice was issued in March 1941 but not followed up by the authorities. Billeting arrangements for the internal transfer of homeless individuals had been put in place should the need arise, as it did after the bombing of Essex Street in 1944 when 345 people had to be rehoused due to the destruction. Hence the 'Blitz Spirit' may have been kept more intact in Colchester due to the relatively low numbers of those 'bombed out' compared with larger conurbations and towns. However, this would be tested when the V1 and V2 rockets came to town between June 1944 and end of the war.

Like all towns Colchester had to endure rationing but had, perhaps due to its experiences in the First World War, planned ahead. A 'Food Control Committee' had been set up before war broke out. Rationing was introduced in January 1940 and, whilst not always popular, was preferred to queuing, as it was meant to ensure a fair distribution of food, and even clothing and (later) furniture. Oddly enough, bread, fruit and vegetables were not rationed but they always seemed to be in short supply. Encouraged to 'grow your own' people often converted gardens and fields into allotments, many of which still survive today. 1942 saw the introduction of coupon cards and some 43,000 'ration books', as they became known, were issued. In addition, 16,000 emergency ration cards were issued to temporary residents, including evacuees and land girls drafted in for service across the county. If it wasn't in the shops then one could always try the black market!

Communal Kitchens or 'British Restaurants' (as Churchill renamed them) were set up nationally in 1940 to provide healthy but cheap food to those who had been bombed out, run out of coupons or required feeding for other reasons. In all, three were opened in Colchester, the first in May 1941 on East Hill in what was then the Ind Coope Brewery. This gave further credence to the notion that beer was in fact nourishment! In January 1942 a central kitchen for cooking such meals, as well as school meals, was set up in Magdalen Street. Meals cost a maximum of 9d, about £1 based on purchasing power in 2008.[16] No doubt they were a much-

[16] https://en.wikipedia.org/wiki/British_Restaurant accessed May 2020

needed resource. They were ostensibly set up to be non-profit-making, and were generally popular with the public and authorities alike. By 1943, there were some 2,160 British Restaurants across the country, serving around 600,000 meals per day.[17]

Petrol was also rationed, though only three garages were available anyway. Sunday buses were cancelled in Autumn 1942 and services cut. Private use was heavily curtailed, though key workers, such as those working for the new EWAC (Essex War Agricultural Committee) were allowed to use vehicles.

Agriculture had stagnated in the eastern region in the inter-war years. In response to wartime needs, increased mechanisation and land drainage was introduced. The new regional committees were asked to oversee and maximise food production at the behest of the Ministry of Agriculture. We know a fair bit about the work of the Colchester District Office, since the local war diarist EJ Rudsdale was appointed secretary to it. The EWAC was not liked by local farmers since it had powers to direct them on what to grow, where to grow it and in what quantities. In addition, failure to comply meant that land could be seized, given to other approved farmers or controlled by the executive committee itself. Draconian powers gave it a devilish reputation. Indeed, disgruntled farmers set up an 'Essex Farmers and Country People's Association' in July 1943 to inquire into the 'high handed injustices, dictatorial methods and wasteful farming of the EWAC'[18] The anger and distrust amongst local farmers made the national newspapers. One farmer remonstrated that the man in charge of cultivating what was previously his land was 'a man I wouldn't trust to judge a baby show.'[19] Others took possession of their land far more seriously and one farmer, a Mr McKerracher from Kelvedon, actually drowned himself.[20]

---

[17] Atkins, Peter J. (2011). "Communal Feeding in War-Time: British Restaurants, 1940-1947 In Ina Zweiniger-
    Bargielowska; et al. (eds.). Food and War in Twentieth Century Europe. Routledge.
[18] Benham 1945 Essex at War p53
[19] Pearson 2010 EJ Rudsdale's Journals of Wartime Colchester p81
[20] Pearson 2010 EJ Rudsdale's Journals of Wartime Colchester p94

Whatever the methods, the results appeared to be impressive. Hervey Benham, editor of a local newspaper and a former CRGS student, wrote: 'Nowhere near Colchester perhaps was the miraculous change in the country scene more apparent than in the district of Wigborough and Peldon. Here one might stand at the harvest of 1943 and see a vast ocean of golden corn stretching almost unbroken from the creeks of Mersea and Tollesbury miles inland…(where) only a few years before the rank grass and bushes grew so thick that a dead sheep might only be revealed by tripping over it.'[21] However, others were competing for use of the land as well: American airfields were feverishly being constructed on erstwhile farming land and crop production actually fell in 1943.

The arrival of the Americans had a big impact on Colchester and its outlying villages. At the end of 1941 there were a mere six operational airfields in Essex but over a two-year period that figure would reach 23 and pretty much all of these were American. By 1943 there were over 100,000 USAAF men based in Britain. By the end of 1944 that figure was 426,000.[22] The airfields were used by the 8th Air Force, and later by the 9th too, sometimes by a bomber group and sometimes by a fighter group, with usage changing over time as groups moved to other airfields. Boxted for example, was home at first, in June 1943, to the 386th Bomb group flying the B-26 Marauder medium range bomber. But in November the airfield was handed over to the 9th Airforce and to the 354th fighter group flying the highly desirable P-51B Mustangs - the first group in the UK to acquire them. Birch airfield was not constructed until spring 1944 but for various reasons it was not used operationally until March 1945 when it was used to drop men of the 6th Airborne Division in operations crossing the Rhine. The airfield used the famous Dakota or C-47 Skytrain which again graced the skies of Essex when a miniature re-run of D-Day was re-enacted in 2019. The famous B-17 Flying Fortress of Memphis Belle legend could be seen at Earls Colne throughout 1943-44. Later, B-26 aircraft would occupy the field. Wormingford was to be the only airfield to be home to a hat-trick of US fighters: the P-47 Thunderbolt, P-51 Mustang

---

[21] Benham 1945 Essex at War p124
[22] Gardiner J. 2010 Wartime Britain 1939-45 p547

and the twin-engine P-38 Lightning, a most effective fighter. American aircraft would dominate the skies of Colchester between 1943 and 1945 and several eyewitness accounts record the masses of aircraft leaving for the D-Day invasion of June 6th 1944. Keith Halley a five-year-old at the time, recalls his mother standing him on the washing-basket to peer out of a window, saying: 'This is the invasion. This is something we've all been waiting for. This is the invasion of Europe. This is something you'll remember all your life.'[23]

Whilst the aircraft they flew might be different, there were some universal elements the Americans brought to the towns and villages they occupied - peanut butter, chewing gum, coke, US cigarettes (highly desirable), jazz, big bands, Glenn Miller, the jitterbug, real chocolate and real stockings. The slick uniforms and slick hair, combined with higher pay than their British counter-parts, gave rise to the humorous, though resentful, adage that the Americans were 'over paid, over sexed and over here.'

Resentment was real, and one account from a Colchester military police female officer noted that: 'We were kept very busy. There were fights every night between the British and the Americans. I thought this was because the Americans had too much money and the British had not enough money. There was jealousy and rivalry between them.'[24] The same was reported of antagonisms between the Australians and Americans in Colchester. Having their own separate social clubs did not aid understanding between the cultures - the American Red Cross had opened a club for US soldiers in Culver Street. To address this, a joint Allies club was set up in Trinity Street, but not until July 1944. There was an American Officers' club in St Nicholas Street and, to the surprise of local residents, a club solely for black troops in Priory Street - the US army was still a segregated one. Many Colcestrians had probably never seen a black man before and would have struggled to decipher an Australian,

[23] Keith Halley www.bbc.co.uk/history/ww2peopleswar/stories/A2357516.shtml accessed May 2020

[24] Elsie Phillips
https://www.bbc.co.uk/history/ww2peopleswar/stories/59/a5314259.shtml accessed May 2020

Canadian, Polish or Czech accent (though the presence of Indian troops was less of shock given Colchester's cavalry background).

American GIs did, in fact, earn almost five times the weekly pay of a British soldier, and in August 1942 the Government introduced an all-round 20% increase in pay for British soldiers.[25] Whilst complaints about pay gradually lessened, a Ministry of Information secret report from July 1944 noted that the wider population held that the Americans had better clothing, clubs and luxuries, and fewer rules and regulations to worry them. The report repeated a complaint that 'our soldier's wives cannot visit Colchester for the weekend, but the Americans' girlfriends can.'[26] On the other hand the regions commented on the friendliness and generosity of the Americans.

But the Americans had other enticements. They put on dances in the aircraft hangers and sent out buses ('passion wagons') to the villages to collect local girls eager to have a night out and be taught how to 'jitterbug.' They put on Christmas concerts for local children, for example at Earls Colne, and provided toys and an American-speaking Santa Claus. In Colchester they paid for local children to attend the Circus. In order to build better relations, they happily accepted offers to spend Christmas Day with local families and would come armed with exotic goods like oranges, evaporated milk, bacon, sugar and coffee – all severely rationed. Younger children were delighted to receive boiled sweets known as hard candy, and chocolate Hershey bars were much desired. 'Got any gum, chum?' became a stock expression for the endless supply of chewing gum to which the Americans had access - not to mention nylon stockings and perfume. Unsurprisingly, relationships blossomed. My own family contributed to the 70,000 or so British GI brides as they were known, when my aunt married an American soldier and emigrated to the States after the war.

---

[25] Gardiner J. 2010 Wartime Britain 1939-45 p552
[26] http://www.moidigital.ac.uk/reports/home-intelligence-reports/home-intelligence-special-reports-inf-1-292-2-#c/idm140465680938368/?hl=Colchester&operator=or 4th July 1944 accessed May 2020

U.S. Fighter Pilots and Essex village Children : A lovely picture taken at a Christmas Party at Wormingford (1944)

But many Americans never did make it back home. In fact, the USAAF 8th Army suffered about half of the US Army Air Force's casualties (47,483 out of 115,332), including more than 26,000 dead.[27] The American war cemetery at Cambridge is testimony to their bravery and sacrifice. An American hangar at Duxford aerodrome shelters one of the few still-flying B-17s.

Apart from airfields, Colchester also provided teams of Royal Observer Corps (ROC) men who spent many cold nights reporting on the paths of incoming bombers and, later, V1 or doodlebug rockets. The

---

[27] https://www.8af.af.mil/About-Us/Fact-Sheets/Display/Article/333794/eighth-air-force-history/ accessed May 2020

plotting centre was situated in Lexden Road. One observer post is still situated out at Great Horkesley and our wartime diarist, EJ Rudsdale, describes how one V1 passed his post at about 500 feet heading west with a 'steady glow and a deep low roar.'[28] He also noted that many townsfolk with a new interest in geography, would discover that Calais (an alleged launch site) was, as the crow flies, nearer to Colchester than it was to London. Ken Brown, a schoolboy whose father had been the Civil Defence Co-ordinator for the town, recalled a song of the time to the tune of 'Annie get your gun' which went: 'First you hear their engines. Then you hear it stop. Then you run for cover and wait for it to pop.' Indeed, he was right about the sequence of detonation. Ken also noted that the blast from one bomb 'brought down our ceiling.'[29]

Between June and October 1944 there were several V1 sightings over the town (up to fifteen in one night in September[30]) and whilst some did crash nearby, the first being at Bakers Hall farm near Bures, luckily only one hit a built-up area - Berechurch Hall Road in November 1944. This blew out the windows of many flats and adjacent houses, but no deaths were reported. Once again, the surrounding villages were not so lucky: four people were killed at Ardleigh in one attack, with villages such as Marks Tey, Nayland, Manningtree and Thorrington also recording V1 impacts.

It was a fairly similar story with the V2 attacks which started in September 1944. These were more sophisticated rockets. Measuring fourteen metres in height, they were powered by a mixture of ethanol, water mixture and liquid oxygen, and carried a warhead of 900kg that could punch a crater 50 feet wide. They were truly the first ballistic missiles and over 1,300 were fired at Britain, killing 2,724 people, (fewer than the V1s) and arriving without visual warning since they hit the speed

[28] Pearson 2010 EJ Rudsdale's Journals of Wartime Colchester p179
[29] Ken Brown
https://www.bbc.co.uk/history/ww2peopleswar/stories/37/a3315737 shtml
accessed May 2020
[30] Benham 1945 Essex at War p70

of sound.[31] The latter fact, however, meant that a double crack was heard up to ten miles away. Although none appear to have hit Colchester, there were some near misses. One landed in Rowhedge, one burst over Brightlingsea and another crashed at Clacton close to the sea, damaging many hotel fronts. These were probably all fired from sites in the Netherlands. Eventually these sites, like the V1 sites in the Pas de Calais, were overrun by Allied forces and the last one fired was on 27th March 1945, landing in Orpington Kent. Colchester must have breathed a sigh of relief. Indeed, there was much alarm at these new rockets. As Rudsdale noted: 'At any moment, without the slightest warning, we may all disappear without trace.'[32] For some months the Government tried to keep them secret, in fear of lowering morale and inducing panic: early explosions were blamed on gas pipe fractures.

In addition to Observers and the ARP, whose numbers touched 800, there were Fire-Watchers, allocated to looking after certain streets (some 281 in Colchester) or buildings within the town itself. When, in July 1941, it was requested that all available males between 18 and 60 register for fire-watch duties, some 7,570 did so. When this order was extended to women in October 1942, a further 8,475 enrolled, though only 2,156 were

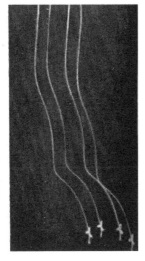

Incendiaries falling. A fphoto taken by a Warden at Old Heath, 1942.

found to be eligible. Several training huts were established across the town and three week-end courses ran from St Helena School. It must be remembered that all these volunteers had had no experience whatsoever in fighting fires of the intensity that could be generated by an incendiary bomb. The NFS (National Fire Service, set up in August 1941) helped train almost

[31] https://www.bbc.com/future/article/20140905-the-nazis-space-age-rocket accessed May 2020
[32] Pearson 2010 EJ Rudsdale's Journals of Wartime Colchester p187

3,000 fireguards and teams for the eight wheelbarrow pumps allocated to the Borough. According to Hervey Benham the average number of fire-watchers on duty at business premises each night in Colchester was 530, with the number of registered fireguards standing at 8,943 by the end of the war.[33] Behind these numbers must have been many nights of broken sleep. The one big raid on the town in February 1944 at St Botolph's meant that their training had been worthwhile.

As well as the NFS and ROC, there were a myriad of other civil defence organisations. There was the ATS (Auxiliary Territorial Service) whose celebrity membership included the current Queen. There was the WLA (Women's Land Army) with some 2,000 strong members in and around Colchester. The WVS (Women's Volunteer Service) helped organise and prepare for evacuations, the distribution of clothing to the needy, the setting up of mobile canteens for ARP workers, those bombed out, and, in Colchester, the running of the ambitious Allies Club from July 1944. They also assisted in helping with food rationing, organising campaigns such as Wings for Victory and ran IIPs (Incident Inquiry Points) to help people locate their families, hopefully alive, after a bomb had hit. Apart from giving their time, WVS members probably gave their blood too. Colchester also ran a successful blood transfusion service, organised in the war by Alec Blaxill JP. In the days after D-Day some 689 residents donated blood. Countless other organisations also existed, perhaps the most esoteric being the 'Colchester Depot for Hospital supplies and comforts for the Services and Prisoners of War'. Run by the triumvirate of Miss Sanders, Lady Benham and Mrs Paxman, they made, moved and delivered countless articles of clothing such as socks (5,000 pairs) gloves (4,000 pairs) and pullovers (3,000) to services' personnel across the globe. In addition, they made POW parcels and saw to it that their relatives had provisions too. This was Colchester's own mini Red Cross.

Like most towns across the UK Colchester's population experienced the war in both general and particular ways. Like all towns it endured rationing, blackouts, air alerts and, like some towns, evacuations. Its men were called up to join the services, or the Home Guard or other defence

---

[33] Benham 1945 Essex at War p112-3

organisations. Its women had to 'make do and mend' but also work in the factories, drive the buses and trains, 'man' observation posts, fire-watch, bring up children, weld engines and help manufacture every aspect of war production. Dr Bensusan-Butt (Colchester's first female doctor) set up day-time nurseries allowing woman to work. The town was bombed but not blitzed, raided but not razed, but suffered the usual privations of hundreds of night-time alerts, broken water and gas pipes, as well as the sapping enemy of broken sleep. It provided hospitals for the injured, homes for refugees and small boats for Dunkirk. In November 1940, the King came to inspect some Army units, the ROC centre and the Australians, whose HQ was in Lexden Road. If he had visited the castle, he would have seen it in use as an air raid shelter at night.

A Home Guard inspection. (November, 1940.)

In its own unique way, the town made other vital contributions. Paxmans employed 1,775 people by February 1943 (404 of whom were women) and had produced over 5,600 engines by the war's end. It was, when combined with the Britannia Works, the biggest producer of engines for the Navy. Every time you see a British made tank, Bren gun carrier, or searchlight in war-time footage, it carries parts manufactured here in Colchester. Indeed, nearly two thirds of all submarine engines and all the tank landing craft engines used in North Africa, Italy and on D-Day originated here.

When the Britannia Works was bombed in 1944, the Government ensured it was quickly rebuilt on an even larger scale.[34] Woods, the

---

[34] Benham 1945 Essex at War p147

famous fan factory, mass produced fans and parts for searchlights, tanks and motors for bombers - in fact 45,000 of them. Indeed, 60,000 feet of timber were used each month just for the packaging of such items. Over 120,000 miles of electrical wiring was used and, over five years, 360,000 machines came off assembly lines. Henry Ford would have felt at home in Colchester! Helped by war production in the town, Britain moved from a nation that could 'take it', as the war propaganda film put it, to a nation that could dish it out too.

Colchester's shipyards (Wivenhoe, Rowhedge and Brightlingsea) did what they had done centuries before – they built wooden ships. The Navy required specific vessels for minesweeping and the yards obliged. Overall, 54 ships of various types were built, in addition to the 200 that were repaired in what had been, pre-war, a derelict dry-dock. Dummy submarines were also made for placement outside Harwich port and Walton-on-the-Naze. They looked real enough to attract the attention of the Luftwaffe and, sadly, on one raid the straw sentry placed on-guard was riddled by machine gun bullets.[35] More significant, but less well known, is that parts of the Mulberry harbour used by the Allies as a floating style pier off the Normandy coast were manufactured at Wivenhoe. Parts of this are still visible today, suggesting that Colchester still provides a steppingstone to the continent.

Colchester's population could celebrate its adoption of a submarine with a Paxman engine, HMS *Unruffled*, whose crew visited the town in December 1943. Indeed, through savings bonds and other war fundraising, the town raised nearly £2,000,000 during the war years. The fundraising 'Wings for Victory' week in May 1943 saw £469,212 raised and in July 1944 the 'Salute the Soldier' week raised £574,212 (the target had been £350,000) - not bad for a town with a population of approximately 52,000 in 1939.[36]

Colchester Garrison, used to the upheavals of war, was the GHQ at the outbreak of war for 4th Infantry Division and had two Officer Cadet Training Units attached to it. Following the retreat from Dunkirk it

---

[35] Johnson D. 1992 East Anglia at War 1939-45 p130
[36] Benham 1945 Essex at War

quickly became an infantry training centre for the new Army that had to be built. Thousands passed through the barracks of the camp before being attached to new regiments. The Cherry Tree sub-camp on Mersea Road became a hospital for the Canadians. Troops must have swelled the numbers in the town and some were billeted with local families, just as had occurred in the First World War. Ack-Ack batteries were set up on Abbey Field and manned by the 8th Essex Battalion of the Home Guard which sported about 2,000 members by the time they stood down in November 1944. They had fired their guns in anger fourteen times over a 21-month period.[37]

The massive construction of the Colchester defences is shown in this picture of the demolition of a strong point on North Hill (October, 1944). Most were disguised to resemble stalls, sheds or kiosks.

The town today still exhibits remnants of its war time architecture in the 78 pillboxes that surround the town, ARP posts and the concrete casements of a large tank trap in Lower Castle park.[38] Abberton Reservoir, now a permanent feature, was used for practice runs
for the bombing of the Moehne and Eder dams in May 1943, led by the charismatic Guy Gibson of 617 Squadron.

---

[37] Benham 1945 Essex at War p104
[38] See Phillips , Andrew, "Retracing the remains of our Stop line." Essex County Standard Feb.8th 2008 28-9

A small, though little reported aspect of wartime Colchester, was the existence of a German POW camp at Berechurch. Not formally established until September 1944, its official title was Camp 186 and at its peak held about 6,000 men. The camp's historian, Colchester resident Ken Free, who remembers the German POWs visiting his church wrote: 'Local newspapers were loath to acknowledge the existence of the camp for some time - presumably due to the need for wartime security and the national policy of non-fraternisation with the prisoners.'[39] One notable inmate was Klaus Kinski who later would become a famous German film actor. He was lucky to have made it to Colchester, as the ship transporting him to England was torpedoed by a U-boat[40] – though perhaps Colchester United fans might have preferred that other famous German POW, Bert Trautmann! Most townsfolk, however, seem to remember the presence of Italian prisoners who began arriving in the area in the last years of the war and worked on local farms. They were not residents of Camp 186, but stayed in hostels or with local farmers, since the majority were 'co-operators', willing to work. No doubt some stayed on after the war.

Overall, the town can be proud of its contributions to victory. It provided numbers of men and women for all the services (Britain was the first country to conscript women for the war effort). It made Herculean efforts to increase food production and help feed itself. It contributed scrap, salvaged waste, raised significant funds and was a pivotal centre of war production, so that the British Army, Navy and Air Force truly stayed moving thanks to parts made in Colchester. It also harboured the planes, pilots and aircraft of the USAAF that contributed so much to the defeat of Germany, and it provided homes and hospitality to men from all corners of the Empire as well as training many of them for battle. Above all that, Colcestrians endured for five long years the deficits that the war brought, both physically and emotionally. They must have welcomed the brief period of rejoicing on May 8th 1945 when the war in Europe was finally declared over.

---

[39] Free 2010 Camp 186 The Lost town at Berechurch p4
[40] *Christian D (2008). Kinski. Die Biographie. Berlin: Aufbau-Verlag P14-16*

Bibliography:

Begent, Andrew 1999: Chelmsford at War. Ian Henry Publications

Benham, Hervey 1945: Essex at War 1st edition Essex County Standard

Duffet R & Zweiniger-Bargielowska (ed) 2011: Food and War in Twentieth Century Europe: Routledge

Free K. 2010: Camp 186, The lost town at Berechurch p4 Amberley Publishing

Gardiner Juliet 2005: Wartime Britain 1939-1945. Headline Book Publishing

Johnson Derek 1992: East Anglia at War. Jarrold Press

Pearson, Catherine. 2010: E.J. Rudsdale's Wartime Colchester. The History Press.

Smith Graham 1996: Essex Airfields in the Second World War. Countryside Books

Vajda F. & Dancey P. 1998: German Aircraft Industry and Production 1933-45. SAE International

My thanks to Catherine Pearson and Andrew Philips who provided sound research advice and an editorial eye that proved invaluable.

THE PRESIDENT WITH HIS GUESTS AFTER LUNCHEON.

Seated : Mr. E. Reeve, Mr. B. H. Kent. J.P., Bishop A. T. Chapman, Mr. G. E. Pepper, Rev. A. W. M. Weatherly, Mr. Horton, Mr. A. T. Daldy, Mr. A. W. Fletcher. Amongs the O.C's are Messrs. L. C. Brock, F. J. Collinge, J. Smith, J. Kent, C. E. Smith, A. J. Berry, N. C. Joscelyne, R. D. Leach, H. Markham, J. H. Nunn, J. M. Newborn, F. G. Lambert, J. D. Sargeant, J. C. Fairbrass, M. G. F. Hall, F. J. Eves, K. S. Cheshire, Q. R. Clarke, E. J. Dunton, O. M. Wightman, A. E. Stanley and L. de P. Henriques. Members of C.R.G.S. staff : Messrs. F. W. Seymour, H. J. Pakenham, J. T. Jones, E. C. Lamb and W. P. T. Casey. Members of C.R.G.S. cricket team : Weatherly, Garside, Quarrell, Bland, Norman, Rouse, Woods, Butcher, Kerry, Bruce, Lamonby and Watson.

Old Colcestrian Society summer reunion – luncheon and cricket match – in 1938.

Five of these OCs died in the Second World War:

EJ Dunton
KB Lamonby
JD Sargeant
PEJ Weatherly
OM Wightman

Paul Woodward

Rex Stephen Slinger

Age:	20
Died:	11th October 1940
Rank:	Second Radio Officer
Service/Regt:	Merchant Navy
Ship/Unit:	MV *Port Gisborne* (London)
Grave/Memorial:	Tower Hill Memorial
Plot/Panel:	Panel 83

Rex Stephen Slinger was born on 2nd October 1920 in Maidenhead, the son of Stephen and Dorothy Slinger (née Falck). His parents ran a succession of pubs and hotels. He joined CRGS from Brentwood Grammar School on 16th September 1932, and was at the school for five terms, during which time his father was the licensee of the Spread Eagle Hotel, Witham.

Rex left the school on 10th April 1934, and a later report in the *Essex Newsman* indicated that he continued his education in Chichester, and at King's School, Taunton, in Somerset. Rex subsequently spent a short time studying in Germany, before returning home in September 1938. By this time, his father had become the proprietor of the Pier Hotel, Southend-on-Sea, with Dorothy acting as the Manageress, while Rex became a cadet member of the Alexandra Yacht Club in Southend.

Merchant Navy Index records indicate that, in order to get his seaman's ID card, Rex gave his date of birth as 2nd October 1917, before serving on board the RMS *Oronsay* as an Assistant Steward/Tourist Waiter. The ship left London on 23rd March 1939, on a voyage to Australia, carrying passengers and mail to Melbourne, Sydney and Brisbane, and arrived back in London on 27th July. The British Postal Service Appointments Book records that, on 17th October 1939, Rex started employment as a Wireless Operator.

Eight months later, Rex returned to the sea, sailing on the 8,390 ton British cargo motor vessel, MV *Port Gisborne*, as the Second Radio Officer, on a voyage to Brisbane, Australia, sailing via Cape Town, Melbourne and Sydney.

On 28th August 1940, the ship left New Zealand for the return voyage, carrying refrigerated and general cargo, which included 2,479 bales of wool and 200 bales of sheepskins.

Passing through the Panama Canal, she stopped in Bermuda from 25th to 28th September, before continuing up the eastern seaboard of the US, to Halifax, Nova Scotia, where the MV *Port Gisborne* joined the convoy HX-77 for the Atlantic crossing back to Belfast and Cardiff.

MV Port Gisborne. Photo: Allen C Green

During the crossing, six ships in the convoy were torpedoed by U-boats. The MV *Port Gisborne* was among three ships sunk by U-48, commanded by Heinrich Bleichrodt. Just after 10pm on 11th October, the *Port Gisborne* was hit near the bridge by a single torpedo from U-48, and sank at position 57.02 N 17.24 W, about 113 miles WSW from the island of Rockall, off the Scottish coast.

The crew abandoned ship in three lifeboats, but one of them capsized in the gale force conditions, and all 26 occupants drowned. The survivors in one of the other lifeboats were picked up by HM Tug *Salvonia* on 22nd October, while the British steam merchant *Alpera* rescued those in the second lifeboat two days later.

The 38 survivors, landed at Greenock in Scotland, included 36 members of the crew, one gunner, and the ship's master, Thomas Kippins, who was later awarded the OBE, and the Lloyd's War Medal, for bravery at sea.

Rex Stephen Slinger was one of the 26 who drowned. In reporting his death, *The Colcestrian* simply stated: 'He will be greatly missed by his friends.' Rex Slinger's sacrifice is commemorated on the Merchant Navy Memorial at Tower Hill, in London.

Edward James Dunton

Age:	22
Died:	7th January 1941
Service Number:	748637
Rank:	Flight Sergeant
Service/Regt:	RAFVR
Ship/Unit:	38 Squadron
Grave/Memorial:	Alamein Memorial, Egypt
Plot/Panel:	Column 243

Edward James Dunton in RAF flying jacket

Edward James Dunton was born on 23rd May 1918, his birth being registered in the district of Wangford, in north-east Suffolk. A sister, Margaret Joyce, was born in 1920, and a younger brother, Earl Anthony Dunton, was born the year following.

Their father, also named Edward, was the son of a pork butcher, who originally hailed from Brome, near Eye, and had begun his working life as a brewer's clerk. In 1915, he married Evelina Ellen Greaves, a midwife working in Lowestoft, although she came originally from Croydon. During WW1, Evelina became a Red Cross nurse, while Edward initially served in the Army, before being transferred to the newly formed Royal Flying Corps.

The Dunton family made their home at Stoke Ash Hall, in Suffolk, and by the late 1920s Edward James Dunton had begun his secondary education at Eye Grammar School. As a boy he was captivated by Arthurian legend, and the romance of the high seas. When his father later became a salesman for the Eastern Counties Farmers Association, selling cattle-feed and other agricultural supplies, the family moved to Wivenhoe, near Colchester.

On 16th September 1932, Edward was admitted to CRGS as a day-scholar and member of School House. He clearly had academic ability, being awarded a certificate for Mathematics in April 1934. Selected as a School Prefect, Edward was awarded Cambridge School Certificates in July and December 1935, and again in December 1936, after which he left the school to follow his father in working for the Eastern Counties Farmers Association, as a clerk.

E J Dunton OCS summer reunion 1938

Edward lived and worked in Felixstowe, *The Colcestrian* publishing his address in December 1937 as 'Rothesay', Cowley Road, Felixstowe. By the following year, he had moved to 'Darley Dale', High Road, Felixstowe, while the rest of the family had moved to 'Pink Cottage', Parsonage Downs, Great Dunmow in Essex, and Edward (Snr) had been promoted to Branch Manager. On the outbreak of war in 1939, he joined the Home Guard, while Evelina became a volunteer nurse with St John's Ambulance.

While at CRGS, Edward enjoyed drama, taking part in two Gilbert and Sullivan operettas at the school. In 1934 he was one of the Chorus of Policemen in 'The Pirates of Penzance', and in 1936 played the more substantial role of Ralph Rackstraw, lover of Josephine, in 'HMS Pinafore', while his brother, Earl, also a student at CRGS, appeared as a member of the chorus of Sir Joseph Porter's sisters, cousins and aunts.

The East Anglian Daily Times correspondent wrote: 'EJ Dunton, as her humble lover, Ralph Rackstraw, earlier gave the impression that he had not the faintest ardour for the fair Josephine, but he showed more ardour in the second act.' However, another newspaper took a different view, writing of Edward's performance: 'He is valiant in wrestling with tenor work which is beyond him, but he makes an ardent lover... and gets his lines over well.'

39

Edward was also an outstanding sportsman, playing 1st XV rugby from 1934 to 1936, first as a wing-forward and later as hooker, captaining the team in 1935 and 1936. *The Colcestrian* describes him as "an excellent captain on the field and an untiring forward – always on the ball and backs up magnificently... remarkably fast and a beautiful defensive player."

Edward Dunton, seated centre in tasselled cap, Captain of 1st XV rugby

He also played for the 1st XI cricket team as wicket-keeper and could be an obdurate batsman when the occasion demanded it. For example, in the 1936 match against the Old Colcestrians, with the CRGS side having lost 8 wickets for 27 runs, he helped the team hold out for an unlikely draw. A good steeplechase runner, Edward was also a strong swimmer, representing the school, and being awarded the Royal Life Saving Society Intermediate Certificate and medal in 1934.

On leaving CRGS, Edward continued to play cricket and rugby for the Old Colcestrians, with the OCs Rugby Notes reporting in December 1938, that 'EJ Dunton is a ferocious, fit, filibustering forward.' However, in June 1939, with tensions in Europe rising, Edward decided to leave his clerical job in Felixstowe, and follow in his father's footsteps by joining the RAF Volunteer Reserve.

Edward started his flying training in early July, at No. 13 Elementary Flying Training School, and lived at 'Altmore House', in Cherry Garden Lane, White Waltham, near Maidenhead. While at EFTS, Edward learned to fly in Miles Magister and Tiger Moth aircraft, and made his first solo flight on 15th November 1939.

On successful completion of his basic flying training, he was sent for advanced training at a Service Flying School, where he finally qualified as a pilot and was awarded his 'wings'. Edward was then posted to No. 11 OTU (Operational Training Unit), at Bassingbourn, near Cambridge. There, flight personnel were formed into night bomber crews, learning together to fly the Vickers Wellington bomber under operational conditions, before being posted to a front-line squadron.

On 12th September 1940, Sergeant Pilot Edward Dunton and his crew arrived at 38 Squadron, based at RAF Marham in Norfolk, which was one of the few in the RAF to use the Vickers Wellington throughout the war. Eight days later, the Dunton crew, flying in Wellington R7854, with Pilot Officer Lane as captain and Edward as 2nd Pilot, took part in an attack on barges in the port of Calais, where the Germans were preparing for the invasion of England. The aircraft was hit by enemy flak, the Navigator was hit in the thigh, and the hydraulic systems were put out of action, forcing the captain to land with the undercarriage retracted.

On 30th September, Sergeant Edward Dunton flew another sortie as 2nd Pilot, this time an attack on Berlin, again with Pilot Officer Lane as captain. The squadron was then stood down from operations, and ordered to prepare for a posting to Fayid, in Egypt. There it was to form part of a night bomber wing, and launch regular night attacks on Italian-held ports along the North African coast, to hamper the movement of supplies to the Italian forces in the Western Desert.

On 12th November, with the RAF Marham Station Band playing them off, 38 Squadron personnel departed from Downham Market railway station aboard a special train. Having been joined by 37 Squadron at Feltwell, they arrived in Glasgow the following morning, and boarded HM Troopship *Franconia*.

Edward Dunton (far left) and his crew

On 15th November they joined a convoy, escorted by light cruisers HMS *Southampton* and HMS *Manchester*, the aircraft carrier HMS *Furious*, as well as a Dido-class cruiser and fourteen destroyers. The convoy arrived in Gibraltar during the afternoon of 21st November, staying for five days, before disembarking at Alexandria, in Egypt, on 30th November. En route, the RAF personnel had the opportunity to watch the Royal Navy in action, as they engaged enemy ships near the coast of Sardinia, sinking a destroyer, and inflicting damaging on a battleship, a cruiser and a destroyer.

Later the same day, the RAF personnel left Alexandria by train, arrived at Fayid at 2300 hrs, and spent the night sleeping on the train. The following morning, the men marched to the camp, and started to prepare the base for operations. Meanwhile, the squadron's aircraft had left Marham on 22nd and 23rd November, and landed in Malta, before flying on to Ismailia. There the aircraft were serviced, and fitted with necessary tropical modifications, before starting to arrive at Fayid airfield on 3rd December 1940.

On 7th December, the squadron received orders that, in co-operation with 37, 70 and 113 Squadrons, and operating from a forward airfield in the Western Desert known as LG60, it was to attack Benina airfield. On 10th December, Edward Dunton flew as 2nd Pilot, as part of Sergeant Clegg's crew, in Wellington P9293, to attacking the airfield at El Adem, near Tobruk. Two days later, they attacked the town and harbour in Tobruk itself, again returning safely.

Further sorties during the rest of December flown by Edward Dunton included the Bardia military HQ and Stores on 14th, Berka and Benina aerodromes (near Benghazi) on 17th & 19th, and the coastal town of Ain El Gazala on 29th of the month. The New Year started quietly for 38 Squadron, but on 6th January 1941, they received orders to provide eight aircraft for an attack on Tobruk. All of the aircraft returned safely, except the Wellington piloted by Sergeants Clegg and Dunton. The Squadron Operational Record Book notes that a radio message was received from the aircraft, reporting engine trouble, but that P9293 'S-Sugar' failed to turn up.

The action report indicates that the skies were clear, there was good visibility over the target, and that fires caused by the bombing could be seen 30 miles away. However, in the moonlight, the crews were met by intense anti-aircraft fire, some of it heavy, and 'S-Sugar' was hit in three places, with the rear fuselage and starboard engine suffering severe damage. The aircraft later crashed into the sea off the Ishaila Rocks, near Sidi Barrani.

In a letter to *The Colcestrian*, Edward Dunton's brother, Earl, later described how, when his brother

> 'was making his bombing run, his port engine was hit and
> set on fire. He carried on and bombed his target. After he
> had finished his bombing and turned away out to sea, his
> other engine was hit and he went into the sea about a mile
> from the shore.'

The only survivor Sergeant AW Roberts, the rear gunner, was picked up by a Royal Navy destroyer. The wreckage of the aircraft was found in shallow water, and two bodies recovered. Sergeants WJE Clegg and PF Wilcock were buried in the El Alamein War Cemetery, while the Alamein

Memorial records the sacrifice of Edward Dunton and the other two members of the crew, who have no known grave.

Edward James Dunton was still just 22 years of age, though the memorials record him as being 23. Just over two weeks later Tobruk was captured by British, Australian and Indian forces. In June 1941, *The Colcestrian* noted that:

> 'In sporting circles and particularly on the rugby field the name of EJ Dunton recalls some vivid memories, but now this brave young man is given as having lost his life while on active service with the RAF.'

In July 1946 the magazine published a poem in memory of Edward Dunton, written by his brother, Earl, who clearly looked up to his elder brother and must have been deeply affected by his death.

Last Flight by E. A. Dunton
In memory of my Brother, and his crew of the Wellington.

> Taking off from his sandy Drome,
> Straight into the setting Sun,
> Thinking all the while of his home,
> And when this war would be won.
>
> Setting his course cross dark'ning sky,
> Bearing slightly to North-West,
> Glancing back to his crew with a sigh
> Knowing they will do their best.
>
> Flying through the moonless night,
> The stars shining high above,
> Not knowing it was his last flight,
> Thinking of those he did love.

His objective was Tobruk,
Scarce half-hour more to fly,
He knew his way there like a book.
Now the flak was marking the sky.

One trial flight across the town
To get his bomb-sight set aright,
Then his bombs drop, down, down and down,
A piece of flak hit his plane on the right.

His star-board engine coughs and sparks
His port not running well.
Then more flak finding its mark.
All seems lost, but who can tell?

His plane now crashing down, and down
Straight for the heavy sea,
Wondering, every second, if he will drown,
All his crew, parachuting! The sea,

The waves, closed fast above the plane,
No one had the chance to save
His body from the gale-lashed Main,
Now rests in an unmarked grave.

Peter Pawsey

Age:	27
Died:	16th February 1941
Rank:	Sub-Lieutenant
Service/Regt:	Royal Navy Volunteer Reserve
Ship/Unit:	HMS *Southsea*
Grave/Memorial:	Wivenhoe (Belle Vue Road) Cemetery
Plot/Panel:	Section F, Grave 51

Peter Pawsey was born on 17th October 1913, the youngest son of Hugh Wake Pawsey and Florence May (née Denton). Hugh Pawsey, having been born on the Isle of Dogs, in London's East End, had gone into the oil-milling/seed-crushing business, eventually becoming the manager of the Owen Parry oil mill in Colchester. In 1900, Hugh married Florence Denton, daughter of Charles Denton, a Colchester solicitor, in the town in 1900.

At the time of Peter's birth, the family were living at 'The Old Rectory', in Brook Street, Colchester,

Peter Pawsey

but by 1924 had moved to 'Ballast Quay House', Elmstead Heath.

One of Peter's brothers, Hugh D Pawsey, also became a solicitor, and joined the same firm, which later became Wittey, Denton and Pawsey of East Stockwell Street. Meanwhile, Peter's eldest brother, Clifford, left his job with British Oil & Cake Mills (Ipswich Branch) in 1929 and, having spent a year farming with his family, joined the rose-growing firm of Benjamin R Cant & Son in 1931.

By then, Clifford was engaged to Diana the younger of two daughters of Cecil & Mildred Cant, the owners of the business. Clifford worked tirelessly for the firm, and dedicated his life to the rose industry. He died in 1997, having received the industry's highest accolade, the Dean Hole Medal, from the Royal National Rose Society.

Peter attended CRGS Junior School, the Pre, before being admitted to the Senior School in September 1924. Despite winning the occasional prize in the junior forms, he doesn't seem to have been particularly academic, failing his Cambridge Local Certificate in 1931.

However, Peter enjoyed success in other areas of his school-life. *The Colcestrian* records that he reguarlyl finished in the top three in sprint races at Sports Days, and represented the school 1st XV at rugby, scoring a try in the match against the Old Colcestrians in 1930. *The Colcestrian* said of him: 'He can run strongly when clear of opposition; his tackling is fair'.

He was also a strong swimmer, gaining two Royal Life Saving Society awards, and was selected as a Prefect, before leaving CRGS, in December 1931, to become articled to Fenn Wright, the Colchester Auctioneers and

Estate Agents. When war broke out, Peter became an Air Raid Warden, until he left Fenn Wright to join the Royal Navy Volunteer Reserve. In 1939, although their father had retired, Peter and his brother Hugh were living with their parents at 'Ten Acres', The Avenue, Wivenhoe.

Peter Pawsey was commissioned as a Sub-Lieutenant in the Royal Navy on 19th April 1940, and assigned as part of the seven-man crew of HMS *Southsea*, an 825-ton paddle steamer, originally used on the Portsmouth to Ryde ferry service, and for excursion trips from Portsmouth. She was requisitioned by the Admiralty during 1939, and equipped with a 12-pounder Anti-Aircraft (AA) gun, as well as two lighter AA guns. After taking part in the evacuation from Dunkirk, HMS *Southsea* was used as a minesweeper and, towards the end of 1940, achieved a measure of fame for shooting down a Luftwaffe Dornier bomber.

At about 1300 hrs on Sunday, 16th February 1941, as HMS *Southsea* came into Tynemouth following a sweep, she struck a mine at the mouth of the River Tyne, between the two piers.

She settled in shallow water, and was eventually beached. The ship was declared to be a 'Constructive Total Loss' and, for a while, was used as a breakwater, before being broken up.

The Paddle Steamer 'Southsea' before the war: Photo J Toomey

HMS *Southsea* sank with the loss of all seven of her crew, including Sub-Lieutenant Peter Pawsey. A report in *The Colcestrian* observed that 'He was 27 years old and had been with Messrs. Fenn, Wright & Co. of Colchester for many years, and held many friends in the farming community'.

Peter Pawsey is buried in Wivenhoe Belle Vue Road Cemetery, in a plot next to his parents' grave. He is also commemorated on the stained-glass window in the CRGS library.

Jack Raymond Cresswell

Age:	20
Died:	17th March 1941
Service Number:	89345
Rank:	Pilot Officer (Pilot)
Service/Regt:	RAF Volunteer Reserve
Ship/Unit:	86 Squadron
Grave/Memorial:	Ipswich Crematorium
Plot/Panel:	Screen Wall, Panel 1

Jack Raymond Cresswell was born on 21st June 1920, in Colchester, the son of Bertram Thomas Cresswell and his wife, Ethel (née Denny), who lived in Hamilton Road, Colchester. The CRGS Admissions Register records his father's occupation as 'Chief Cashier to the Colchester Corporation'.

Jack received his early education at Canterbury Road Council Primary School, and was admitted to CRGS, as a day-scholar in Form Upper IIIA, on 17th September 1931. There are few details of Jack's time in the school, but *The Colcestrian* carried a report, in December 1932 edition, that Jack had won a Royal Drawing Society Honours award, and a 'Junior Foundation Scholarship' Consolation Prize.

Jack was also credited as the compiler of crosswords which appeared in the July 1935 and April 1936 editions of the magazine. He received a further mention in December 1936, when it reported that Jack had passed the Cambridge School Certificate examination the previous July, and again the following spring for his part in the 'Chorus of Sisters, Cousins and Aunts' for the school production of 'HMS Pinafore'.

He left Form Upper VIA of CRGS on 5th February 1937, and started work at British Xylonite Ltd., the Brantham-based plastics manufacturer, as a laboratory assistant. In the 1939 Census Register records that he was living at home with his parents, in Hamilton Road, Colchester, and still working as a laboratory assistant.

Jack Cresswell, fifth from the left, on a CRGS scout trip to France
One of the two Dobbies pictured here also died in the Second World War

It appears that Jack joined the RAF shortly after the outbreak of war, with his commission being reported in *The London Gazette* on 21st January 1941, with effect from 6th December 1940 when, as Pilot Officer Jack Cresswell, he was posted to 86 Squadron, which had just been reformed at Gosport.

Flying Blenheim light bombers, the squadron trained for convoy escort duties at RAF Leuchars, before it moved to RAF Wattisham in March 1941, with one flight of aircraft being deployed to Ipswich Airport (known as RAF Nacton).

Before the Squadron could officially become operational, two aircraft on a training flight, Z5808 and V5464, collided and crashed just to the east of Gayton Road Station, near King's Lynn, in Norfolk. Both aircraft were a 'total loss', and all six crew were killed.

Poignantly, the June 1941 edition of *The Colcestrian*, in addition to carrying the sad news of Jack Cresswell's death, printed the following letter, which he had penned in February of that year:

Our news has its tragic side, as will be seen by the announcements at the end, but it seems fitting to give the following extract from a letter received in February last from the late Jack Cresswell as a typical expression of the young men whom we know :

" It seems years now since we used to enjoy ourselves in Big School each week playing, or doing our best to play, badminton. Much has happened to me in that time, and I must say I have enjoyed it all, having passed through the ranks of the R.A.F. from the lowliest rank of AC2 to the now exalted position of P/O. My training as a pilot has been most interesting, and I have enjoyed every minute of it—it is a grand life.

" I am at present in a Coastal Command squadron flying Bristol ' Blenheim IV ' (long nose) ; it is grand fun and they are marvellous aircraft."

The Colcestrian also noted that Jack had been a member of St Mary's Church choir in Colchester, and was well-known as a 'tennis player of repute' in local circles, and that he would be greatly missed.

The sacrifice made by Pilot Officer Jack Raymond Cresswell is commemorated on the Screen Wall in Ipswich Crematorium (see biography of Francis Edensor Richardson for image) and on the memorial window in the CRGS library.

"Number" Crossword.

By J. R. CRESSWELL.

All Unclued Words are Numbers.

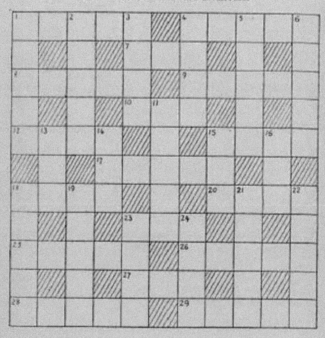

CLUES ACROSS.	CLUES DOWN.
7. Feminine name.	1. Curved sword.
8. Title.	2. Border.
9. 1 coin (Anag.).	4. Not to succeed.
10. 45 inches.	5. Napkin used at the Eucharist.
12. Observed.	6. Sailing vessel.
15. The current month.	11. Berry.
18. Width.	13. Yelp.
20. Office of the sixth hour.	14. Lair.
25. Three masted vessel.	15. Possessive.
28. Port on the Red Sea.	19. For pictures.
29. Cinders.	21. Soil.
	22. Plants.
	23. Having sight.
	24. Volcano.

The solution is on page 2648.

One of Jack's many crosswords

52

Paul Sydney Hirst

Age:	25
Died:	17th May 1941
Service Number:	76581
Rank:	Flying Officer
Service/Regt:	RAF Volunteer Reserve
Ship/Unit:	252 Squadron
Grave/Memorial:	Phaleron Cemetery, Athens, Greece (Originally buried in Heliopolis Civil Cemetery, Athens)
Plot/Panel:	Plot 5, Row C, Grave 7

Paul Sydney Hirst was born on 19th April 1915 at Manor Park, West Ham, the fourth of five sons born to Bertram Layton Hirst, and his wife Dora Louisa (née Shepherd-Smith). Paul was baptised at St Gabriel Church, Aldersbrook (Wanstead) on 16th May, possibly by his father, who was a Clerk in Holy Orders.

His father had been born on 27th August 1874, at Farnley Tyas, in Yorkshire, and had married Dora in July 1906 at Bedford. Martin Bertram Hirst was born on 23rd December 1907, David George on 29th July 1909 and Archie on 28th April 1911. The youngest son, Philip, was born in Colchester on 8th June 1925, while Bertram Hirst was the minister at St James' Church, in Colchester.

Paul Hirst was admitted to CRGS on 5th May 1924, as a day-scholar, having previously been educated at the County High School, Colchester. From reports in *The Colcestrian*, Paul appears to have followed in the footsteps of his older brother, David, who was very successful in his Higher Certificate examination in 1926, won an Open Exhibition in History at Keble College, Oxford, and went on to become a chemist.

During his four years at the School, Paul Hirst was awarded three Form Certificates, and a Junior Foundation Scholarship. He left CRGS on 27th July 1928, following his father's death, and continued his education at St Edmund's School, Canterbury.

In the 1939 Register Paul Hirst is recorded as lodging with a family in Wall Hill Lane, Meriden, in the West Midlands. His occupation is listed as 'RAFVR Sergeant 740586', which suggests that he had probably joined the RAF earlier in the year, gained his 'wings', and was continuing his training locally. On 19th January 1940, *The London Gazette* reported that he had been commissioned as a Pilot Officer in the RAF with effect from 24th December 1939.

Having been disbanded after the end of the Great War, 252 Squadron was reformed on 21st November 1940, at RAF Bircham Newton, near King's Lynn in Norfolk. Ten days later, the squadron moved to RAF Chivenor, in Devon. Operating as a Coastal Command unit, it was initially assigned twenty twin-engine Bristol Beaufighter 1C aircraft, although delays in their arrival, the unserviceability of the few Blenheims made available for training purposes, and the weather, severely limited training flights for several weeks.

The Squadron Operational Record Book (ORB) Summary of Events records that, on 10th December 1940, 'Pilot Officer PS Hirst (76581) arrived on posting from No. 4 Bombing and Gunnery School (near Stranraer, in Scotland), for flying duties.' On 28th February 1941, *The London Gazette* reported that Paul Hirst had been promoted to Flying Officer with effect from 24th December 1940.

Temporarily using Blenheim aircraft, 252 Squadron continued training throughout the winter, eventually receiving its first three Coastal Command Beaufighter aircraft, including T3228, on 8th March 1941. Further Beaufighters arrived during the rest of the month, although many were lacking radios, wing guns and other essential equipment.

By the end of March, the progress made with training, and aircraft fitting-out, meant that the squadron had ten aircraft at operational status. On 3rd April 1941, just as Germany was invading Greece, a first detachment of eleven aircraft flew to RAF Aldergrove, in Northern Ireland, where 'A' Flight would provide convoy protection patrols.

Two days later a second flight, consisting of a further ten Beaufighter aircraft proceeded to Aldergrove, completing 252 Squadron's relocation, and enabling it to commence operational flying immediately as part of No. 15 Group. Eleven days later, the squadron recorded its first success, when a Beaufighter shot down a four-engine German Focke-Wolf 'Kondor' patrol aircraft.

Over the next couple of weeks, Flying Officer Paul Hirst and his Observer/Navigator, Sergeant Eric Payton, flew frequent convoy escort and anti-aircraft patrols into the northern Atlantic, and over the Irish Sea. On 23rd April, having received information that it might be sent to Malta at short notice, the squadron was stood down from operations, all leave was cancelled, and personnel on leave were recalled. Six days later, fifteen aircraft left Aldergrove, flying via St Eval, in Cornwall, and Gibraltar, for a one-month deployment in the Mediterranean. However, since one Beaufighter had to return to St Eval with engine trouble, and another disappeared en route, just thirteen aircraft left Gibraltar on 3rd May to fly on to Malta, where they landed at RAF Luqa.

Having reported on a number of sorties by 252 Squadron aircraft since their arrival from the UK, the Malta War Diary reports that on Saturday 17th May 1941, Beaufighters of 252 Squadron launched a dawn operation against aerodromes in Greece. Flying Beaufighter 1C T3228, the RAF crew of Hirst and Payton were shot down by flak while attacking Hassani airfield (also known as Kalamaki or Hellinikon), south-west of Athens, and crashed just beyond airfield, in the Athens suburb of Heliopolis.

The bodies of Flying Officer Paul Sydney Hirst and Sergeant Eric Richard Payton (643867) were originally buried in the nearby cemetery at Heliopolis (Ilioupoli), in SE Athens. On 16th July 1945, following the end of the war in Europe, their remains were re-interred in the Phaleron Military Cemetery.

Gerald Graham Garrard

Age:	25
Died:	21st May 1941
Rank:	Lieutenant
Service/Regt:	Royal Naval Volunteer Reserve
Ship/Unit:	HMS *Juno*
Grave/Memorial:	Royal Naval Memorial, Chatham
Plot/Panel:	Panel 50, Column 1

 Gerald Graham Garrard was born in North London on 13th June 1915, the younger son of Arthur Christie Garrard and his wife Louisa E Mary (née Alston) of Winchmore Hill in London. Gerald's older brother, Raymond, later followed their father into business as a master builder and decorator, while older sister, Lema Maryllia, became a hospital nurse.

Having been previously educated at Winchmore Council School, Gerald was admitted to CRGS on 5th May 1925, as boarder and member of School House. While he was only at the school for two years, Gerald was later remembered in *The Colcestrian* for his 'very pleasing personality'.

During his brief stay at CRGS, Gerald demonstrated both academic and sporting abilities, winning a Mathematics prize shortly after his arrival, being awarded a Form Certificate the following year, and being part of the winning team for the Under-12 4x110 yard sprint relay. He also played a role in the Chorus for the school drama production of 'The Pirates of Penzance'

Gerald Garrard left CRGS on 23rd July 1927, and continued his education at Merchant Taylor's School, which was then located in Central London. During his time there, it appears that Gerald focused his studies on Science and Maths and took an active interest in shooting, in which he was awarded his Second Colours.

He left Merchant Taylor's School in 1931, having passed his School Certificate, and was articled to a chartered accountant. In December 1935, *The Colcestrian* noted that he had passed the 'Intermediate Examination of the Institute of Chartered Accountants', while *The Taylorian* reported two years later, that Gerald had passed the Institute's final exam.

From naval records, it would appear that Gerald enrolled in the Royal Navy Volunteer Reserve in London on 17th October 1938, and received his commission on 5th August 1939. He then appears to have been called up for active service in late 1940, and sent to the Naval Base at Alexandria, in Egypt, where he joined the ship's company of HMS *Juno* (F46), a British Royal Navy 'J' Class Destroyer, providing cover for Allied merchant convoys in the eastern Mediterranean, and seeking to attack enemy shipping.

During March 1941, HMS *Juno* sailed from the Greek port of Piraeus, to join Force D of the Mediterranean Fleet, and took part in the Battle of Matapan, in which the Royal Navy inflicted the Italian Navy's greatest defeat at sea. Following the battle, *Juno* continued to carry out convoy escort duties and attacks on Italian merchant shipping throughout April and into May, when it returned the naval base at Alexandria.

HMS Juno (F46)

HMS *Juno* was deployed on 17th May with cruisers HMS *Naiad* and HMAS *Perth* (of the Royal Australian Navy), and, to intercept Axis craft on their way to Crete, as part of the German sea-borne invasion of the island.

On 21st May 1941, while heading towards the Kaso Strait, about 30 miles south-east of Crete, HMS *Juno* was attacked from high level by five Italian CANT Z1007 medium bomber aircraft of 50° Gruppo of the Italian Regia Aeronautica, led by Lt. Mario Morassutti.

During the course of the attack, HMS *Juno* was hit by three bombs, which caused the ship to split in half astern of the bridge structure, and she sank in less than two minutes. Although the destroyers *Nubian*, *Kandahar* and *Kingston* were able to pick up 96 survivors from the water, five of those rescued died later, and 116 of the *Juno's* crew, including Gerald Garrard, were declared 'Missing Presumed Killed'.

The sacrifice of Lieutenant Gerald Graham Garrard RNVR is commemorated on the Royal Navy Memorial at Chatham.

Linocut by J. B. Watson, 4A.

From The Colcestrian, July 1940

Owen Maurice Wightman

Age:	20
Died:	30th June 1941
Rank:	Midshipman (Acting Sub-Lieutenant)
Service/Regt:	RN Fleet Air Arm
Ship/Unit:	807 Sq. (HMS *Ark Royal*)
Grave/Memorial:	North Front Cemetery, Gibraltar
Plot/Panel:	Plot 2, Row H, Grave 7

Owen Maurice Wightman was born in Hackney on 16th March 1921, the son of (Ughtred) Cecil Maurice Wightman. His father, who was born in the district of Wangford, in Suffolk, was a journalist who had married Owen's mother, Doris Thelma Johnson, in Chelmsford in 1919. When Owen entered CRGS in September 1932, the family were living at 'Myrtle Villa' on Wivenhoe High Street. His younger brother, Raymond, also attended the school.

At CRGS Owen was an accomplished sportsman who played 1st team rugby and cricket. He is prominent in rugby match reports in *The Colcestrian* as an aggressive hooker who could score tries. For the 1st XI cricket team he was a medium pace bowler 'with a low arm action who does not do much with the ball but bowls with determination to a good length. Not a polished batsman, but impresses in defence and can hit the loose ball hard - very safe hands.' He sometimes opened the bowling and took a respectable number of wickets. After CRGS he joined the Old Colcestrians' Rugby Club.

Owen left the school at Easter 1938 after passing his Cambridge School Certificate the previous year, taking a job with the Railway company, LNER. By now the family had moved to 49 Athelstan Road, Colchester – very close to the CRGS playing fields. This may well have been due to Owen's prowess on the sports field. His father is described in *The Colcestrian* as an enthusiastic supporter of school sport, who seldom missed a match and provided changing facilities for visiting referees in his own house! On his death in 1956 his wife presented a cup in his name – the Wightman Cup – to be awarded to the winner of the House rugby matches.

Owen's job with the LNER did not last long and on 1st July 1939 he decided to join the Fleet Air Arm of the Royal Navy. He did his elementary flying training at No. 14 EFTS Elmdon, before going on to No. 7 FTS Peterborough for the No. 7 (Fleet Air Arm) course from December 1939 to May 1940. On 15th June 1940, having attained the rank of Midshipman, he was assigned to the RAF. After converting to Hurricanes, he was posted to 151 Squadron at North Weald on 1st July, only to be thrown into action almost immediately in the Battle of Britain.

On 9th July 151 Squadron formed part of a force which was scrambled to deal with concentrations of enemy aircraft operating off the Thames Estuary. They encountered a very strong force of He 111 and Ju 88 bombers with a fighter escort of Me 109 and Me ll0 aircraft. Estimates put the total force of enemy aircraft as being approximately 100 and flying in an effective battle formation.

In the battle which took place, which was very vicious, 151 Squadron were successful. Midshipman Owen Wightman claimed a Me 109 destroyed over Margate, but was then shot down himself over the Thames Estuary. He bailed out into the sea, and fortunately was picked up by a trawler and landed at Sheerness.

On 15th September Owen was posted back to the Fleet Air Arm, joining 807 Squadron. The unit embarked on HMS *Ark Royal* in early May 1941 for deployment to the Mediterranean. On 30th June 1941 *Ark Royal* was preparing to fly off 26 Hurricanes to Malta. The first nine were flown off without problems; however, the tenth aircraft crashed into the bridge structure during take-off and a long-range fuel tank fell off, starting a fire on the flight deck. The accident, which caused the deaths of twelve and injured ten, prevented the last six aircraft from being flown off.

Owen Maurice Wightman, by then an Acting Sub-Lieutenant, was one of those killed. *The Colcestrian* recorded in December 1941: 'Sub-Lieut. (A) O Wightman, RN, at the age of 20 years was killed on active service. He was always a very popular fellow, and obtained his rugby cap and cricket cap while at CRGS.'

The inscription on his grave reads:

WORTHY OF EVERLASTING REMEMBRANCE

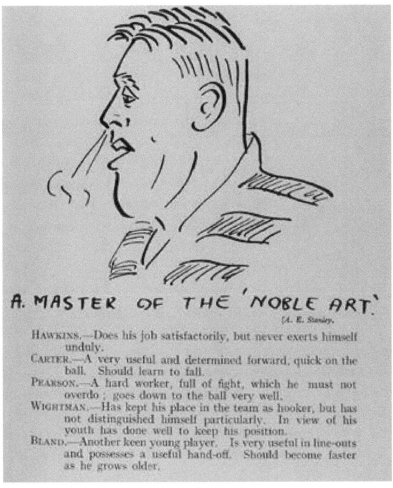

A. MASTER OF THE 'NOBLE ART'

[A. E. Stanley.

HAWKINS.—Does his job satisfactorily, but never exerts himself unduly.

CARTER.—A very useful and determined forward, quick on the ball. Should learn to fall.

PEARSON.—A hard worker, full of fight, which he must not overdo ; goes down to the ball very well.

WIGHTMAN.—Has kept his place in the team as hooker, but has not distinguished himself particularly. In view of his youth has done well to keep his position.

BLAND.—Another keen young player. Is very useful in line-outs and possesses a useful hand-off. Should become faster as he grows older.

Comments and cartoon in The Colcestrian on the CRGS rugby team, including two teammates who died in the war, Pearson and Wightman, December 1935

Kenneth Coney

Age:	20
Died:	6th July 1941
Service Number:	755735
Rank:	Flight Sergeant
Service/Regt:	RAF Volunteer Reserve
Ship/Unit:	49 Squadron
Grave/Memorial:	Runnymede Memorial
Plot/Panel:	Panel 35

Kenneth Coney

Kenneth Coney was born on 6th November 1920 to Alfred Henry and Dorothy Evelyn Coney (née Reid), in Colchester. His father was employed as a bank cashier, and Kenneth also had an older brother, Gordon Frederick, born in 1919, and a sister, Pamela, born in June 1928. His parents were living in Creffield Road, Colchester when he was born, but later moved to Ireton Road.

Kenneth received his early education in the CRGS Junior School, being listed among the 'New Boys', with AC Dier and KB Lamonby, in *The Colcestrian* published in December 1927, before entering the Senior School on 16th January, 1930 as a day-scholar.

Having won prizes for reading while in the Pre, Kenneth was awarded a Senior School Form Prize in the Summer Term of 1930. In April 1931, *The Colcestrian* reported that he had taken part in the school production of 'Ruddigore', as one of the 'Chorus of Professional Bridesmaids and Fisherwomen'. Kenneth Coney left CRGS in April 1934, to continue his education at Bishops Stortford College.

At the outbreak of war, in September 1939, Kenneth was recorded as living at Coulsdon, in Surrey. It would seem likely that he joined the RAF about the time that war broke out, since, having completed his RAF flying training with 106 Squadron, on 27th Oct 1940, Sergeant K Coney was posted to 49 Squadron, based at RAF Scampton in Lincolnshire.

During the following eight months, Kenneth Coney flew, as a member of 49 Squadron, on nearly 30 operational sorties against targets in France and Germany.

On 6th July 1941, between 2220 and 2250 hrs, ten aircraft of 49 Squadron took off from RAF Scampton, to form part of a force of 88 Hampdens and 21 Wellington aircraft, in an attack on the German battlecruisers *Scharnhorst* and *Gneisenau*, then moored in the dockyard at Brest.

Although one aircraft was forced to return early, due to engine trouble, the remaining 49 Squadron aircraft pressed home their attack on the target, in perfect and cloudless weather.

Hampden AD739, with Flight Sergeant Kenneth Coney included in its crew of four, was among ten aircraft from 49 Squadron to successfully bomb the dock area, although a smoke screen in the target area prevented the bombing of the German warships being observed.

Unfortunately, AD739 was the only 49 Squadron aircraft not to return from the raid, with Pilot Officer Henderson and his crew apparently having crashed into the sea off the Dutch coast, the victims of enemy flak.

The crew of Hampden AD739 (EA-A) on that final flight was as follows:

82170	P/O A.J. Henderson	Pilot
740123	F/Sgt. I.M.T. Fisher	Navigator
750570	F/Sgt. H. Aldridge	Wireless Operator/Air Gunner
755735	F/Sgt. K. Coney	Wireless Operator/Air Gunner

Poignantly, in the hours before taking off, Kenneth Coney had related to another Old Colcestrian that this trip was the last of his tour, after which he was due to be rested from operational duties and withdrawn from front-line service.

Alan Claude Dier

Age:	21
Died:	7th July 1941
Service Number:	40090
Rank:	Flight Lieutenant
Service/Regt:	RAF
Ship/Unit:	24 Elementary Flight Training School (EFTS)
Grave/Memorial:	Luton Church Burial Ground, Bedfordshire
Plot/Panel:	Section 3, Row D, Grave 20

Alan Claude Dier was born in Guildford, Surrey on 28th August 1919, the second of three sons of Spencer and Emma Violet May Dier (née Monk). Alan's older brother, Kenneth Spencer Dier, was born on 12th March 1915, also in Guildford, while his younger brother, Robin Spencer Dier, was born at Braintree on 14th November 1926.

Alan Dier was admitted to the Senior School on 2nd May 1929, as a day-scholar and member of School House, having previously been educated in the CRGS Junior School. The family then lived at 'Witham House' in Witham, where his father managed a bank.

While at CRGS, Alan showed a great aptitude for sport, as an athlete as well as playing for the school at both rugby and cricket. As well as being awarded Half Colours for rugby, he received his Full Colours for cricket in 1933, regularly opening the batting, taking part in the bowling attack, going on to become to captain the school First XI. Early in his school cricket career *The Colcestrian* noted that: 'He could make a good bat, and a dangerous fast bowler, if he wishes. He is a good fielder, and never slacks', and later noted that, as a captain, 'Dier has himself set an excellent example, and has used good judgment in setting his field and changing his bowling.'

In addition to his sporting success, Alan Dier also played an active part in the school Gilbert & Sullivan productions, excelling in the 1931 production of 'Ruddigore' and appearing in the Pirate Chorus of the 1934 production of 'The Pirates of Penzance'. In his final year, Alan was appointed as a School Prefect, but was unsuccessful in both his attempts to pass the Cambridge School Certificate examination.

When Alan Dier left CRGS on 24th July 1936, it was noted that his intention was to join the RAF. Having completed his initial training, he was selected for flying training, and received his 'wings' on 5th September 1937. His rank of Pilot Officer in the Royal Air Force was confirmed on 12th July 1938, with early RAF flying career appearing to have been spent with 106 Squadron, based at Thornaby in North Yorkshire, which had re-formed on 1st June 1938, as part of No. 5 Group, and equipped with Fairey Battle light bombers.

On 8th April 1939, Alan Dier was returning to Thornaby following a training flight in Fairey Battle K7563 but forgot to lower the undercarriage during his approach to the airfield. The aircraft was badly damaged in the resultant belly landing and was written off. The pilot was uninjured. During May 1939, the squadron was re-equipped with twin-engine Handley Page Hampdens, using Avro Ansons to assist in the conversion to the new aircraft. After spending the early part of the summer training with its new aircraft, 106 Squadron left RAF Thornaby on 19th August 1939, for a two week armament training detachment at RAF Evanton, before the outbreak of war in early September resulted in the squadron being ordered to RAF Cottesmore.

106 Squadron flew training sorties day and night throughout September, which continued when it returned to North Yorkshire on 6th October, with a move to RAF Finningley. For example, one entry in the squadron Operational Record Book (ORB), for 18th October 1939, indicates that Pilot Officer Dier left RAF Finningley in Hampden L4180 at 1415 hrs, to fly a cross-country route, and returned at 1710 hrs.

Alan Dier carried out further training flights, including flying an Avro Anson to RAF Cottesmore and back on 23rd October 1939, and a lunchtime flight the following day, in Hampden L4180, to carry out bombsight practice. That evening, he took off again, this time in Hampden L4175, to practice night flying and landings.

The 106 Squadron 'Summary of Events' for October 1939 records that

> 'Hampden L4175, Pilot Officer AC Dier, crashed whilst attempting to land on flare path during solo flying practice. Pilot sustained broken thigh, and shock. Aircraft destroyed by fire. This is the second aircraft destroyed in a similar way. The fire started in a small way under one of the engines, and then quickly spread to the whole aircraft. An automatic fire extinguisher fitted to the engine would probably have prevented this.'

Another report indicates that the crash was caused by the aircraft hitting trees on its approach to the airfield.

The details of Alan Dier's RAF career following his injury are unclear. It is known that he was promoted to Flying Officer with effect from 12th March 1940, and that he received a further promotion, to Flight Lieutenant, on 12th March 1941. It would seem possible that he did not return to operational flying with 106 Squadron, but instead trained as a flying instructor, before being posted to No. 24 EFTS, based at RAF Luton Airport.

On the 7th July 1941, Flight Lieutenant AC Dier was detailed to give flying lessons to Leading Aircraftman (Pilot under training) Herbert Hearne, in Miles Magister L5984. During the flight, L5984 collided in mid-air with another 24 EFTS aircraft, Tiger Moth T7113. Both aircraft crashed, with the Magister being destroyed by fire, and all three pilots killed. Aged just 21 years, Flight Lieutenant Alan Dier was buried in the Luton Church Burial Ground, Bedfordshire, where his gravestone carries the inscription:

Treasured memories of a dearly loved son

Alan Claude Dier is also commemorated on the memorial window in the CRGS library.

SOMEWHERE IN HOSPITAL.

The Headmaster, C.R.G.S.   March 16th.

Dear Sir,

During the last three years since leaving C.R.G.S. I have been serving as an officer in the Royal Air Force in squadrons in many parts of England.

At the present time I am in an Air Force Hospital with a broken leg following an air crash at night, in which I was very lucky to be dragged out of a burning aircraft.

During the many weeks I have been in hospital I have often thought about the old School and how I have lost touch with School activities, and so feeling a very real loss for something which, looking back now, I treasure very much indeed. I should very much like to hear from old friends. Of course, I have had no *Colcestrian* for a long time, so I have no address list to refer to. I should be very pleased to receive the next copy of the *Colcestrian*.

With very best wishes to all " past and present."

Yours sincerely,

ALAN C. DIER,
Flying Officer R.A.F.

" Lychgate House,"
Shrub End,
Colchester.
June 8th, 1940.

Alan reminiscing about the school, June 1940

Ronald Sycamore Frost

Age:	29
Died:	20th August 1941
Rank:	Lieutenant
Service/Regt:	Royal Naval Reserve (RNR)
Ship/Unit:	HM Submarine P33
Grave/Memorial:	Royal Navy Memorial, Portsmouth
Plot/Panel:	Bay 6, Panel 5

Ronald was born in 'Albany Villa' on 4th August 1909, the son of George William Frost, and his wife Edith Elizabeth (née Sycamore), who were married at All Saints' Church in Brightlingsea on 14th October 1908. Ronald was the last of his branch of the family to be born in Tollesbury and was fortunate to survive an attack of polio when 18 months of age, apparently with no long-term effects. On the night of the 1911 census, Ronald and his mother were recorded as staying with his maternal grandparents, Edward Isaac ('Syc') and Elizabeth Rosetta Sycamore, in Nelson Street, Brightlingsea.

Ronald Sycamore Frost

Having received his early education at a private school, and spent most of his childhood in Brightlingsea, Ronald entered Colchester Royal Grammar School on 9th May 1919, as a boarder, and member of School House. In the school Admissions Register, his father's occupation was noted as 'Steward', and the family's home address as 'White Lodge', in Brightlingsea.

The references to Ronald in *The Colcestrian* suggest that he was both athletic, and academically able. He seems to have taken an active interest in the school Scout Troop, qualifying for both his 'Tenderfoot' and '2nd

Class' badges in 1922, gaining his '1st Class' badge the following year, and going on to become a King's Scout in 1924. He also represented School House at rugby, and was part of the winning School House 4x220 yards relay team on Sports Day.

Ronald Frost on his first day of school in 1919 (courtesy of David Frost)

Ronald's sister Marie was born on 21st June 1923, but, within a year, his father had passed away in hospital. Although the family home was recorded as the 'Castle Club', in Rochester, George Frost was buried in the churchyard of 'All Saints', in Brightlingsea. Less than a year later, Ronald left CRGS, and (unsurprisingly, given his family's sea-faring tradition) was sent to continue his education at HMS *Worcester*, a former two-decker sailing ship, moored at Greenhithe, where he entered the Incorporated Thames Nautical Training College (ITNTC) on 7th May 1925. A cheque stub in his grandfather's cheque book shows that 'Syc' paid £29/8/11 for 'Ronald's outfit'.

Ronald was sponsored on his two-year course by the Peninsular and Oriental Steam Navigation Company (P&O), which contributed half of the annual fees of £140. He left HMS *Worcester* on 14th April 1927, with a First-Class Extra Certificate for both scholastic and seamanship work.

A contemporary scholar recalled that: 'HMS *Worcester* was a rough place, the Captain Superintendent, Sayers, was a rough type and so was the Chief Officer, PT Perkins. Corporal punishment was the order of the day and senior boys persecuted their juniors. A tarred, two-and-a-half-inch rope was always used.'

The account goes on to describe Ronald Frost as 'a dark boy, black-haired and with a bronzed skin. He was always cheerful, seldom without a grin on his face.' In a competition to name the *Worcester's* first motorboat, he won with 'GOZLIKELL', although it was considered too 'undignified' to be adopted. Another story tells of a boat race being instituted, with six crews taking part in a knockout competition. Each member of the winning crew, including Ronald Frost, was given a silver oar.

Ronald was keen to join the Royal Naval Reserve (RNR), and so, after leaving HMS *Worcester* on 1st May 1927, he started six months' training as a Midshipman in HMS *Marlborough*, a WW1 'Ironclad' battleship, in Portland. In December 1927, at the end of his RNR training, Ronald joined the Merchant Navy as a cadet, sailing from London to the Far East and Japan on board the SS *Khyber*.

Over the next nine years, Ronald made many more such voyages to the Far East, Asia and Australia. He also passed several exams for promotion, rising to the position of 3rd Officer of the SS *Hororata* by the mid-1930s. During this time in his Merchant Navy career, Ronald also spent several periods with the RNR, which included submarine training at HMS *Dolphin*, as well as time spent at sea in surface ships, and submarines.

During 1936, Ronald met Betty Lillian Brewer, who worked in the 'rag trade', and was the daughter of James Brewer, a meat purveyor. In September 1937, having returned from a voyage to New Zealand, Ronald and Betty were married at Caxton Hall, in London. The couple flew to Brussels for a brief honeymoon, before Ronald returned to spend a month training with the RNR, as Navigating Officer of HM Submarine H33, based at Portland. Returning to the merchant fleet, Ronald made two voyages to Australia, and one to New Zealand, as 2nd Officer of SS *Turakina*, before taking the exam for his Master's ticket.

On 3rd August 1939, Ronald was mobilised by the Royal Navy, and assigned to the submarine HMS *Oberon*. Six months later, he was assigned to HMS *Talisman*, then being commissioned on Merseyside. The ship's First Lieutenant during her trials, and first patrol, well remembers Ronald from his time on board: 'He was entirely imperturbable and generally had a wicked grin on his face. He was a brilliant navigator.'

On 3rd October 1940, Ronald was posted again, this time as First Lieutenant on HM Submarine L26, based at Dundee. In a letter to his sister, Ronald wrote 'Life is not very exciting at the moment and apart from two cinema shows a week there is nothing at all to do.' However, the skipper of the ship seems to remember things a bit differently…

> 'We had a few excitements, including being bombed at the mouth of the Forth and losing our compass. We were in thick mist and somehow navigated back to Dundee thanks to Ronnie. Still always cheerful, he was no stranger to practical jokes in Rosyth, where, among other things, he pinched some silver from a destroyer, and had a hilarious time returning it without being caught… There was never a dull moment with Ronnie around.'

In April 1941, Ronald was posted as First Lieutenant on the U-class submarine P33 during her sea trials. When she was commissioned on 30th May, although Ronald had been selected for 'The Perisher' Submarine Command Course, the unavailability of another officer for P33 meant that he stayed with the ship when the P33 was attached to the 10th Submarine Flotilla, based at HMS *St Angelo*, in Malta.

The P33 left the Holy Loch base at 0600 hrs on Tuesday 17th June 1941. Escorted by HMY *Cutty Sark*, and with fighter protection, she sailed south, past the Scilly Isles and Cape St Vincent, where German and Italian submarines were known to operate, until she reached Cape Spartel, at the entrance to the Straits of Gibraltar, on 25th June.

P33 left Gibraltar three days later and arrived at the Lazaretto submarine base in Malta on 6th July 1941. She left Malta on 11th July, to join HMS *Unbeaten* (N93), which was already at sea, with orders for them to intercept an Italian convoy. Originally, it was intended that HMS *Ursula* (N59) should also take part in the mission, but she was unable to put to sea, due to a defect.

With the convoy passing far to the west of the waiting submarines, P33 was then ordered to sail south, to intercept another convoy off the heavily-fortified island of Pantelleria, an island between Sicily and North Africa. At 1407 hrs on 15th July, P33 sighted an important enemy convoy, consisting of a small number of merchant ships, heavily escorted by

71

maritime aircraft, and a flotilla of destroyers and MAS anti-submarine torpedo boats from the Italian Regia Marina.

Twenty minutes later, having passed through the destroyer screen undetected, the P33 fired a spread of four torpedoes at the Italian MN *Barbarigo*, hitting her with at least one torpedo, and sinking her. Shortly after the P33 had fired the last torpedo, two MAS boats counter-attacked with depth charges, and were soon joined by a third boat. Meanwhile, P33 had dived, and gone into her 'Silent Routine', in an effort to avoid the counter-attack.

For the next 90 minutes, the destroyers and MAS boats carried out a series of persistent and accurate depth charge attacks on P33, scattering more than 100 depth charges across the area, with over 50 explosions being counted very close to the submarine. The main ballast pump, a main electric propulsion motor, the main lighting, steering and hydroplanes were all put out of action by the battering.

As P33 spiralled downwards, out of control, the pressure hull creaked, rivets sprang, and the stern glands and hull valves leaked alarmingly as she reached a depth of 350 feet, deeper than any U-class submarine had successfully dived before. Fortunately, under the skilful handling of Ronald Frost, and her skipper, Lt RD Whiteway-Wilkinson DSC, the crew were able to trim the main ballast before it was too late and regain control. Eventually the enemy ships withdrew, either having run out of depth charges, or believing that the submarine had sunk. P33 surfaced five hours later, after repairing the worst of the damage caused by the explosions. Despite extensive damage, including a distorted pressure hull, the P33 was able to limp back to Malta, to be repaired.

On Wednesday 6th August, with the repairs completed, P33 left Malta again, to patrol the area around Sicily. A few days later, having been joined by P32 and HMS *Unique*, the three submarines were ordered to intercept an Italian troop convoy, bound for the Libyan port of Tripoli. Patrolling the area to the west of Tripoli, P33 later reported her position as seventeen miles WNW of Tripoli lighthouse, while *Unique* had taken up position twelve miles north of the port, about eight miles from P33, and twelve miles from P32.

At about noon on 18th August, the crew of P32 heard a series of explosions to the west, suggesting that Italian anti-submarine craft were carrying out a sustained depth charge attack, or were conducting a 'sweep' of the area off Tripoli, in preparation for the arrival of a convoy. Attempts were made by HMS *Unique* and P32 to contact P33 by underwater telephone, but neither received an answer.

While the official Italian war record suggests that P33 was sunk by an Italian MAS boat on 23rd August, near Pantelleria, the exact circumstances of her loss have never been determined. It seems more likely that the P33, which became overdue on 20th August, was sunk in the depth charge attack on the 18th August, heard by P32 and HMS *Unique*.

Ronald's wife, Betty, was officially informed that P33 was overdue on 29th August 1941. Red Cross enquiries into an unsubstantiated report of a number of sailors being held in Athens, and the possibility that they might be submariners, revealed nothing.

The Colcestrian later published a notice that his son, David, had been born on March 9th 1942 and, commented that "Ronald Sycamore Frost was dearly loved by all who knew him, and he brought great honour to the old school which was so dear to him".

Ronald was awarded the 1939-45 War Medal, 1939-45 Star, Atlantic Star and Africa Star. He is remembered on his father's grave and a tile in All Saints' Church, Brightlingsea, as well as the Royal Navy war memorial at Southsea, the HMS *Worcester* Memorial (in the crypt of All Hallows' Church near the Tower of London), and the Submarine Museum in Gosport.

Arthur Robert Fitch

Age:	25
Died:	3rd September 1941
Service Number:	65581
Rank:	Pilot Officer
Service/Regt:	RAF Volunteer Reserve
Ship/Unit:	40 Squadron
Grave/Memorial:	Middelkerke Communal Cemetery
Plot/Panel:	Row A. Grave 7

Arthur Robert Fitch was born on 11th November 1915, the second child of Frank Arthur Fitch, an automobile electrical engineer, and his wife Mabel (née Issard), of St. Osyth, Essex. Arthur had an older brother Clement, born in June 1914, a younger brother, John, who died very shortly after being born at the end of 1917, and a sister, Joan, born in June 1919.

Having received his early education at Holland Road Council School, Clacton-on-Sea, Arthur Fitch was admitted to Form Upper IIIᶜ of CRGS on 17th September 1926, as a day-scholar, and member of Dugard House.

While at the school, Fitch enjoyed success academically and was a keen sportsman, taking part in a wide range of sports. He played regularly for the school 1st XV at rugby, as well as enjoying success on the athletics field and in the swimming pool. In December 1931, *The Colcestrian* reported that AR Fitch had been selected as a CRGS Prefect.

Arthur left Form Upper Vᴬ of CRGS on 22nd July 1932, having passed the Cambridge School Certificate with Honours, and thus gaining exemption from the London Matriculation examination. With a view to entering Holy Orders, Arthur Fitch entered King's College, London in 1933, as a Theological student, where he acquired the nickname 'Bo'.

The December 1935 of *The Colcestrian* reported that Arthur had passed the London University Intermediate Bachelor of Divinity examination, and gained College Colours for Boxing.

Two years later, *The Colcestrian*, reported that Arthur Fitch was now living at St Mark's Vicarage in Silvertown, London E16, where he was a curate 'working in slum parishes', and serving the local community as an ARP (Air Raid Precautions) Warden.

After two years in the dockland parish of St Mark's, Silvertown, Rev. Arthur Fitch moved to St Mary's Church, at Prittlewell, near Southend in Essex. On the day that France fell, in June 1940, Arthur Fitch went to his vicar, and asked to be allowed to leave the Church in order to train as an RAF pilot. He said that he knew what it meant for an ordained man to join the armed forces, but felt that it was his duty to volunteer.

Having joined the RAF, Arthur Fitch completed his flying training at No. 20 Operational Training Unit (OTU) at RAF Lossiemouth, in Scotland, and was commissioned as a Pilot Officer in the RAF on 4th May 1941. His first posting was to No. 40 Squadron at RAF Alconbury, where he arrived on 25th May 1941.

As part of No. 3 Group RAF, 40 Squadron had moved to Alconbury in February 1941, and operated twin-engine Vickers Wellingtons in the night bombing role, attacking targets in France, the Low Countries and Germany.

Initially, Pilot Officer Fitch flew as the 2nd pilot on a number of bombing raids. The first mission was to Hamburg on 21st July, taking off at 2255 hrs in Wellington 1c Z8782-H, and returning to base at 0252 hrs. Two further missions followed that, both as second pilot, to Mannheim on 22nd July, and then to Kiel on 24th July.

Fitch flew one further operation as 2nd pilot, on 2nd August, in a raid on Bremen. His first operation as captain was on 8th August 1941, when Fitch piloted R1168-B on a bombing raid to the docks at Boulogne. He flew further missions throughout that month, to Hannover on 12th August, and to Karlsruhe on 25th August, in a mission which had to be abandoned due to adverse weather conditions.

On 28th August, while at the controls of Wellington T2701, Arthur Fitch crashed, although there were no casualties. In their last operation that month, an attack on Cologne, the crew were forced to divert to RAF Wyton, without setting course for the target, when the front gunner realised he had forgotten his helmet!

Taking a brief respite between raids, from his duties as a bomber pilot, Arthur Fitch would often go down to Southend-on-Sea, and his beloved St Mary's. The church would fill to capacity as word went round that Reverend Fitch was to read the lessons.

One summer evening, on his last visit to his congregation, these solemn words from Ecclesiastes Chapter 9, verse 10 echoed round the quiet old church of St Mary's, Southend, as Pilot Officer Fitch addressed his congregation for what was to be the last time:

> 'Whatsoever thy hand findeth to do, do it with thy might:
> for there is no work, no device, nor knowledge, nor
> wisdom, in the grave whither thou goest.'

A few hours later, he was in the air again, heading for Germany, never to return.

On 2nd September 1941, Arthur Fitch and his crew took off from Alconbury at 2010 hrs, flying Wellington 1c R1030 'BL-R', on a bombing raid to Frankfurt. As they pressed home their attack, the aircraft was hit by anti-aircraft fire. With great skill, Fitch nursed the plane back across Europe, and over the North Sea, to the English east coast, only a few miles from his hometown.

With the Wellington suffering from worsening engine trouble, Fitch knew that he had to land the aircraft quickly. Realising that he was over a town, and not wishing to endanger the lives of those below, Fitch turned the aircraft around, shouted to his crew to bail out, and headed towards the North Sea.

The Wireless Operator, Sergeant Robertson, bravely stayed at his post, constantly signalling their position. Before the two men could follow the rest of the crew, and parachute to safety, the aircraft broke up in mid-air, and plunged into the sea, about ten miles off the port of Harwich. Pilot Officer Kinniburgh, and Sergeants Stabler, Delgado and Parslow were rescued by a British trawler.

Sergeant Robertson's body was washed ashore at Vlissingen (Flushing), in Holland, and eventually re-patriated to Scotland, where he was buried in his parents' hometown of Cupar, in Fife.

The body of Pilot Officer Rev. Arthur Robert Fitch was found on the Belgian coast, and was buried in the local cemetery at Middelkerke, where his grave (pictured below) carries the inscription:

A Christian life, sincere and true
He sacrificed that life to save his crew

Arthur Fitch is also commemorated in King's College Chapel, and on St. Mary's War Memorial, in Southend-on-Sea.

Francis Edensor Richardson

Age:	23
Died:	15th September 1941
Service Number:	755737
Rank:	Flight Sergeant
Service/Regt:	RAF Volunteer Reserve
Ship/Unit:	236 Squadron
Grave/Memorial:	Ipswich Crematorium
Plot/Panel:	Screen Wall

Francis Edensor Richardson was born on 6th April 1918, the son of Francis Edensor Fleetwood (FEF) Richardson, and his wife, Evelyn Victoria (née Rhodes), who had been born in Scarborough, although her mother came from Worlingworth, Suffolk. Francis EF Richardson originated from Bramshall, Staffordshire, where his father was a prosperous farmer.

Evelyn's father had died while she was still a young child in the 1890s and, with her mother, she moved back to Worlingworth to live on a farm owned by Evelyn's grandmother. In 1904, her mother had married again, to farmer Henry Howlett, who lived at 'The Priory', in Little Horkesley, near Colchester.

In the summer of 1911, Evelyn married Francis EF Richardson at Lexden, and together they set up home at Scotland Hall Farm, in Stoke-by-Nayland, where a daughter, Joan Hesketh Richardson, was born on 29th May 1912. Two sons followed, with Kenneth Francis Richardson being born on 1st October 1914, and Francis Edensor Richardson arriving on 6th April 1918.

However, in August 1924, Francis EF Richardson died at the relatively young age of 44 years, and was buried at his family home in Bramshall,

Staffordshire. Evelyn, widowed and with three young children, left Scotland Farm, and moved to 'The Homestead', in Boxted.

Francis Edensor Richardson attended the CRGS Preparatory School (the Pre) from 1924, moving up to Senior School in January 1928. The Admissions Register shows that he was absent for the Autumn Term in 1930, because his mother 'had gone to British Columbia, taking her son with her.'

Francis' career at CRGS appears to have been undistinguished academically, but he was a fine sportsman. He played cricket as a batsman for the 1st and 2nd XIs, but it was at rugby that he excelled. He played for the 1st XV as full-back, and *The Colcestrian* describes him as 'one of the most reliable players in the side', praising his 'coolness and resource at full-back'.

The review of the 1936 season states: 'he can look back on practically every game with the satisfaction of knowing his work at full-back has been well done. In some of the games his performance alone was the redeeming feature.'

On leaving CRGS in 1936, Francis embarked on a career as an auctioneer but appears to have given this up to travel, his name appearing as arriving from Melbourne, Australia, on board SS *Mooltan* on 30th September 1938.

In the 1939 Census Register his mother and brother were living at 'Harts Lodge', Harts Lane, Tendring. Evelyn is described as 'retired, living on private means' (presumably the sale of Scotland Hall Farm) and Kenneth, aged 25, is engaged in 'tractor ploughing'.

Francis then joined the RAF Volunteer Reserve, trained as a Wireless Operator/Air Gunner, and was posted to 236 Squadron, which had been reformed at RAF Stradishall on 31 October 1939, and was equipped with Bristol Blenheim aircraft. From August 1940 it operated from bases in the south-west, carrying out convoy escort duties, and anti-shipping patrols, over the Channel and the Irish Sea.

It was on one such operation that Francis Edensor Richardson was to lose his life. A Blenheim IV V5567 (code letters ND-L) took off from Carew Cheriton, in Pembrokeshire, at 1642 hrs on 15th September 1941 to escort a convoy, code name 'Camel'. The crew comprised Sgt. Blackie, Sgt. McNichol and Flt. Sgt. FE Richardson.

Due to bad weather and wireless transmission failure, the plane ran out of fuel at 2320 hrs and was abandoned one mile north-east of Bodorgan (Anglesey). The crew baled out and Blackie and Nichol landed safely, but Francis Edensor Richardson's body was later recovered from the sea at West Tarbert, on the Mull of Galloway.

In addition to his name appearing on the stained-glass window in the CRGS Memorial Library, Flight Sergeant Francis Edensor Richardson, who appears to have been living at 'The King's Arms', Hadleigh, is commemorated on the War Memorials at Hadleigh and Ipswich (pictured below).

Jack Bendall

Age:	20
Died:	17th September 1941
Service Number:	745763
Rank:	Flight Sergeant
Service/Regt:	RAF Volunteer Reserve
Ship/Unit:	105 Squadron
Grave/Memorial:	Malta Memorial
Plot/Panel:	Panel 1, Column 1

Malta Memorial

Born 3rd October 1920, the youngest child of Albert George Bendall and his wife, Florence Elizabeth (née Kettle) of High Street, Kelvedon, Essex. Jack, whose father was a railway clerk, had an elder brother, Frederick, and an older sister, Esther.

Having received his early education at Kelvedon Church of England Boys' School, Jack was admitted to CRGS, as a day-scholar, on 16th September 1932, and left the school on 23rd July 1937, following his brother in taking up a career in farming near Kelvedon.

Jack Bendall joined the RAFVR as a Sergeant Pilot in April 1939, training at weekends in Southend. Having attended a course at Coventry, he was mobilised on September 1st 1939, and sent to Peterborough for training as a Sergeant Pilot. Receiving his 'wings' at the end of 1939, Jack arrived at 98 Squadron in May 1940, and flew single-engine Fairey Battle light bomber aircraft in the UK, France and Iceland during his six-month posting with the squadron.

On 20th November 1940, he was posted to 88 Squadron, then based at RAF Sydenham in Belfast docks (now the George Best City Airport), where he continued to fly Battle aircraft on coastal patrol duties over the Irish Sea and Western Approaches, as well as training on twin-engine Blenheim bomber aircraft.

In the summer of 1941, 88 Squadron moved to RAF Swanton Morley, in Norfolk. Very shortly afterwards, on 22nd July 1941, Jack was posted from 88 Squadron to 105 Squadron. Three days later, 105 Squadron sent a detachment of twelve Blenheim IV bombers from Swanton Morley, flying via Portreath and Gibraltar, to a new base at Luqa Airfield, in Malta. Ten of the twelve aircraft, including Jack's, arrived safely on 28th July 1941, but one aircraft diverted to neutral Portugal, and was interned, while another was delayed in Gibraltar, and arrived in Malta two days after the main party.

On 1st August, Sergeant J Bendall, and his crew, were in one of three Blenheims to attack Axis shipping in the harbour on the Italian island of Lampedpusa, about 100 miles west of Malta. Flying in tight formation with the flight leader, Jack Bendall's aircraft attacked a group of two merchant vessels and a destroyer with 500lb bombs, and appeared to have secured a hit.

Over the next few weeks, Jack Bendall and his crew flew a number of sorties against enemy ships in the Mediterranean, including the sinking of a merchant vessel in the Ionian Sea on 11th September, and scoring two direct hits on another ship the following day, causing a large fire on board.

On 17th September, three Blenheim aircraft of 105 Squadron, and another from 107 Squadron, took off from Luqa airfield in Malta, to attack an Axis convoy consisting of a small merchant vessel, a tug, and two schooners, which had been spotted near the Tunisian coast, heading towards Tripoli. One schooner was left a mass of flames, and the other seen to blow up, and disintegrate.

However, two of the Blenheims were lost as they swooped to make their low-level attack on the ships. Bendall's aircraft collided with the mast of a schooner, and crashed into the sea, instantly killing the pilot and his crew. A second Blenheim, flown by Pilot Officer Peter Robinson of

107 Squadron, was hit by anti-aircraft fire and burst into flames, again killing all three of the crew.

The crew of Flight Sergeant Jack Bendall's Blenheim were Wireless Operator/Air Gunner Flight Sergeant Alexander Brown, aged 19, and Observer Sergeant Charles Hill. They are all commemorated on the RAF Memorial on the island of Malta (pictured below).

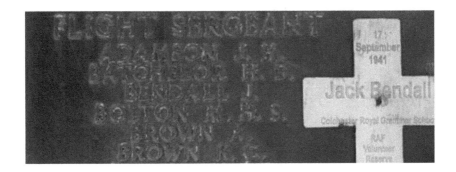

Douglas John Ashcroft

Age:	22
Died:	9th December 1941
Service Number:	920530
Rank:	Sergeant (Observer)
Service/Regt:	RAF Volunteer Reserve
Ship/Unit:	143 Squadron
Grave/Memorial:	Tripoli War Cemetery, Libya (Originally Misurata Marina Cemetery; re-buried 30th November, 1944)
Plot/Panel:	Grave 5.D.3

Douglas John Ashcroft

John Douglas Ashcroft (or Douglas John as he became known) was born on 16th November 1919, the second child, and only son, of John and Annie Elizabeth Ashcroft (née Mole) of Collingwood Road, in Colchester. It appears that Douglas, whose father was a tailor, had six sisters: Lavinia (b.1917), Joan (b.1921), Pauline (b.1924), Sheila (b.1925), Estelle (b.1929) and Margaret Una (b.1934).

Having received his early education at Lexden Council School, Douglas was admitted to CRGS on 7th September 1931, as a member of Dugard House. In December 1932, *The Colcestrian* reported that he had gained three or more certificates from the Royal Drawing Society, at least one of which was an Honours Certificate. He was also accomplished at athletics, finishing 3rd in the Junior Steeplechase in the spring of 1933. Three years later, *The Colcestrian* reported that Douglas had received a certificate for Mathematics.

Having been unsuccessful in his Cambridge School Certificate exam, Douglas left the school on 24th July 1936, and took up employment as a clerk. Later, he moved on, to become a floor walker at Messrs. Marks & Spencer's in Romford.

In April 1940, Douglas joined the RAF and, after initial basic training, was selected for flying training as a Wireless Operator/Air Observer. On 15th July 1941 he was posted from the RAF base at Gosport to 143 Squadron, then based at RAF Thornaby in Yorkshire, for training on Beaufighter aircraft.

Soon after his arrival at Thornaby, the squadron moved to RAF Dyce, near Aberdeen, where Douglas completed his operational training. A month later the crews being trained at Dyce were sent to the Middle East, although the available RAF records provide no information as to the specific base to which Douglas was posted.

Less than four months later, the 143 Squadron Operational Record Book (ORB) noted that Flying Officer DA Smith RCAF and Sergeant JD Ashcroft had been reported missing by the BPO RAF Mediterranean, in cypher message 759, dated 7th December 1941.

In July 1942, *The Colcestrian* reported:

> 'Mystery surrounds the fate of a young Colchester airman, Sergeant Observer Douglas Ashcroft, whose parents, Mr & Mrs J Ashcroft, of 132 Maldon Road, have had contradictory reports of his whereabouts and fate since last year. Mrs Ashcroft has heard from neighbours that her son's name has twice been given over the Italian radio as being a prisoner-of-war, but she has received information, originating from the Red Cross, that he has been killed, and buried at a place called Misurata, and she has received a letter offering condolences from the Red Cross.'

From information now available, it would seem likely that Bristol Beaufighter Ic T4756, took off from an airfield on Malta on 6th December 1941, piloted by Canadian Flying Officer Douglas A Smith (42899), and with Sergeant Douglas John Ashcroft (920530) as Wireless Operator/Observer. The crew of T4756 had previously claimed two enemy aircraft shot down over North Africa. However, it seems that while taking part in a raid on Misurata, the aircraft was bought down by enemy gunfire, and was reported missing the following day.

From Commonwealth War Graves Commission (CWGC) records, it would seem that both men survived the crash, but later died of their injuries, with Douglas Ashcroft's death being recorded as 9th December 1941, while Douglas Smith died five days later. Although both were buried in the Misurata cemetery, they were later re-interred in the CWGC military cemetery in Tripoli.

Sergeant Douglas John Ashcroft's grave in Tripoli carries the inscription:

He lives with us in memory yet, we loved him too dearly to
ever forget

From The Colcestrian

John Cedric Addy

Age:	21
Died:	17th January 1942
Service Number:	748538
Rank:	Flight Sergeant (Pilot)
Service/Regt:	RAF Volunteer Reserve
Ship/Unit:	27 OTU (Operational Training Unit)
Grave/Memorial:	St Patrick's Churchyard, Jurby, Isle of Man
Plot/Panel:	Grave 340

John Cedric Addy was born on 23rd January 1920, the eldest son of Guy Cedric & Jessie Addy (née Oakley), at Ightham, near Tonbridge in Kent. John's father was a poultry farmer, and the family was living at Mayland, near Chelmsford, when John was admitted to CRGS on 29th April 1931. John, and his younger brother, Kenneth, both joined School House.

John left CRGS two years later, to continue his education at Lindisfarne College at Westcliff-on-Sea. In April 1939, while living in Southend, John Addy obtained his pilot's licence, flying an AVRO Cadet, and became a pre-war member of the Royal Aero Club.

In the 1939 Register, John was recorded as living with his parents in Southend, while his occupation was given as RAF Flight Sergeant.

After flying training, John joined 103 Squadron, at RAF Bircham Newton in Nottinghamshire, in March 1941. Over the next three months, John Addy flew thirteen missions as second pilot in the crew of a twin-engine Wellington bomber, flying at night and using dead reckoning to navigate their way to their targets.

In June 1941, having successfully completed a number of training flights, he was promoted to command his own aircraft and crew. Unfortunately, his time as an aircraft captain began inauspiciously, when he was forced to turn back from his first operational sortie, a raid on Duisburg, due to severe technical trouble.

However, Flight Sergeant John Addy went on to command his aircraft on a further twelve missions, attacking targets throughout Germany and northern France, including a raid on Hamburg on 2nd August 1941. Despite his Wellington being severely hit by flak, and the loss of one engine, John managed to nurse the plane home, and made a forced landing. The bomb aimer, Squadron Leader RN Ayles DFC DFM, commented in his logbook:

> The Wellington ran into trouble on the way to Hamburg. Hit by flak at Delmenhorst. Kite holed in 80 places. Jettisoned bombs and returned to make forced landing at Bircham Newton. Port motor cutting on landing.

For his actions that night, and for showing conspicuous bravery throughout his 25 operational flights with 103 Squadron, Sergeant Pilot Addy was awarded the Distinguished Flying Medal (DFM) on 24th October 1941. The citation read:

> Since joining the squadron in March 1941, this NCO has been outstanding by his consistent keenness as his operational record shows. He has, since becoming a captain, only abandoned his mission twice; once by unavoidable engine trouble and, on the second occasion, his aircraft was seriously hit by flak over Delmonhurst and one engine put out of commission.

> On this occasion, Sergeant Addy jettisoned his bombs and by skilful piloting brought his aircraft safely back to Bircham Newton. By his determination in the air and his quiet coolness on the ground, Sergeant Addy sets a particularly fine example to the remaining aircrews of the squadron. I have every confidence in this NCO as a pilot and strongly recommend him for the award of the Distinguished Flying Medal which I consider his fine record deserves.

After completing his tour of duty with 103 Squadron, John Addy was posted to No. 27 Operational Training Unit, based at RAF Lichfield in Staffordshire, where he helped to train bomber crews, mainly from the Commonwealth and, in particular, Australia.

However, despite the boredom of flying up and down the Irish Sea, the training of new crews was not without its risks, and some of the instructors did not survive this 'rest' period away from the front-line.

The Avro Anson was the first low-wing monoplane, with twin engines and retractable undercarriage to enter RAF service. By the outbreak of World War 2, the Anson was deemed to be unsuitable for front-line combat, but was used in large numbers as a multi-engine aircrew trainer, and became a mainstay of RAF crew training.

On the evening of Saturday, 17th January 1942, piloted by Flight Sergeant John Addy, and with a crew of seven on board, Avro Anson N5030 took off from RAF Lichfield on a night navigational and meteorological exercise, including the Isle of Man as one of its waypoints.

The full crew list was as follows:

748538	F/Sgt. John Cedric Addy	DFM RAFVR Pilot
581409	WO Andrew Steel Patterson	RAF Observer
407839	Sgt. Joseph Howe Levett	RAAF Observer (u/t)
403561	Sgt. Nicholas Dan	RAAF Observer/Bomb Aimer
617247	F/Sgt. Henry Johnston	DFM RAF Wireless Operator
R56323	F/Sgt. Edward Carroll McManaman	RCAF Air Gunner
	Mr Glynn Halford Civilian	Meteorologist

Flying across the Irish Sea at an altitude of 1800 feet, the aircraft approached the cloud-covered slopes of Snaefell, on the Isle of Man, which rises to a height of 2,038 feet. At approximately 1940 hrs, the aircraft crashed on the western slope of Snaefell, bouncing along the ground until it hit a rise. Although the crash caused extensive mechanical damage, the aircraft did not catch fire.

However, it was not until 1000 hrs the following day that the alarm was raised, when Sergeant Levett was spotted on a nearby road. He reported that three of the crew were dead, and that three other survivors were sheltering in the wreckage from the snowy weather conditions.

The four men to survive the crash were picked up later that day and admitted to the island's military hospital at Douglas. However, only Sergeant Levett was to survive the war, returning to his native Australia in 1943, having been discharged from the RAAF after being injured in another training accident, near Sheffield.

Two of the men who died on the slopes of Snaefell were Flight Sergeant John Addy and Air Gunner Edward McManaman. They were both laid to rest in the graveyard of St Patrick's Church, in Jurby, on the Isle of Man. The third person to die in the crash was eighteen-year old civilian meteorologist Mr Glyn Halford, who was buried in his hometown of Pontypool, in Wales.

Flight Sergeant John Cedric Addy DFM is commemorated on a war memorial tablet in Greenstead Green Church, and on the CRGS Memorial to the Fallen of the Second World War in the school library.

James Walker Leach

Age: 31
Died: 14th February 1942
Service Number: 1392375
Rank: Leading Aircraftman (Pilot)
Service/Regt: RAFVR
Grave/Memorial: Kidlington Burial Ground, Oxfordshire
Plot/Panel: Ref. Section B, Grave 6

James 'Jim' Walker Leach was born on 10th August 1910 in Hong Kong. His father Robert Walker Leach was a marine engineer who had been born in Singapore in 1883; his mother Alice (née LeFevre) was born in 1886 in Hackney, London. She and Robert were married at St Peter's Church, Alresford, in 1906, before going out to live in the Far East.

James Walker Leach

Jim had two brothers: Robert 'Rob' LeFevre Leach, born in Hong Kong in 1908, and Richard 'Dick' Dennington Leach, born in 1911. A sister, Daphne Geraldine, followed in 1913. All the children were educated at boarding schools in England, with the boys attending CRGS. Jim was admitted in September 1923 from Elmstead Council School. Alice's side of the family owned Fen Farm, Elmstead Market; Jim lived there while at Elmstead School and, while at CRGS, the boys spent school holidays there. Their parents appear to have returned to England to visit them on one occasion, at least.

It is clear from *The Colcestrian* that all the boys were extremely sports-orientated. Like his brothers, Jim was an excellent rugby player and represented the 1st XV. He also played cricket for the 1st and 2nd XIs and invariably competed strongly in the swimming sports, including diving.

He was also a member of the school scouts, part of the 3rd Colchester Scout Troop, and even took part, with success, in a boxing competition.

In 1926 Jim's parents visited England. They returned to the Far East, to Singapore, where they were now living, on the *Kao Mara*, taking Rob, who had already left CRGS, and Daphne back with them. Jim followed after he left the school in 1927.

By the end of that year both Jim and Dick were living with their parents at a house named 'East Anglia', at 6 Oxley Rise, Singapore. Rob's address is given in *The Colcestrian* as being the Sea View Hotel. By 1929 Rob was working for Blunn & Co. an import/export company, in Kuala Lumpur, while Jim was employed on the Raja Musa Estate, Kuala Selangor, in Malaya (north-west of Kuala Lumpur) as the Assistant Manager of a Rubber Plantation. According to relatives, Jim was a keen 'ladies' man' and apparently enjoyed many conquests amongst ex-pats' wives at the tennis club!

6 Oxley Rise, Singapore

The brothers clearly had great affection for CRGS, since throughout the 1930s they all wrote letters back to the school. These were invariably published in *The Colcestrian* and they give an interesting insight into the 'gung-ho' attitude to life of the colonial British in Malaya and Singapore at that time.

A letter from Jim in 1931 finds him playing inter-state rugby for Selangor against Perak A, with Rob on the opposition team (Perak A won 11-8). Jim reports that Rob had also made the full Singapore team, so he was clearly the more talented player. He says, with what seems like boyish enthusiasm: 'Rob, Dick and I are all of the opinion that we have yet to find a game we like better than rugger.'

Another letter, in 1933, sees Rob donating two six-foot long blowpipes to CRGS. They were hung in the Big School (now the Hall) and Rob had composed an informative inscription for the benefit of the students which read as follows:

SAKAI BLOWPIPES

Killing range up to 80 yards
Poison is employed only for killing animals; for birds the darts are left unpoisoned
The darts in this case are not poisoned
The poison is derived from the IPOH tree and is very deadly
The blowpipe barrel is cased by bamboo for protection against heat or accident. The carvings on it are tribal.

Also in 1933, we hear that Jim has an adventurous plan to sail his Chinese junk the 8,000 miles from Singapore to London. A letter from another OC in Singapore, RE Cox (who was to die in a Japanese POW camp) gives a detailed account of what happened. The junk was called the *Soon Lee*; Jim's voyage, which began in February, lasted just three weeks and was plagued by bad weather and near misses with other ships. He and his two companions were forced to give up on reaching Penang, in north-west Malaya, with broken rigging, torn sails, leaks and a sprung mast.

JIM'S JUNK
"SOON LEE"

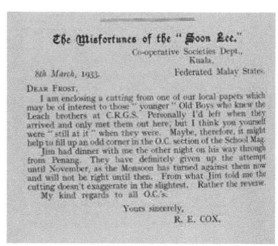

The Misfortunes of the "Soon Lee."

Co-operative Societies Dept.,
Kuala,
8th March, 1933.   Federated Malay States.

DEAR FROST,
    I am enclosing a cutting from one of our local papers which
may be of interest to those "younger" Old Boys who knew the
Leach brothers at C.R.G.S. Personally I'd left when they
arrived and only met them out here, but I think you yourself
were "still at it" when they were. Maybe, therefore, it might
help to fill up an odd corner in the O.C. section of the School Mag.
    Jim had dinner with me the other night on his way through
from Penang. They have definitely given up the attempt
until November, as the Monsoon has turned against them now
and will not be right until then. From what Jim told me the
cutting doesn't exaggerate in the slightest. Rather the reverse.
    My kind regards to all O.C.'s.
                            Yours sincerely,
                                R. E. COX.

The Soon Lee

However, Jim was not the sort to be put off by a few 'minor' problems like these. By 1937 he had hatched a new version of his plan. This time he and another friend, a Mr EJC Edwards, would take a ten-ton yacht, named *Mat Ali* belonging to Edwards, lashed to deck of a steamer, the *City of Derby*, to Port Said at the top end of the Suez Canal. From there, joined by a Mr E Fesq, they would sail it across the Mediterranean, via Greece and some Italian ports, then through France via the canal system, which included 123 locks, to Bordeaux. From there it would be just a short hop into the Channel and across to Mr Edwards' house in Falmouth, Cornwall - and the total sailing distance would now be reduced to a mere 3,100 miles.

Amazingly, the plan succeeded and they completed the journey from Port Said to Falmouth in 74 days. The story was covered by a Singapore newspaper, The *Straits Times*. On 20th August 1937, the paper reported the arrival of the *Mat Ali* in Falmouth and gave an account of the voyage. One of the most ominous sights noted by Jim and his friends was the preparation being made in the Italian ports at which they stopped: many were being fortified and dredged to allow access for battle-cruisers; the people to whom they spoke all believed that war was imminent and put on an outward display of loyalty to Mussolini.

The paper also reported that at Bordeaux Jim was left on his own for a time. Mr Fesq's trip ended there and Mr Edwards could wait no longer to see his wife in England, taking a flight to be with her for a few days, then flying back to Bordeaux to re-join Jim. The two of them then managed to navigate their way through thick fog into the Channel and eventually reached Falmouth, whereupon Jim apparently changed his clothes and caught the first train to London. He is quoted as saying: 'We had a great trip and called at over 30 out-of-the-way ports.' When asked how he was returning to Malaya, he replied, 'I am going to go on the biggest boat I can find. And if there isn't a big one, I'll walk.'

Before he left England, however, Jim made a point of visiting CRGS. *The Colcestrian* of April 1938 records this visit, saying poignantly that 'he felt like a lost soul', though adding, a bit more reassuringly, that he was cheered by seeing Mr Cape, Headmaster during his time at the school, and other members of staff who had known him. We are not told whether he examined the blowpipes donated by Rob which were hanging in the Hall, but we can probably imagine that he would have done so.

The *Straits Times* article reporting his voyage was headed 'NEVER AGAIN, THEY DECLARE'. However, on reflection Jim must have thought that this was not quite the right attitude, as when the newspaper reported his arrival back in Singapore on 23rd December 1937, he is quoted as saying: 'Edwards and I would do it again if we had the opportunity.'

Earlier in 1937, before departing on his epic voyage, Jim had written a long letter to *The Colcestrian* explaining his job in Malaya - the process of manufacturing rubber from latex. Now that he had seen the situation in Europe at first hand, however, he seems to have increasingly turned his mind to the possibility of war and the threat from Japan. In 1938 *The Colcestrian* reports him as being 'a corporal in the machine-gunners'. In June 1941, with Britain now at war with Germany, his brother Dick says in another letter to the magazine: 'you'll be interested to hear that brother Rob drives a tank in his leisure moments, and Jim, I understand, is joining the Air Force at Singapore.'

This was the time when the Japanese had Malaya, and ultimately Singapore, clearly in their sights, so Jim was sent back to England to train as a pilot at RAF Kidlington in Oxfordshire. On 14th February 1942, with his training completed, he embarked on his first solo flight. At some point he lost control of the aircraft. It crashed and he was killed.

Reporting his death, *The Colcestrian* describes him as 'a most courageous person who felt the call to serve his country', telling its readers, 'He was buried with full military honours.' With tragic irony, on the day after he died, Singapore surrendered to the Japanese.

Both his brothers survived the war. Dick was also in the RAF, based in England, while Rob, who had remained in the Far East, spent three and a half years in the infamous Japanese Prisoner of War camp at Changi in Singapore, during which time he kept a diary written on Red Cross parcel wrappings. After his liberation, he was re-united with his wife and children in Perth, Western Australia, where his parents had also taken refuge (though his father had died in 1942). He was awarded the DCM for having rescued Australian soldiers, including a senior officer, pinned down by the Japanese. He had used his armoured car as a shield for them to retreat behind and went in under fire several times to get them all out. He returned to Malaya in 1946, and by 1953 was again writing to *The Colcestrian,* this time on the subject of the Communist insurgency there. Dick appears to have stayed in England and died in Eastbourne in 1995.

Robert Humphrey Page

Age:	30
Died:	15th February 1942
Rank:	Captain
Service/Regt:	British Overseas Airways Corporation
Grave/Memorial:	Runnymede Memorial
Plot/Panel:	Reference Panel 288

(Robert) Humphrey Page was born on 27th October 1911, the only child of Robert Page, 55, a farmer from Clacton and Margaret May Page, née Moult. She had been born in Manchester and, at 26, was almost 30 years younger than her husband. The 1901 census records her as a sixteen-year-old Assistant and Teacher at The Convent, Grange Road, Beccles, so it appears that she may have been preparing for life as a nun when she met and married Robert.

Robert Page was a prosperous farmer – he and Margaret had two servants at the time of the 1911 census, just before Humphrey's birth. In the 1860s and 1870s, Robert's father, also a farmer, employed between 20 and 25 men and boys on his farm.

Humphrey Page attended the Pre at CRGS from 1919, entering the Senior School as a boarder in May 1922. By then his father had retired and the family were living at 'The Gables', Tendring. Humphrey's interests at CRGS seem to have been mainly athletic. *The Colcestrian* records him successfully participating in cross-country running and steeple-chases, and at Sports Days he had success in relays and the half-mile. He was also a member of the scouts and captained the School House junior rugby team.

On leaving CRGS in April 1925, Humphrey Page went on to the Royal Nautical College at Pangbourne, before changing tack and switching to Cranwell RAF College. While serving with the RAF No. 97 Squadron in 1936 he had a remarkable escape when his aircraft crashed into the sea. It was the early hours of the morning of 19th February and his Heyford biplane bomber was running very low of fuel during a training exercise in low cloud off the Northern French coast. Despite circling the area, Flight Officer Page was unable to find anywhere to land and so was forced to ditch in the Channel, off Sainte-Adresse, near Le Havre. The plane struck the water close to the shore, about 250 yards from the Regatta Palace. The noise of the crash could easily be heard by the local population.

Two local men, M. Tanguy, a well-known swimmer, and M. Grieu, the chief pilot of the Havre Aero Club, went to the aid of the crew in a canoe. Cars in the area drew up with their headlights on to help. When they reached the plane, it had already started to sink, but all four crew were still alive. They reached Humphrey Page first and were able to pull him from the water, but the canoe then overturned and all three men had to swim ashore. This meant that they were unable to rescue the other three crew, who all disappeared, presumed drowned, while trying to swim to safety.

The incident was widely reported in the press and prompted questions in Parliament. The Under-Secretary for Air told the House of Commons that the aircraft had been in communication with the Andover Wireless Station throughout and, because of the conditions, had been given bearings to return to Northolt rather than its own base at Boscombe Down. He also stated that pilots needed to be given more training in low cloud conditions.

Later in 1936 Humphrey left the RAF to join the civil airline, Imperial Airways Ltd. In 1939 Imperial was merged with British Airways to form BOAC (British Overseas Airways Corporation), the new state passenger airline. BOAC continued to operate during the war, despite the threat from enemy action – not least because of the continuing need to transport important civil and military personnel around the globe. Capt. Humphrey Page flew both the Empire Service to various points in Africa and Asia and the Atlantic Ferry Service to the US and Canada.

Ironically, however, it was not enemy fire which was to be his nemesis. On 15th February 1942 he was flying a BOAC B-24 Liberator, with five crew and four passengers, non-stop from Cairo to England. Because of strong headwinds, the normal approach for friendly aircraft, via the Bay of Biscay around Brittany and approaching the Channel from the west, would have meant running out of fuel. Humphrey Page therefore suggested the more daring plan of flying directly across Europe by night. The Air Ministry in London approved the route, RAF Transport Command were against it, while BOAC appeared to be in favour. On 14th February Humphrey Page asked BOAC to confirm its position and, after receiving no reply, made the fateful decision to go ahead.

At 0813 hrs on the morning of 15th February, the aircraft entered the Channel near St. Malo, initially registering as 'hostile' on British radar screens. Two Polish Spitfire pilots, based in Exeter, were sent to investigate. At that time there were not many B-24 Liberators around. The pilots presumed it to be a four-engine Focke-Wulf 200, and further suspicions were aroused when one of them saw a bright flash coming from a glass turret and the aircraft turned and dived into a cloud.

Both Spitfires opened fire, hitting the Liberator's starboard engine and sending it crashing into the sea. The time was 0850 hrs. Just eleven minutes earlier, but unbeknown to the Spitfire pilots, its identification status had been changed to 'friendly'. The Liberator was just five miles from the Eddystone Lighthouse near Plymouth. All nine crew and passengers were lost without trace.

Among the passengers was Lt. Col. Townsend 'Tim' Griffiss, a senior USAAF Officer. He had been seconded to London in 1941 on the staff of General James Chaney, coordinating US military co-operation with the UK on the assumption that the US would at some point join the war. Having worked on the implementation of the crucial 'lend/lease' deal of 1940, by which Britain leased some of its military bases to the US in return for the loan of 50 US destroyers, and the strategically vital US occupation of Iceland, he was now returning to London, via Tehran and Cairo, from the USSR, where he had been discussing sending US-built aircraft to the Soviets via Alaska and Siberia, rather than on Artic convoys from the UK.

Griffiss, now a 'forgotten hero' of WW2, was the first USAAF airman to be killed in the war. Before his posting to London, he had been, from 1935-38, Assistant Military Attaché in France, Spain and Germany. This allowed him to observe the Spanish Civil War - seen as a testing-ground for the military technology that would decide the next world war. His detailed despatches provided crucial information about the new German planes, and helped to dispel the then fashionable theory that powerfully armed 'flying fortress' bombers could win a war by themselves.

Such was Griffiss's stature that the British HQ of the USAAF, set up in the summer of 1942, was named 'Camp Griffiss'. The circumstances of his death were a major embarrassment for the UK Air Ministry. A Court of Enquiry was set up and placed blame on the Spitfire pilots for their failure to identify Humphrey Page's Liberator as 'friendly'. However, the controllers on the ground, who knew a Liberator would be arriving on a path over occupied France, were also reprimanded for not warning the Exeter fighter sector. The question of why the Liberator was not immediately recognised as a friendly aircraft went unanswered – either its friend-or-foe identification transmitter was not working or had not been turned on. One of the Enquiry's key recommendation stated: 'In view of the important personages carried in civil aircraft, more attention should be paid to the identification of civil aircraft.'

Francis Newton Pope

Age:	25
Died:	20th March 1942
Service Number:	100069
Rank:	Pilot Officer
Service/Regt:	RAFVR
Ship/Unit:	104 Sq.
Grave/Memorial:	Alamein Memorial, Egypt
Plot/Panel:	Reference Column 249

Francis Newton Pope was born on 9th March 1917, the son of Francis Arthur and Minnie Maud Pope, née Newton. His mother came from Halstead, one of four sisters who were all silk weavers, while Francis Arthur Pope was born in Hornsey. For a time in his youth he was an assistant to his uncle, Arthur G Pope, an artist/sculptor who lived and worked in Bournemouth. He then worked for his father, Thomas, a painter and decorator who had moved to 6 Constantine Road, Colchester.

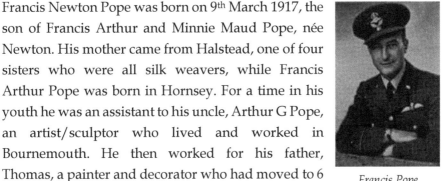

Francis Pope

After marrying Minnie Newton, Francis Arthur Pope sought to improve the family's prospects by becoming an Insurance Agent for the Co-op. Eventually he would become President of the Colchester Co-operative Society. The family moved to 'Kelmscott', Bourne Road, Colchester and were doing sufficiently well by September 1928 to send Francis Newton from Old Heath School to CRGS. He remained at the school until February 1934, passing his Cambridge Local Certificate in July 1933. He then became a pupil to Mr Eves, of Bensusan-Butt, Eves and Co. Chartered Accountants. *The Colcestrian* reports that 'he was keen on sports, and played for the Casuals Tennis Club and the Nomads Cricket Club. One of his favourite pastimes was boating and he spent many hours at Mersea in pursuit of this hobby.'

After passing his final examinations to qualify as a Chartered Accountant, Francis Newton Pope joined the RAF Volunteer Reserve in September 1940. Following training, he received his commission to the rank of Pilot Officer (on probation) on 1st July 1941 and was assigned to 104 Squadron, based in Driffield, Yorkshire. The squadron was equipped with the Vickers Wellington bomber and had begun night bombing operations in May 1941 as part of No. 4 Group RAF.

Vickers Wellington bomber

On 12th September 1941 Francis was involved in an accident when an aircraft he was piloting suffered engine failure at around 1700 hrs. He attempted to force-land the aircraft near Middleton on the Wolds but ran through a number of hedges and ditches and across a road before the aircraft stopped. As a result of this incident Cat.E2/FA damage was recorded.

In October 1941, a detachment from 104 squadron was sent to Luqa in Malta, moving to Kabrit in Egypt in January 1942. Francis was part of this deployment. However, on 20th March 1942 his Wellington (possibly Z8510) was lost off Greece while on a bombing mission He was 25 years old and is commemorated on the Alamein Memorial in Egypt.

Frederick John Finch

Age:	22
Died:	11th June 1942
Service Number:	2341177
Rank:	Signaller
Service/Regt:	Royal Signals
Ship/Unit:	18th (Eastern) Division
Grave/Memorial:	Kranji War Cemetery, Singapore (Originally Changi Cemetery - 3 L/12 017192 B-C-7. re-buried 21.04.46)
Plot/Panel:	Grave 9.B.15

Frederick John Finch was born, near Colchester, on 12th February 1920, the only son of Frederick Donald and Mabel Finch. A younger sister, Margaret, was born five years later.

His early education was at the Inworth Council School, near Tiptree, where his father, himself a former pupil of CRGS, was the schoolmaster. The family were living at 'Mechi House', in Church Road, Tiptree when Frederick entered CRGS, as a day-scholar in Form Upper IIIb, on 17th September 1931. A prize-winning pupil, he left the school, from Form IVb, on 8th April 1936, entering into an apprenticeship with Messrs. Reeman & Dansie, auctioneers and estate agents.

Frederick continued to live with his family until, shortly after the outbreak of war, he joined the Army, where he trained as a signaller in the Royal Corps of Signals. As part of the 18th (Eastern) Infantry Division, Frederick left Britain during October 1941, bound for Egypt.

In early December, the Japanese Empire launched their surprise raid on the US Navy moored in Pearl Harbour, and simultaneously invaded Malaya. The 18th Division having arrived in South Africa, and preparing themselves for the final stage of their journey, were diverted to India, and then sent on to reinforce British forces facing the Japanese in Singapore.

Upon arriving on the island, in late January 1942, the Division was deployed to the north-eastern side, where it was not directly involved in facing the initial Japanese attack. However, after the Japanese established a beachhead in the north-west sector, the Division was split up, and

Roberts Hospital, Changi

deployed piecemeal in the battle, before it regrouped for the final stand in the city of Singapore, repulsing several Japanese attacks, until the garrison was forced to surrender to the Japanese on 15th February 1942.

During the three years of captivity that followed, over one-third of the division's personnel were to die from starvation, ill-treatment, or execution by the Japanese army.

In July 1946, *The Colcestrian* reported that Mr & Mrs Finch had finally received news of their son, who had been reported missing after the fall of Singapore on 15th February 1942. The report indicated that Frederick had been captured by the Imperial Japanese Army at the time of the British surrender, but had then been held in the notorious Changi Camp. There, as with many of his fellow servicemen, he had to suffer appalling conditions, and eventually died, of dysentery, in Roberts' Hospital on 11th June, 1942.

An eye-witness account of the conditions in the hospital, reported:

The battle casualties, some desperately ill, many minus a limb, were quartered on the ground floor, the "less" sick on the upper floors. With the septic system damaged and with no water for flushing anyway, men suffering from dysentery had to stagger down several flights of stairs to an outside latrine...

The report continued: 'Mr Finch has been missed, and will be mourned by a large circle of friends, with whom he was very popular.' Having been initially buried in Changi British Military Cemetery, Frederick's remains were re-interred shortly after the war ended, in the main Kranji War Cemetery, in the north of the island of Singapore.

Kranji War Cemetery (Photo credit: Royal Air Force Changi Association)

Gordon Frederick Studley

Age:	25
Died:	22nd July 1942
Service Number:	1310593
Rank:	Wireless Operator/Air Gunner (Sergeant)
Service/Regt:	RAFVR
Ship/Unit:	55 Sq.
Grave/Memorial:	Tel El Kebir War Memorial Cemetery, Egypt
Plot/Panel:	Ref. 1.M.10

Gordon Frederick Studley was born on 22nd August 1916. His father, Albert, was a grocer and master draper who originally came from East Bergholt. He had started his working life as an errand boy, working his way up to owning and running the general store in Birch. His wife, Gordon's mother, Alice Julia Studley, was the daughter of Frederick Playle of Foundry Farm, Griston, in Norfolk. Gordon had two older brothers, George William, (1912-85) and Richard Ernest, (1914-2004), who both also attended CRGS. Richard emigrated to Queensland, Australia in 1958, where he lived until his death in Brisbane in 2004. The family lived in a house in Birch named 'Gristonia', no doubt after Alice's birthplace.

Gordon attended Birch (C of E) School, then CRGS from September 1928 to July 1932. His parents were supportive of school financially and otherwise. They contributed to the pavilion fund in 1929 and are mentioned in *The Colcestrian* as attending social and other functions.

On leaving CRGS Gordon initially helped in his father's business. He then joined Spencer, Turner and Boldero Ltd, a big linen draper's in London, founded circa 1855 when three independent Master drapers joined together to form one larger firm. From this date on the business expanded rapidly, eventually employing several hundred assistants and needle-women, based at 70 Lisson Grove. However, the drapery business started to decline towards the latter part of the 19th century and to compensate for the loss in trade, Spencer, Turner & Boldero diversified to become wholesale traders in a wide variety of products, including carpets and furniture. The company is last recorded in 1969.

By the late 1930s Gordon was living in a staff hostel at 130 Harrow Road, W2, and was a warehouseman and salesman (of fancy goods). However, in 1940 he left Spencer, Turner & Boldero to join the RAF Volunteer Reserve. Around the same time, he got married to Lena Florence Hawthorn. The couple set up home in Marylebone, London.

In the RAF Gordon trained as a Wireless Operator, then an Air Gunner. He passed out in August 1941 with rank of Sergeant and was sent to 55 Squadron. This was a bomber squadron based at Ismailia in Egypt, which had been patrolling shipping over the Gulf of Suez. When Italy declared war in June 1940, it switched to operations against targets in Libya, participating in the first attack by the RAF on the Italian air force base at El Adem on 11th June 1940, in which eighteen aircraft were destroyed or damaged on the ground, against the loss of just three British planes. In September 1941 it was switched to anti-shipping operations until it was withdrawn from these in March 1942 for conversion from Blenheims to Baltimores. It then returned to its previous bombing role.

Tragically, however, Gordon Studley was killed in a flying accident while on active service in North Africa on 22nd July 1942. During a formation practice exercise, while flying low over the landing ground, the Baltimore, of which he was a crew member, struck the surface and burst into flames. The incident took place at Qassassin, six miles NW of Abu Sueir in Egypt. All four crew were killed.

He is buried at Tel El Kebir Cemetery, Egypt. The inscription chosen by his wife, Lena, and parents reads:

Deep in our hearts your memory is kept,
we who loved you will never forget

He is also commemorated on Birch War Memorial at St Peter's Church, Birch.

A few months after Gordon's death, towards the end of 1942, Lena gave birth to Gordon's posthumous daughter, Gloria.

Patrick Campbell Sayce

Age:	22
Died:	27th July 1942
Service Number:	84331
Rank:	Flying Officer (Pilot)
Service/Regt:	RAFVR
Ship/Unit:	No. 1 (Coastal) Operational Training Unit
Grave/Memorial:	Runnymede Memorial
Plot/Panel:	Ref. Panel 67

Patrick Campbell Sayce

Patrick Campbell Sayce was born on 16th March 1920, son of Claud Nicholson Sayce and Constance Elsie (née Campbell). Patrick had an elder brother, Joseph Ernest, born in 1918 and a sister Constance Hazel, born on 16th February 1915. The family lived at 'St Kilda', Fronks Avenue, Dovercourt.

Patrick's father, Claud, was a seaman who had been born in Melbourne, Australia in 1884. He came over to England, qualifying as a Second Mate in the Merchant Service in 1908 and a ship's Master in 1911. In 1913 he married Patrick's mother, who hailed from West Ham. When the First World War broke out, he joined the Royal Navy, serving on a number of battleships, most notably HMS *Venerable*.

After the war, the family settled in Dovercourt where Claud worked as a nautical pilot. Both Joseph and Patrick attended CRGS. Patrick joined the school from Harwich County High in September 1932 and left in July 1936. He achieved his Cambridge Certificate in 1936 and, perhaps unsurprisingly, appears to have been a strong swimmer.

On leaving CRGS Patrick went to work for an insurance broker. However, this was soon interrupted by the outbreak of war and he followed his brother into the RAF. Joseph was assigned to 151 Squadron, based in North Weald, and survived the war. Their sister, Constance Hazel Sayce, who had been working as a hotel receptionist and bookkeeper in Poole, also did war service for the WRNS in a secretarial capacity, at Belfast, Chatham and even on a delegation to Washington DC.

Patrick joined No. 1 (Coastal) Operational Training Unit. This unit originally started out life as the RAF Coastal Command Landplane Pilots Pool based at RAF Silloth in Cumbria, training crews for landplanes flying Avro Ansons, Lockheed Hudsons, Bristol Blenheims and Bristol Beauforts. However, during April 1940 the unit was renamed to No. 1 (Coastal) Operational Training Unit and before long, with the creation of more OTUs, the unit started to specialise in training Hudson crews.

At some point in 1941/1942 Patrick met and married Jesse Fraser Hepburn in Edinburgh. He may have been attached for a time to an RAF base in the area. She was the daughter of Jean Hepburn, housekeeper at 'Shore House', Kinghorn, in Fife, just to the north of Edinburgh. Jean and Jesse are recorded as making a trip to New York from Glasgow in 1922, when Jesse was barely a year old. They returned in 1924.

As fate was to have it, the marriage between Patrick and Jesse did not last long. On July 27th 1942 Patrick piloted a Mosquito W4067 from RAF Heston in Hounslow on a photographic reconnaissance mission to Bergen and Stavanger in Nazi-controlled Norway. His plane was lost, probably shot down by German Navy anti-aircraft fire, although a Luftwaffe pilot based in the area named Josef Gruber did claim the credit. The aircraft crashed into North Sea off Walcheren in Holland. Both Patrick Campbell Sayce, the pilot, and George Thomas Thornton, the observer, were killed.

Patrick's story, however, does not quite end there. His wife, Jesse, was pregnant at the time of his death and on 15th March 1943 she gave birth to a daughter in Fife, whom she named Denise Patricia Nilsine Campbell Sayce. Denise spent much of her childhood between Wimbledon, London and Dovercourt, Essex where she often stayed with her beloved Gran Sayce. While Denise sadly never met her father, she got to know much about him. She went on to become a successful actress and model in the 1960s (stage name: Fiona Frazer) and rubbed shoulders with much of the London jet set. During this time, she met her husband Ken Mallett. They together moved to his native Toronto, Canada and had two children Tania and Jason (who, apparently, bears a striking resemblance to Patrick).

This scroll commemorates

Flying Officer P. C. Sayce
Royal Air Force

held in honour as one who
served King and Country in
the world war of 1939-1945
and gave his life to save
mankind from tyranny. May
his sacrifice help to bring
the peace and freedom for
which he died.

Photograph courtesy of Jason Mallett, grandson of Patrick Sayce

Eric Alfred Stone

Age:	19
Died:	18th August 1942
Service Number:	C/JX 318777
Rank:	Ordinary Seaman
Service/Regt:	Royal Navy
Ship/Unit:	HM Motor Torpedo Boat 218
Grave/Memorial:	Royal Navy Memorial, Chatham
Plot/Panel:	Panel 58, Column 1

Eric Alfred Stone

Eric Alfred Stone was born on 6th January 1923, the son of Eric Richard and Ivy Florris (née Brown), who had married in 1920. Both his father and grandfather were boat builders, his father having been born in Erith, Kent, on 9th July 1890, before his father moved the family to 13 Lower Park Road, Brightlingsea. According to the 1911 census, the household included two servants, suggesting that they were prosperous.

After their marriage, Eric and Ivy lived at 9 Regent Road, Brightlingsea, before moving to 92 Church Road. After starting his education at the local Methodist School, Eric Alfred Stone entered CRGS as a day-scholar on 18th September 1934. Receiving a partial remission of fees from Essex County Council, he obtained his Cambridge School Certificate before leaving the school on 29th July 1939. As *The Colcestrian* later reported, Eric was 'greatly interested in small boat sailing and often took the wheel in Colne Yacht Club and Brightlingsea Sailing Club Races'. After leaving CRGS, Eric was employed at Barclays Bank in Colchester and, when war broke out 'did good service in the control and report centre of the ARP' (Air Raid Precautions organisation).

Early in 1942, Eric joined the Royal Navy and, after initial training, was assigned to HM Coastal Forces, as part of the crew of HMS MTB 218. A Vosper, 70-foot motor torpedo boat, fitted with three V12 marine engines, and capable of about 37 knots, MTB 218 was armed with two 21-inch torpedo tubes, two 0.5" machine guns, two 0.303" machine guns, and four depth charges. Commissioned on 9th June 1941, MTB 218 was part of the Royal Navy 5th MTB flotilla, based in Dover, patrolling the northern section of the English Channel.

On the night of 17th/18th August, MTB 218 was one of a number of boats based at Dover that took part in a major action off the French coast. Under the overall command of Lieutenant CLG Philpotts, the MTBs spread out along the Dunkirk channel, and sought to attack the enemy convoy as it passed. The plan succeeded, in that an escort vessel and a merchant ship were sunk, but the Royal Navy also lost MTB 43 to enemy gunfire.

HMS Motor Torpedo Boat 218 (NavyPhotos)

MTB 218 was hit, and her engine-room badly damaged, but still her skipper brought her in for another attack. However, as she was taking on water fast, the attack had to be abandoned, and she started to struggle back to port until, finally, the engines flooded and stopped. As MTB 218 drifted helplessly, she struck a mine and blew up, and all six crew were lost, including Ordinary Seaman Eric Alfred Stone, who had been due to sit for a commission just two weeks later.

Sub-Lieutenant Malcolm J Ball, MTB 218's captain, who had previously been awarded the Distinguished Service Cross for his actions while a midshipman on the destroyer HMS *Scimitar* at Dunkirk, would posthumously be 'Mentioned in Dispatches' for the actions of his command that night.

In addition to being commemorated on the Chatham Naval Memorial, and a memorial tile in All Saints' Church, Brightlingsea, Eric's name is also included on the memorial window in the CRGS library.

THE CHURCH ON THE KNOLL

Very many years ago they built
A little church upon an Essex knoll.
A goodly church it was. I liked it well.
It boasted many noble monuments
Of mediæval warriors and their wives.
The armoured knights were clamped in shining metal,
Their hands were clasped in prayer, and at their feet
A bestial abortion vanquished lay.
It was a sign that these brave men
The Cross had borne and battled for the Faith.
Their ladies, sweet and gentle, slept there too,
With folded hands and rosary entwined.
The brasses shone ; the stone was hard and cold ;
The old oak knights shone less, they dully glowed.

The sunlight streamed in from the East,
Golden, flickering through the trees ;
The wooden cover of the ancient font,
With little saints in little spindly nooks,
Was warm with filtering autumn light.
It was a prayerful, hallowed, dusty place.

One night this year the German bombers came
And hurled to earth their God-outraging iron.

The baleful sunlight glowed upon
A shambling low ruin. The tower,
The nave, God's altar, font and
All the good old mediæval men
Were flat upon the earth.
The winter moonlight silver-plates
A grey, deserted, but still prayerful place.

The knoll has lost its church.

J. A. Fitch, 6b.

Poem published in The Colcestrian, December 1940

113

Arthur Gordon Flory

Age:	27
Died:	19th August 1942
Rank:	Acting Lieutenant
Service/Regt:	Royal Navy
Ship/Unit:	HM Motor Launch 291
Grave/Memorial:	Royal Navy Memorial, Portsmouth
Plot/Panel:	Panel 71, Column 1

Gordon Flory

Arthur Gordon Flory, who was usually known as 'Gordon', was born on 16th May 1915, the son of Arthur Edwin Flory, a builder, and his wife Dorothy Rose Jennie (née Cooper), who lived at 'The White House', in Victoria Road, Colchester. Gordon was educated at CRGS Junior School, before moving up into the Senior School on 27th April 1926, as a day-scholar in Parr House.

Gordon joined the school Scout Troop during the Autumn Term 1926 and played an active role in scouting throughout his association with the school. He was also a very good swimmer, achieving success in competitive swimming and diving, as well as being awarded his Royal Life Saving Society Proficiency Certificate & Bronze Medallion, and the OC Memorial Gold Medal for swimming. Gordon also played junior House football

Academically, he showed a great talent for art, regularly passing the annual Royal Drawing Society Examinations, as well as being successful in the School Mathematics Exam. Gordon also regularly appeared in the Chorus for school productions of Gilbert & Sullivan, including appearances in 'The Pirates of Penzance', 'Utopia Limited' and 'Ruddigore'.

Gordon Flory left CRGS on 24th July 1931, and started work helping in his father's building business. In his spare time, he played an active role in the Old Colcestrian Society, especially when it came to swimming competitions against the school, although he was also known to turn out for the OC tug-of-war team. As well as being responsible for founding the 26th Colchester Sea Scout Troop, Gordon also enjoyed sailing, and was a member of the local branch of the Royal Observer Corps.

In March 1940, Gordon Flory found himself in the Royal Navy and, after initial training, he was posted to Southsea, as part of the Royal Navy Patrol Service. There, as he wrote in a letter to *The Colcestrian*, published in December 1940, he found himself serving under another OC, Hervey Benham, undertaking 'experimental minesweeping and mine recovery', and seemingly enjoying his naval career!

THE PATROL SERVICE

18, Sussex Road,
Southsea.
28th November, 1940.

Dear Norman Joscelyne,

HOW very easy it is to ask for news and, under these conditions, how much more difficult to give it. Nevertheless, I will try and tell you in a few words what sort of life we naval "gentlemen" lead, trying at the same time not to provoke the blue pencil.

Long before it was thought the scenes of 1914-18 would again be enacted the sea has had a great fascination for me, so when the time came to discard the grey slacks and sports jacket and don a uniform it didn't take me long to make up my mind as to which service I should enter.

In March I found myself in bell-bottom trousers, in the R.N. Patrol Service—the branch of the Navy which mans the minesweeping trawlers and many patrol yachts—and for a short time was attached to a flotilla in a port a few miles from Colchester. For there our "ship" was ordered down to a port somewhere on the South Coast.

To any fellow with a liking for the sea, I can thoroughly recommend the R.S. for the thing follows from most when

My particular branch of this service deals with experimental minesweeping and mine recovery. One of which knocks all the other branches on the head for interest (and excitement). All of us are aware this war is going to be a battle of science to a large extent, which makes it all the more interesting for us, when we have to try out all the weird and wonderful gadgets the long-haired scientific gentlemen give us to play with.

In the course of carrying out these experiments Jerry invites us to some very delightful creeks and places around our coasts (and sometimes a little further away). The fact these little voyages are so enjoyed is mainly due to the crew consisting of 50 per cent. O.C.s. Rather a high percentage you may very well say. Perhaps I should add our crew numbers four. Hervey Benham, with whom I have done a great deal of yachting (and sea scouting) is the "skipper." My fellow seaman was a sea scouter friend of mine some time prior to our joining up. Having a crew as we have overcomes a great danger of becoming tired of each other's company, as is very easily done on small craft.

115

Gordon writing to The Colcestrian about his naval career

During May 1941, Gordon Flory was selected for a naval commission. He was initially posted to HMS *King Alfred*, a shore establishment at Hove in Sussex, where he met five other OCs – 'Adey', 'Hardy' Frost, Peter Neate, 'Breeze' and 'Paul'. After twelve weeks training at HMS *King Alfred* Gordon Flory emerged as a Temporary Acting Probationary Sub-Lieutenant

Arthur Gordon Flory received his commission into the Royal Navy on 14th August 1941, and was sent to HMS *St Christopher*, the Coastal Forces shore base near Fort William, for operational training. During the training, which lasted several weeks, recruits were trained to operate the different types of high-speed, inshore patrol craft used by the Royal Navy, learning the skills needed to sail them, as well as undertaking such activities as firing torpedoes from MTBs, or live-firing the guns.

As the year drew to a close, Gordon completed his training and, as a full-fledged Sub-Lieutenant, was assigned as 1st Lieutenant, i.e. second-in-command, to Lieutenant James Basil Colegate Lumsden, better known as 'Jimmy', who was the skipper of HM Motor Launch (ML) 291, a Fairmile 'B' Class boat which had been commissioned on 30th September 1941. Over 100 feet in length, a displacement of 85 tons, and a crew of sixteen, ML 291 was capable of sailing at 20 knots. Her main armament was a 3-pounder gun, although she was also equipped with two .303" machine guns for defence.

During the summer of 1942, with the Allies unable to open a Second Front in Europe, it was decided to mount a large-scale raid on the French coast, in order to try and ease the pressure on the Russian Army, being attacked by the Nazis on the Eastern Front. The plan, code-named 'Operation Jubilee', involved Canadian troops, with the support of British commandos, launching an assault on the German defences around the port of Dieppe, in northern France.

On the 18th August 1942, over 6,000 troops, on board a fleet of more than 200 ships, comprised of escort destroyers, coastal forces and landing craft, sailed from ports along the English south coast. The following morning, landings were attempted against heavy defensive gunfire and, while one flanking attack by commandos achieved some success, a second flanking attack failed, as did a frontal assault by tanks.

By midday it was decided that the force should attempt to withdraw. Based on her ship's log, it is believed that, while under constant air attack from the Lufwaffe, ML291 not only opened fire on an enemy trawler, but later steered a passage through a minefield to successfully extract soldiers from Green Beach.

The crew of ML291 also picked up survivors and enemy airmen from the water, whom they transferred to HMS *Berkeley* before returning to search for further survivors. It was during this action that Sub Lieutenant Arthur G Flory was severely wounded and taken on board HMS *Berkeley*.

HMS Berkeley after being bombed at Dieppe

However, during one of the attacks, HMS *Berkeley* was struck by bombs dropped by German Focke-Wulf Fw190s. She sustained two direct hits on her starboard side, forward of the bridge, which broke her back, and damaged her beyond control.

The ship was abandoned, and later scuttled by torpedoes from the escort destroyer HMS *Albrighton*. Seventeen men of the Royal Navy died in the attack on HMS *Berkeley*, including Sub-Lieutenant AG Flory.

The raid on Dieppe resulted in severe casualties, particularly among the Canadian forces, the loss of over 100 RAF aircraft, and the sinking of 33 landing craft, in addition to HMS *Berkeley*. However, the Allies learned important lessons about the difficulties of attempting to take a well-defended port in Occupied Europe, which were used to shape the planning of the Allied landings in Normandy, which took place on D-Day, 6th June 1944.

On 2nd October 1942, *The London Gazette* published an announcement, that Sub-Lieutenant Arthur Gordon Flory had been posthumously awarded a Mention in Dispatches for his actions at Dieppe on 19th August 1942.

Two months later, *The Colcestrian* carried an obituary for Sub-Lieutenant AG Flory, in which it recalled his universal popularity as a Scoutmaster, his efforts in establishing the Mersea headquarters of the Sea Scouts, and his performances in the scout 'Gang Shows'. It concluded by stating that 'he was one of the most promising of the younger leaders, not only in the scout movement, but in the life of Colchester generally, and he will be very widely missed and mourned.'

The sacrifice made by Arthur Gordon Flory is commemorated on the Royal Navy Memorial at Chatham. His loss is also remembered on his parents' grave in Colchester Borough Cemetery.

Herbert Vincent Winch

Age:	31
Died:	28th August 1942
Service Number:	962373
Rank:	Sergeant
Service/Regt:	RAF Volunteer Reserve
Ship/Unit:	44 (Rhodesia) Squadron
Grave/Memorial:	Reichswald Cemetery
Plot/Panel:	Collective Grave 24. C. 12-18

Herbert Winch was born on 9th December 1910, the eighth child of Frederick Clappison Winch and his wife, Lillian Rose Winch, of Colchester, Essex. Frederick Winch (known as 'Clappy') was a Licensed Wines and Spirits Merchant, with a shop in Head Street, Colchester.

Herbert had five older brothers, Wilfred, Harold, Leonard, Donald and Quinton, and two older sisters, Lilian and Olive. Gordon Winch, Herbert's younger brother and fellow CRGS pupil, was born late in 1912.

The family was living in Capel Road when, on 16th September 1921, Herbert was admitted to Form Lower III at the school,

Herbert Vincent Winch

as a member of Parr House. He left CRGS, from the Form Upper V, on 26th July 1929, intending to train for service with the Indian Police.

Of exceptional physique, he was a fine rugby football player, and played regularly for the school First XV, being awarded his colours in 1927, and captaining the team during the next season. The following year, *The Colcestrian* also recorded Herbert's appointment as a School Prefect.

After leaving the school, Herbert joined the Old Colcestrian Society, and continued his rugby career playing for the OCs. However, beside playing rugby, Herbert's other main love was the sea, and his smack-yacht, *Nellie*, which he owned with his younger brother Gordon, and was kept at West Mersea.

Winch family wine and spirit shop, Head Street

For a while, Herbert worked with his father in the family wine and spirit merchant business in Head Street, before sailing to Sydney, Australia on 28th May 1932, on board SS *Orsova*, where Herbert remained for five years, working as a sheep farmer near 'The Rock', in New South Wales.

He returned to England on 20th June 1937, on board SS *Largs Bay*, living again at the family home in Colchester, and working with his father in the wine and spirit business.

After the outbreak of the Second World War, Herbert joined the RAF, qualifying as a Wireless Operator/Air Gunner in the autumn of 1941. He was then sent to No. 16 Operational Training Unit (OTU), based at RAF Upper Heyford in Oxfordshire, for night bomber training, and on 26th December 1941, Herbert was posted to the newly-formed 455 Squadron, at RAF Swinderby in Lincolnshire, which was equipped with the Handley Page Hampden light bomber.

Four months later, 455 Squadron was transferred to RAF Coastal Command and, having completed eight missions with the squadron, on 26th April 1942, Herbert was posted to No. 44 (Rhodesia) Squadron, based at RAF Waddington at Great Steeping in Lincolnshire. While with the squadron, which was the first to convert completely to flying the new, four-engine Avro Lancaster heavy bomber, Herbert flew a further ten missions between May and July 1942, including the first two 'Thousand Bomber' raids, before being rested.

Herbert returned to operations on the night of 27th August 1942, when his aircraft, Lancaster W4124 (KM-D), piloted by New Zealander Russell H Suckling, was part of a force of 306 aircraft which attacked the city of Kassel, in the German industrial heartland of the Ruhr Valley.

There was little cloud over Kassel, enabling the Pathfinder Force (PFF) to illuminate the area well, which led to widespread damage being caused, especially to the south-west of the city. Nearly 500 buildings were destroyed or seriously damaged, including three factories belonging to the Henschel Aircraft Company. A number of military establishments were also hit.

During the attack, it appears that the aircraft was shot down by a Luftwaffe night-fighter, piloted by Oberleutnant Viktor Bauer, of VII/NJG1, and crashed at Haltern, near Munster in Germany, at 0026 hrs on 28th August 1942.

The other crew members of the ill-fated aircraft were:

1259470	Sgt. Edward C. Allen	Air Bomber	age 22
521924	Sgt. Thomas Bickers	Flight Engineer	age 33
R/91312	Flt. Sgt. Allen F. Christie (RCAF)	Air Gunner	age 20
1112721	Sgt. Albert E. Johnson	W.Op/Air Gunner	
1027453	Sgt. Miles Rowbottom	Navigator	age 27
411469	F/O Russell H Suckling	Pilot	age 26

Initially, the crew were buried in the Rheine-Koenigsesch Cemetery, but were re-interred after the war, on 26th March 1947, in Reichswald Forest War Cemetery.

(Both photographs courtesy of Mersea Museum and Pauline Winch)

James Douglas Sargeant

Age:	22
Died:	6th September 1942
Service Number:	656315
Rank:	Sergeant
Service/Regt:	RAF
Ship/Unit:	51 Sq.
Grave/Memorial:	Runnymede Memorial
Plot/Panel:	Reference Panel 93

James ('Jim') Douglas Sargeant was born on 6th October 1919, son of Nelson Sargeant and May Alice (née Bennell), of 10 Capel Road, Colchester. Nelson was born in Workington, Cumberland in 1887, though by 1911 he was boarding at 151 Butt Road, Colchester, and working as a clerk in the Town Clerk's Office. May Bennell lived at 24 Rawstorn Road, Colchester, and worked as a milliner. Her father, Charles, was a stonemason. Nelson and May married in 1913 and had two children, with Peter Charles following Jim in 1923.

Jim came to CRGS from St John's Green Council School in April 1931 and left at the end of September, 1936. He passed his Cambridge School Certificate and was a keen cricketer who played for the 1st and 2nd XIs, as well as for the OCs against the school after leaving. By then he was working as a clerk for the Essex and Suffolk Fire Insurance Society in the High Street.

Following the outbreak of war, Jim joined the RAF Volunteer Reserve. *The Colcestrian* of July 1941 records him as a Leading Aircraftman with the RAF, and suggests he was in Canada for some time at least, maybe for training and possibly to bring US-built planes over to Britain. He was assigned to 51 Squadron, which for most of the war acted as a night bomber unit as part of Bomber Command, and promoted to Sergeant. In February 1942, the squadron was used to carry British paratroops on their first raid on occupied France. Then, from May to October 1942, it was loaned to Coastal Command to fly patrols over the Bay of Biscay against German U-boats.

On 6th September 1942 Jim Sargeant was among the crew of an AW 38 Whitley bomber, Z9387, which set off from RAF Chivenor in Devon on an anti-submarine patrol over the Bay of Biscay. At 1926 hrs the plane disappeared completely. No trace of it was ever found and eventually all those on board were presumed to have been killed in action.

Jim Sargeant was 22 years of age. He is commemorated on both the Essex and Suffolk Fire Office and the Colchester Town Hall War Memorials. His brother, Peter, served in the Royal Navy during the war and survived. However, there was some confusion on the part of *The Colcestrian* which on more than one occasion reported him as being long-term missing. This was much to the annoyance of his father who wrote to the magazine in 1944 to set the record straight.

"Essex and Suffolk" Fire Office's Dedication Tablet: Centre.
Colchester Town Hall, Essex. *Courtesy/© of Heather Anne Johnson.*

Dennis Wilford Willsmore

Age:	23
Died:	1st October 1942
Service Number:	6018275
Rank:	Rifleman
Service/Regt:	King's Royal Rifle Corps
Ship/Unit:	1st Battalion
Grave/Memorial:	Alamein Memorial, Egypt
Plot/Panel:	Reference Column 68

Dennis Wilford Willsmore was born on 11th October 1918, the son of Wilford Willsmore, a Police Constable, of 5 Claudius Road, Colchester. Wilford was from Layer-de-la Haye, and in 1911 at the age of 26 and already in the Police Force, he married Alice Rose Mallett. She was a servant in the home of Elizabeth Ann Smythies of 55 Lexden Road, Colchester, wife of Palmer K Smythies, a retired naval captain.

Dennis had two older brothers, Clifford William, born in 1912, who would become a mechanical engineer, and Leslie Reuben, born in 1915, who was to be a commercial clerk. Their father, Wilford, left the Police to join the Grenadier Guards during WW1, returning to the Force after the war. Alice and he continued to live on Claudius Road during Wilford's retirement, and until their deaths in 1952 and 1953, respectively.

Dennis came to CRGS from Canterbury Road Council School in September 1930. He received total exemption from fees from Essex LEA, so must have been academically able. He also had an interest in horticulture; he was a member of the CRGS Horticultural Society and received a number of prizes in 1932 for the vegetables he grew.

Dennis left CRGS in July 1935, having passed his Cambridge School Certificate. The Admissions Register states under 'Occupation on Leaving': 'Nothing at present, hoping for a Clerkship under Colchester Corporation'. This, however, appears not to have materialised and instead he joined the staff of Barclays Bank at Walton-on-the-Naze.

Following the outbreak of war, Dennis joined the 1st Battalion of the King's Royal Rifle Corps. This battalion was deployed to North Africa and saw action throughout the Western Desert Campaign as part of the 7th Armoured Division. Initially the Division helped stave off Italian attacks on Egypt, then advanced into Libya to take Tobruk. By 1942, however, Axis forces were revived under Rommel and his Afrika Korps.

Dennis almost certainly fought in the Battle of Gazala, 26th May to 30th June 1942. This was an attempt to hold the advance of the Rommel's forces, in which the 1st Battalion of the King's Royal Rifles fought throughout. However, the Allies were now in retreat. Tobruk finally fell to Rommel on 20th June, with the Eighth Army falling back to Alamein on 3rd July to await his final attack.

Rommel launched this attack on the night of 30th/31st August. However, after three days of intensive fighting with heavy losses, all attacks were foiled. General Montgomery counter-attacked on 3rd September and severe fighting continued until the 7th, when the Allied front was re-established and the battle then stopped. The 1st Battalion was fighting on the southern flank of this battle from the first to the last, delaying the enemy advance and then harassing their retreat.

Dennis Willsmore died on 1st October 1942, so he did not live to take part in Second Battle of Alamein, later that month, which finally ended Rommel's hopes of wresting control of Egypt from the British. *The Colcestrian* records that, before his death, 'he had previously been wounded', presumably at some point in the fighting which ended on 7th September. He was 23 years old at the time of his death.

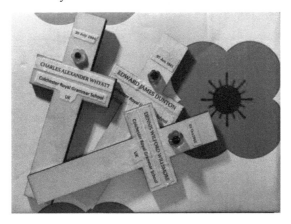

Philip Edward Gerald Sayer

Age:	37
Died:	21st October 1942
Rank:	Flying Officer (Chief Test Pilot)
Service/Regt:	Reserve of Air Force Officers (Class A)

Gerry Sayer was born in Colchester on 5th February 1905. He was the only son of Wing Commander Edward James Sayer MC and his wife, Ethel Jane (née Hellyar), from Cornwall. He had two sisters, Ethel Gwendoline (known as Gladys) who was a year older, and Ghita Alice, three years younger. In 1911 the family were living in 'Alexandrich', Irvine Road, Colchester, close to the CRGS playing fields.

Gerry came to CRGS as a day-scholar in January 1915, from the Wesleyan School. The family were now living at 44 North Hill, Colchester. (Just a few years later, in 1923, the remains of a Roman mosaic floor were unearthed in the garden of this house). His father, a Lieutenant in the Essex Yeomanry, was serving in WW1 at the time. In 1917 Gerry became a boarder and, as the war ended, the rest of the family moved to India where his father was now stationed with the rank of Major. During the school holidays, Gerry lived in digs in Head Street. He left in December 1920 to join the rest of his family and complete his education at St Joseph's College, Nainital, in India.

The Colcestrian describes him as 'well remembered by both masters and pupils of that time. He was very popular and well liked.' The Headmaster, Harry Cape, described him as a good all-rounder; a good footballer and a keen cricketer, whose hobby was science, especially physics.

With his education completed, Gerry initially had the desire to go to Sandhurst. However, he switched to the Royal Air Force, which he joined on 30th June 1924, and was granted a short service, five-year commission with the rank of probationary Pilot Officer. Posted to No. 29 Squadron, based at RAF Duxford, Cambridgeshire, he was promoted to Flying Officer on 30th March 1926. He learnt to fly in an Avro 504K and later flew Sopwith Snipes, before becoming a test pilot at RAF Martlesham Heath, Suffolk, the home of the Aeroplane and Armament Experimental Establishment.

In January 1929, Gerry became engaged to May Violet Ellen Wallace-Smyth, daughter of the vicar of Bures. They were married on 7th June 1930 at Holy Innocents Church, Lamarsh. In the following year, the couple had a daughter, June.

Gerry was transferred to the Reserve of Air Force Officers (Class A) on 2nd March 1929 to become second test pilot with Hawker Aircraft, assistant to Group Captain PWS (George) Bulman (who first flew the Hurricane on 6th November 1935). In 1930 he competed in the 1930 King's Cup Air Race, averaging 108.4 miles per hour over the course and coming in 23rd place.

In 1934 Hawker took over the Gloster Aircraft Company and Gerry was appointed chief test pilot in the November of that year. He tested Gladiators, Hurricanes and Typhoons. On 2nd March 1937 on completion of service, he relinquished his reserve commission and was permitted to retain his rank.

On 15th May 1941 at 1945 hrs, Gerry took off from RAF Cranwell, near Sleaford, Lincolnshire in the Gloster E28/39 (W4041/G) powered by the W1 engine and flew for seventeen minutes at over 500 miles per hour, impossible for other aircraft at the time in level flight. This constituted the first successful flight in a jet-propelled plane, though his first actual flight in the E28/39 had consisted of some short hops of between 100 and 200 yards at Hucclecote on the 7th April 1941 while the aircraft was still fitted with its first W1X (Taxi only) engine. Over the next thirteen days Gerry completed a further ten hours of test flights at altitudes up to 25,000 feet with the longest of just under an hour with its maximum load of 81 gallons. His Gloster aircraft has been in the Science Museum since 1946.

Gerry Sayer was awarded the OBE in the 1942 New Year's Honours List for his work with the Gloster company. However, on 21st October 1942 he set out from RAF Acklington, Northumberland, in a Hawker

Typhoon and accompanied by another Typhoon, to carry out tests of a gunsight involving gun-firing into the Druridge Bay Ranges. Neither aircraft returned, and it was assumed that they had collided over the bay. His replacement as Gloster's test pilot, Michael Daunt, said of him:

> 'As a test pilot he was one of the foremost in the country. He had a terrific ability of being able to fly extremely well and smoothly, but he had also the type of orderly brain that never misses a detail.'

Linocut.   D. Garwood, Vb.

From The Colcestrian, July 1943

Horace Ian Coe

Age:	24
Died:	9th November 1942
Service Number:	D/SR 934
Rank:	Leading Seaman
Service/Regt:	Royal Navy
Ship/Unit:	HMS *Cromer*
Grave/Memorial:	Plymouth Naval Memorial
Plot/Panel:	Panel 63, Column 3

Horace Coe was born on 30th October 1918, at Swaffham in Norfolk, the elder of two sons of Francis Clifford and Margaret 'Peggy' Coe (née Ribbands). Horace's younger brother, William Richard Coe, was born on 11th January 1926, and later also attended CRGS, before enlisting in the Royal Engineers, and training as an armourer.

When Horace was admitted to CRGS as a day-scholar on 17th January 1933, the school Admissions Register noted that he had previously been educated at Eye Grammar School, and that the family lived in Frinton-on-Sea, Essex, where Francis Coe was a postmaster.

Horace passed the Cambridge School Certificate examination in July 1935, and again in December the same year. He left CRGS on 14th March 1936, joining the Old Colcestrian Society, and working in the Accounts Section of Frinton Urban District Council. When war started, Horace soon enlisted, joining the Royal Navy in October 1939. Although the list of OC members' addresses in the December 1939 issue of *The Colcestrian* still gives the family home in Frinton-on-Sea as a correspondence address, it does reflect his new status in the Royal Navy.

After Horace completed his training, some of which was spent at HMS *Iron Duke*, a decommissioned battleship being used as a base ship at Scapa Flow, he served or a while on the newly-built battleship, HMS *Duke of York*, before volunteering for service on the minesweeper HMS *Cromer* (J128).

In December 1941, HMS *Cromer* was among eight 'Bangor' class minesweepers transferred from the 9th Minesweeping Flotilla to the 14th Flotilla, based at Rosyth, with responsibility for keeping the North Sea clear of mines, and ensure the safe passage of convoys from the Thames Estuary as far north as Aberdeen.

While he was deployed in Scotland, Horace became friendly with a young Wren (member of the Women's Royal Naval Service) and, on 2nd February 1942, married 23-year-old Beatrice Eveline Esson White, at St Andrew's Cathedral in her hometown of Aberdeen. A month after the wedding, however, the 14th Minesweeping Flotilla was transferred to the Mediterranean Fleet, due to the number of Royal Navy ships lost in the defence of Crete and Greece, and the need to provide anti-submarine convoy defence in support of the garrisons on Malta and at Tobruk.

HMS *Cromer*, with Horace on board, initially sailed to Gibraltar, but was then re-routed via the Cape of Good Hope and the Red Sea. On their arrival at Durban, in South Africa, HMS *Romney, Cromer, Cromarty* and *Poole* were detached from the Flotilla, assigned to provide the Eastern Fleet with minesweeping support in the Indian Ocean, especially during 'Operation Ironclad' – the seizure of the port of Diego Suarez, near the northern tip of the island of Madagascar.

The landings, on 5th May 1942, were part of the British campaign to capture Vichy French-controlled ports on the island, in order to deny them to the Imperial Japanese Navy and prevent a threat to the Allied shipping routes. During the operation, the minesweepers cleared mines in Amararata Bay and Courier Bay, to ensure a safe anchorage for the disembarkation of troops from Landing Ships.

Once released from 'Ironclad', the four minesweepers sailed to Kilindini, a port on the Kenyan coast, which became their base for the next four months, as they provided convoy defence in the Indian Ocean. On 22nd September 1942, the four ships left Kilindini, and set sail for Egypt.

They arrived in Aden, at the entrance to the Red Sea, on Monday 5th October, and soon re-joined the 14th Flotilla base at Alexandria. From there they carried out minesweeping duties off the Egyptian and Libyan coasts, to ensure the safe passage of supply convoys supporting Allied forces in the Western Desert, and especially the garrison at Tobruk.

On 9th November 1942, HMS *Cromer* sailed from Alexandria, accompanied by HMS *Cromarty* and HMS *Boston*, to clear the route for a coastal convoy heading for the port of Bardia, in Eastern Libya, and particularly the approaches to Mersa Matruh. The flotilla later reported having swept up 46 mines in that one day.

Unfortunately, at 1715 hrs, HMS *Cromer* detonated a magnetic mine at position 31°27'N, 27°16'E, 46 nautical miles west of Mersa Matruh, which was floating just below the surface, having been laid four months previously by the destroyers *Antonio Pigafetta* and *Giovanni da Verazzano*, as part of an Italian minefield in the area.

Although HMS *Cromarty* and *Boston* were able to rescue four officers and 32 ratings, nine of whom were seriously wounded, the loss of HMS *Cromer* resulted in 43 other members of the crew being declared 'Missing, Presumed Killed'.

Among those who perished was Leading Seaman Horace Ian Raymond Coe, leaving his wife (who died in 2000, having never remarried), his parents and brother to mourn their loss. Having no grave but the sea, Horace is commemorated on the Plymouth Naval Memorial, and on the stained-glass commemorative window in the CRGS library.

From The Colcestrian, December 1941

Robert Ray Sargent

Age:	22
Died:	20th November 1942
Service Number:	121372
Rank:	Flying Officer (Pilot)
Service/Regt:	RAF
Ship/Unit:	254 Sq.
Grave/Memorial:	Runnymede Memorial
Plot/Panel:	Reference Panel 67

Robert Ray Sargent was born in 1920, the son of Robert and Kathleen Ray Sargent (née Bentall) of 47 Hedingham Road, Halstead. His father was a solicitor's managing clerk, who had been born in 1862, and was 26 years older than Robert's mother. They were married at St Andrew's Church in Halstead in 1914. Robert had an elder sister, Phyllis, who was born in 1917.

After the outbreak of war, Robert joined the RAF. He trained as a pilot and was assigned to 254 Squadron. This was initially formed as a shipping protection squadron and spent the first part of the war on largely defensive duties. However, on November 16th 1942, 254 Sqn. flew into North Coates, Lincolnshire, to become part of North Coates Strike Wing, along with Squadrons 143 and 236. They were tasked with flying the Beaufighter bomber and the Torbeau torpedo bomber to attack enemy shipping in the North Sea.

The first operation of the Strike Wing took place on 20th November 1942 when Beaufighters from 236 and 254 Squadrons took off to attack a convoy of twelve to sixteen ships heading towards Rotterdam. The weather was poor, the squadrons lost contact with each other and the convoy was protected by Focke-Wulf Fw 190 fighters. As a result, only three enemy ships were damaged. Three Beaufighters were shot down and four so badly damaged that they crashed or made forced landings.

Pilot Officer Robert Ray Sargent's Bristol Beaufighter took off from North Coates at 1505 hrs on 20th November as part of this operation. Just under an hour later it was shot down into the North Sea by ships' flak 8km west of the Hook of Holland. Both crew members, pilot Robert Ray Sargent and his navigator, Sgt. C Heskel, were killed.

From The Colcestrian

Ivan Henry Bland

Age:	19
Died:	27th March 1943
Service Number:	C/JX 355221
Rank:	Ordinary Seaman
Service/Regt:	Royal Navy
Ship/Unit:	HMS *Dasher* (D37)
Grave/Memorial:	Chatham Naval Memorial
Plot/Panel:	Panel 70, Column 2

Ivan Henry Bland was born on 30th August 1923, the son of John Julian Bland and his wife Winifred Maud (née Hocking) of Wellesley Road, Colchester. John Bland had served in the Royal Army Service Corps during the Great War. The CRGS Admissions Register records his occupation as a 'Commission Agent', while the 1939 Register lists him as a 'Cinema Director and Turf Accountant'.

Ivan Henry Bland

One of a band of brothers, who became well-known in local sporting circles, Ivan Bland entered the CRGS Preparatory School (the Pre) for the Autumn term of 1929, transferring to the Senior School on 1st April 1933, as a day-scholar and member of Parr House.

During his time at CRGS, Ivan played a full part in school life, excelling at sport, as well as achieving academic success. He showed himself to be a proficient swimmer, being awarded a Bar to his Royal Life Saving Society Bronze Medallion, and a capable steeplechase runner. He represented the school at cricket and was awarded Full Colours for playing rugby with the First XV. As well as his sporting achievements, Ivan was part of the backstage team for school drama productions and was appointed as Form Rep. and School Prefect.

After leaving CRGS in the first half of 1941, to become a student farmer near Birch, Ivan joined the Old Colcestrian Society, and was an 'ever-present' in the OC rugby XV during the autumn of the same year. A report in *The Colcestrian* indicates that Ivan Bland joined the Royal Navy during 1942, in which two of his brothers, Edwin and Richard also served during the war. Ivan was eventually posted, as an Ordinary Seaman, to HMS *Dasher* - an American merchant ship, which had been converted into an 'Archer Class' escort aircraft carrier and commissioned into the Royal Navy in July 1942.

Having taken part in 'Operation Torch', the Allied invasion of French North Africa, and ferried aircraft in the Mediterranean, HMS *Dasher* returned to the Firth of Clyde in Glasgow in November 1942. In January

HMS Dasher Picture: Royal Navy/PA Wire

1943, having had her flight deck extended, and her air defences improved, *Dasher* returned to active duty with the Home Fleet, at Scapa Flow.

In mid-February, she escorted a convoy to Russia, but had to divert to Iceland, for repairs to the flight deck, which had been damaged by the heavy seas. A few days later, HMS *Dasher* returned to Scapa Flow, disembarked her aircraft, and continued to the Clyde, where new aircraft came on board, and preparations for the next operation began.

On Saturday 27th March, having escorted another convoy earlier in the month, the crew of HMS *Dasher* prepared for a night torpedo strike against the German pocket battleship *Tirpitz*, then at anchor in a Norwegian fjord, by carrying out exercises with her aircraft. Just before 1700 hrs, her newly-appointed captain announced that the day's exercises were complete, and that shore leave would be granted on arrival back at Greenock.

Almost immediately, there was a tremendous explosion, and the ship's two-ton aircraft lift shot 60 feet into the air, falling into the sea behind the ship. HMS *Dasher* lurched, quickly came to a halt as her engines stopped, and started to go down at the stern as she began to take on water. Below decks was plunged into darkness as all electrical power was lost, and thick black smoke and flames poured from the hole where the lift had been.

As the fire in the hangar deck intensified, and ammunition began explode, all those that were able began jumping overboard from anywhere they could reach. Nearby Royal Navy ships responded immediately to the emergency, while other vessels along the River Clyde, rushed to assist in rescuing survivors from the cold waters and the burning oil. Despite the heroic efforts of the rescuers, 379 of the 528 men on board perished.

A cloak of secrecy surrounded the loss of HMS *Dasher*, with survivors being told never to talk of the matter, and details of the incident not being made public until after the war. Recent information indicates that, after the accident, the ship was run aground on Ardrossan North beach, where she remained for a week, before being taken out into the Clyde, and scuttled. To this day, there are unconfirmed reports of a large number of bodies being recovered from the shores of the Firth of Clyde, and buried in a mass grave near Ardrossan, the site of which has yet to be established. With the final resting place of many who died in the incident still unknown, a memorial stone has been erected in Ardrossan to commemorate all those who lost their lives in the sinking of HMS *Dasher*. Meanwhile, the personal sacrifice of Ordinary Seaman Ivan Henry Bland is commemorated on the Royal Navy Memorial at Chatham, and the commemorative window in the CRGS library.

Roy Valentine Whitehead

Age:	30
Died:	30th March 1943
Service Number:	41086
Rank:	Squadron Leader (Pilot)
Service/Regt:	RAF
Ship/Unit:	Photographic Reconnaissance Unit
Grave/Memorial:	Brookwood Military Cemetery, Surrey
Plot/Panel:	Ref. 23.B.13

Roy Whitehead
(courtesy of unithistories.com)

Roy Valentine Whitehead was born on 8th January 1913 in Portsmouth. His father, Ambrose Smith Valentine Whitehead, had been born in 1867 in Walton-on-the-Hill in Liverpool, and was an engineer in the Royal Navy from 1890 to 1902. His occupation after that is not clear, but within a few years he had married the much younger Elizabeth Williams, born in Dunedin, New Zealand on 2nd May 1886. They lived at 4 North End Avenue, Portsmouth, though on the day of the 1911 census Ambrose was absent from the family home. This might suggest that his work still involved travelling. The census records Elizabeth, a son, Noel Ambrose Whitehead, then aged six months, who was Roy's older brother, and a domestic servant. A sister, Nora, was born on 18th February 1912,

The family moved to 15 Lower Park Road, Brightlingsea, and both Noel and Roy attended CRGS. Roy entered the school in September 1924 from the Wesleyan School, Brightlingsea. He was initially granted total exemption from fees by Essex LEA. However, this was withdrawn in 1928, presumably because his academic performance was not up to scratch – he failed his Cambridge School Certificate twice, in July and December 1929. He was, however, a keen rugby player, and his record suggests a lively, intelligent student who was perhaps not really motivated by academic studies.

The CRGS Admissions Register states that, at the time of his leaving the school in June 1930, he was on the waiting list for a post at the British Petroleum Company (BP). However, this may not have materialised, as *The Colcestrian* records that he went to work for Stanford & Son, Auctioneers and Estate Agents in Colchester. In October 1937 Roy's father, Ambrose, died at the age of 70. The family were now living at 66 Ladysmith Avenue, Brightlingsea.

The following year, 1938, Roy joined the RAF. By 1939 his mother, Elizabeth, had moved away from Essex. She was living off her private means in a house named 'Mersea', on The Avenue, Durham, with Roy's sister, Nora.

Asleep in the Officers' Mess: Roy Whitehead in the centre.
Courtesy of lionsroarmagazine.com

Following the outbreak of war, Roy was flying bombers. In December 1941, *The London Gazette* records his award of the DFC and he became a Squadron Leader. RAF life seems to have suited him well. In 1942 he married Joan Mary Jones, who came from Oxford, the marriage being registered there in the second quarter, April-June. They had a child 'Joey', born before Roy's death.

His mother appears to have moved again, this time to Surrey, as *The Colcestrian* of July 1943 records that:

> 'Mrs E Whitehead, of 'Shatsford', Firwood Drive, Camberley had been informed of the death of her son, Squadron Leader Roy Valentine Whitehead DFC, killed in action. On leaving CRGS, Roy had gone to work for Messrs. Stanford & Son, auctioneers and estate agents. His forceful personality and cheery disposition had gained him a host of friends in Colchester and the surrounding district. He had been keen on rugger and other games, and had joined the RAF in 1938.'

The *Essex County Standard* describes him as 'a rugby player of local reputation.'

In December 1943 Roy's brother, Major Noel Whitehead, serving in the Far East wrote to *The Colcestrian* about Roy:

> 'After flying bombers right through the Battle of Britain and long thereafter, he went to the PRU (Photographic Reconnaissance Unit) on Super Spitfires, with no guns. A grand job. In 1943 he became test pilot on super first aircraft for PRU work at Farnborough. He was killed instantly on 30th March 1943 when his Super Spitfire crashed on take-off in very bad weather.'

During WW2, Farnborough airfield was run by the Royal Aircraft Establishment (RAE) and used for the testing and development of new aircraft, and this was Roy's new role. In fact, Roy's plane crashed at RAF

Benson in Oxfordshire, as it took off to return to Farnborough. He encountered severe down-draught in the course of a low-level circuit of the airfield and one of the wings hit a hut. The plane crashed onto others on the ground belonging to 542 Squadron, with the result that F/Lt BJ McMaster DFC and LAC Bedford who were on the ground were both killed, along with Roy Whitehead himself. The plane was burnt out and an aircraft of 542 Squadron was also slightly burnt. In his letter to *The Colcestrian*, Noel Whitehead seems to have confused this (BJ) McMaster with a (WW) McMaster who had attended CRGS, stating: 'I hear that MacMaster (sic), who was a great friend of Roy's, another OC and DFC whom I knew well, was watching Roy take off and was killed instantly by a piece of Roy's aircraft which flew off and struck his head'. (This may well be the reason why the name of WW McMaster is erroneously recorded on the CRGS WW2 memorial window in the library.)

Noel Whitehead survived the war, and went on to work for Shell, becoming a senior executive for International Sales. He retired to Mersea, and in 1967-68 was President of the Old Colcestrian Society. He lived at 'Tideways', 4 Rosebank Road, West Mersea until his death in 1983.

Leonard Roy Cunningham

Age:	23
Died:	11th April 1943
Service Number:	643601
Rank:	Sergeant (Air Gunner)
Service/Regt:	RAF
Ship/Unit:	75 Squadron (NZ)
Grave/Memorial:	Rheinberg War Cemetery, Germany
Plot/Panel:	Plot 18, Row E, Collective Grave 4 -7

Leonard Roy Cunningham was born on 22nd September 1919, and appears to have been the only child of Leonard B Cunningham, a shopkeeper, and his wife Gertrude Florence (née Flynn), who had married in Kingston, Surrey in the autumn of 1912.

In late 1925, Leonard's mother married again, in Wandsworth, London, to Ernest William Oxenbury. Having previously been educated at the Selhurst Grammar School for Boys, in Croydon, and with the family having moved to 'The White House', on East Hill, Colchester, Leonard entered CRGS on 17th January 1933, as a day-scholar in Form Lower IVᴮ. Unfortunately, Leonard's time at CRGS was all too brief, and he left the school on 7th October 1933. However, he must have created an impression, because in an address in December 1944, his name was among those that the Headmaster asked his audience to remember as having been missing for some time.

Available records reveal almost nothing of Leonard's life in the intervening ten years, until his appearance as an RAF Air Gunner in the crew captained by Sergeant John Webb among the aircrew of 75 Squadron (NZ). This squadron, which was constantly engaged against Germany from 1940 to VE day and flew more sorties than any other Allied heavy bomber squadron, consisted almost entirely of New Zealand personnel. The squadron was based at RAF Newmarket, and equipped with Short Stirling III, four-engine heavy bombers, which it flew from a grass strip on the famous Rowley Mile Racecourse.

The squadron Operational Record Book (ORB), and a website dedicated to the memory of those who flew with the unit, record three missions flown by the Webb crew during April 1943.

On their first mission, the Webb crew took off from RAF Newmarket at 2040 hrs on 4th April 1943, flying Stirling III W7513 'AA-G' on a raid against targets in Kiel. On this occasion, four of the crews were forced to return early due to engine trouble. With Kiel completely obscured by cloud, the remaining five aircraft successfully bombed the target, despite opposition from enemy searchlights and heavy anti-aircraft fire.

Four days later, the Webb crew took off from Newmarket in Stirling III BF337, as one of nine aircraft sent to attack Duisburg with 1,000-lb bombs. Four of the aircraft returned to base early, due to severe icing conditions, which prevented them from gaining height.

However, despite electrical storms and rain, the remaining aircraft braved heavy enemy anti-aircraft fire, and successfully bombed the target through 10/10ths cloud, with large fires visible below the cloud. The Webb crew returned safely to Newmarket, landing at 0035 hrs on 9th April 1943.

On their last mission, the Webb crew, flying Stirling III BF456 'AA-J', took off from RAF Newmarket at 0006 hrs on 11th April 1943, as one of twelve detailed to attack Frankfurt. Three of the squadron's aircraft were forced to return early, as they were unable to maintain height.

Eight crews reported that they had successfully dropped their bombs in the target area, which was obscured by thick cloud. On this occasion the enemy anti-aircraft fire and searchlights were ineffective.

Stirling III BF456 'AA-J', flying at an altitude of about 16,000 feet above the town of Bacharach in the Rhine Valley, was intercepted at about 0135 hrs GMT by a Messerschmitt Bf 110 night fighter, flown by Luftwaffe pilot Lieutenant Heinz-Martin Hadeball of 12./NJG 4. The Stirling, captained by Sergeant Webb, crashed near the village of Steeg, just south of Bacharach, killing all on board.

The crew were originally buried in Rheinböllen Cemetery, but were re-interred on 2nd April 1948 in Plot 18, Row B of Rheinberg War Cemetery, eleven miles NW of Duisburg (picture below).

Herbert Donald Dixon

Age:	29
Died:	16th April 1943
Service Number:	125643
Rank:	Flying Officer (Bomb Aimer)
Service/Regt:	RAF Volunteer Reserve
Ship/Unit:	78 Squadron
Grave/Memorial:	Roye New British Cemetery, France
Plot/Panel:	Plot 1, Row AA, Grave 16

Herbert Donald Dixon was born on 18th September 1913, the son of Reverend Herbert Henry Dixon, and his wife Jessie Maud (née Dixon). Rev. Dixon was Master of Grenville House at Dulwich College, where he had begun teaching in September 1909, later becoming an officer in the College's Officer Training Corps and reaching the rank of Captain in 1924.

Herbert Donald Dixon was educated at Dulwich College from 1927 to 1932, before going up to Magdalen College, Cambridge, where he gained a 2nd Class Honours Geography Tripos degree, before spending a further year training as a teacher at Oxford University.

Herbert worked at CRGS for three weeks in January and February 1937. He then taught in the Junior department of Felsted School throughout the Summer Term, before officially joining the CRGS staff on 1st September 1937. He soon gained a reputation as 'a highly-strung Scripture-cum-Geography Master', and was given the nickname of 'Tusker'.

While at the school, as well as being Assistant House Master for School House, Herbert took a keen interest in games, becoming Assistant

Scoutmaster and Cubmaster in the school Scout Troop. *The Colcestrian* also reported his involvement in stage managing and prompting for the school production of 'A Midsummer Night's Dream' in March 1939. At the end of the Summer Term in 1940, Herbert Dixon became the ninth master to leave the school to serve in the Armed Forces, when he joined the RAF.

Having completed his initial Flying Training in America, Sergeant Herbert Donald Dixon returned to the UK, was commissioned as a Pilot Officer in the RAF on 5th July 1942, and then posted to an Operational Training Unit (OTU) to become part of a new, five-man bomber crew.

After crews had completed their training together on twin-engine bomber aircraft, such as the Vickers Wellington, or Armstrong Whitley, they were then sent to a Heavy Conversion Unit (HCU). There they were joined by two additional air gunners and trained to fly the four-engine Handley-Page Halifax heavy bomber, before being posted to a front-line squadron to commence active service operations.

Pilot Officer Herbert Dixon was promoted to Flying Officer on 5th January 1943, and was posted to 78 Squadron, based at RAF Linton-on-Ouse in Yorkshire, as part of a Halifax bomber crew, captained by Sergeant William Illingworth.

On 2nd April 1943, the Illingworth crew took off from the Linton-on-Ouse airfield at 1922 hrs, to attack the U-boat pens and dockyards at St Nazaire, on the Atlantic coast of France. The crew reported that they were able to identify the target by the nearby river, and by the red and green flares which had been dropped by the Pathfinder Force (PFF). The crew reported that, having dropped their bombs from a height of 14,000 feet, the glow of the fires could still be seen as they departed the French coast, and they returned safely to base, landing at 0253 hrs the following morning.

Two weeks later, the crew again took off from RAF Linton-on-Ouse at 2115 hrs, as one of three aircraft from 78 Squadron in a force of 271 aircraft sent to bomb Mannheim. On this occasion the Illingworth crew were flying in a Halifax II JB780 MP-F, which was on loan from 76 Squadron. One of 78 Squadron's aircraft returned to base early, after it had been held in a cone of 30 searchlights and hit by heavy enemy anti-aircraft fire.

Halifax II JB780 failed to return from the raid, having crashed at 0336 hrs on the morning of 17th April 1943. The aircraft was shot down on the way back from the target, by a Luftwaffe night-fighter, flown by Hauptmann Hans Karl Kamp of 7/NJG 4. The Halifax came down between Goyencourt and Roye, in northern France, killing all of the crew, who were buried in the New British Cemetery at Roye.

The sacrifice made by Flying Officer Herbert Donald Dixon is remembered on the war memorial inside the Parish Church of St Mannacus and St Dunstan in Manaccan, Cornwall, where his father served as minister after leaving Dulwich College. Herbert's gravestone, in Roye cemetery (pictured below), carries the inscription:

Grant him, O Lord, eternal rest;
and may light perpetual shine upon him

Leslie Newell Goldspink

Age:	22
Died:	9th May 1943
Service Number:	131557
Rank:	Flying Officer (Air Gunner)
Service/Regt:	RAF Volunteer Reserve
Ship/Unit:	150 Squadron
Grave/Memorial:	The Malta Memorial
Plot/Panel:	Panel 6 Column 2

Leslie Newell Whittingham Goldspink was born in Aston, Warwickshire on 26th April 1921, the son of Frederick Wickham Goldspink, and his wife Miriam (née Barber). His father was a licensed grocer, having served as a driver in the Royal Flying Corps during the Great War. Leslie, whose last forename may relate to Whittingham Hall, in Fressingfield, Suffolk, the home of his paternal grandparents, also had a younger brother, Anthony G Goldspink, who was born two years after him, also in Aston.

Malta Memorial

After the family had moved to Suffolk and set up business in Manningtree, Leslie and Anthony were both admitted to CRGS on 14th September 1938, as day-scholars. Leslie, who had previously attended Stowmarket County Secondary School, entered the 6th Form, and appears to have had a good sense of humour, contributing to a number of witty articles in *The Colcestrian*. He was listed in the magazine as a member of the Local Defence Volunteer (LDV) Force in the Manningtree area and also awarded the Bronze Medallion of the Royal Life Saving Society

Leslie left CRGS in the summer of 1940, and later followed in his father's footsteps, by joining the RAF. Selected for training as a member of Bomber Command flight crew, he was commissioned as a Pilot Officer Air Gunner on 25th September 1942. On 18th June 1943, *The London Gazette* published, posthumously, notice of his promotion to Flying Officer with effect from 25th March 1943.

From available records, it would seem that, at some point in his short flying career (possibly while at an Operational Training Unit), Flying Officer Leslie Goldspink became part of the crew of a Vickers Wellington, captained by Sergeant Donald Rayment. It would seem likely that the crew was posted to 150 Squadron, which had re-equipped with Vickers Wellingtons in October 1940, and been posted to the Mediterranean in December 1942. There it flew from its base at Blida, in Algeria, against targets in Tunisia and Sardinia.

Arriving at the squadron during March 1943, the Rayment crew commenced their operational sorties on 10th April 1943, as one of ten aircraft from 150 Squadron which attacked Monserrato airfield, to the north-east of Cagliari, in Sardinia. Taking off between at 1800 hrs, the attack was well concentrated, and all the aircraft returned safely, although two stragglers found the ground defences active.

Four days later, Sgt Rayment and his crew took part in the squadron's largest effort to date, when twelve aircraft again attacked aerodromes and landing grounds in Southern Sardinia. The raid by 150 Squadron was co-ordinated with a follow-up attack by twelve aircraft from 142 Squadron, which bombed the enemy bases at Villacidro, Decamonamou and Elmas again, an hour and a half later.

On the evening of 17th April, the crew were part of a ten-strong force which attacked docks and marshalling yards at Tunis. Conditions over the target were good, enabling a concentrated attack to be made. One aircraft was hit by flak over Tunis, and the fuel tanks damaged, although the pilot managed to keep the plane in the air until it ran out of fuel, when he was forced to ditch in the sea. The crew took to the dinghy, were picked up by a destroyer 36 hours later, and taken to Gibraltar, suffering from exposure. Due to bad weather at Blida, the remaining aircraft diverted to an airfield at Maison Blanche.

In the very early hours of 29th April, the Rayment crew was one of twelve to attack El Aouina airfield near Tunis. After getting airborne, the aircraft encountered much thundery cloud. The intense darkness made it difficult to pin-point the target, but one of the crews managed to place a 'stick' of incendiaries across the aerodrome, thus providing an aiming point for the other aircraft. All the aircraft landed safely back at base, with the exception of one crew who landed at Bone.

Later the same day, the Rayment crew attacked Bizerte/Sidi Ahmed airfield NW of Tunis, as part of a raid by a force of ten aircraft from 150 Squadron. Taking off at midnight, the crews faced only light flak as they attacked the target three hours later, although they again experienced poor visibility over the target. One aircraft crashed during the return flight, killing all the crew, but the remaining nine returned safely to base, landing after a second six-hour flight within one day.

Due to adverse weather conditions, 150 Squadron was stood down for the first four days of May, but on the 5th May the squadron moved to the airfield at Fontaine Chaude, near the village of Pasteur, 60 miles south of Bone. There, operating at an altitude of 3,000 feet (900m) above sea level, it was combined with 142 Squadron to form 330 Wing, within 205 Group. The following day, five aircraft had to be withdrawn from the initial squadron complement of eleven aircraft for an attack on Trapani docks, in Sicily.   However, among the six remaining crews to take off from Fontaine Chaude just before midnight, was the Rayment crew, flying in Wellington DF731 'S-Sugar'.

There was much cloud, and an electrical storm, on the way to the target. Bad visibility in the target area made it very difficult to pinpoint the aiming point, with the aircraft also encountering very active heavy and light anti-aircraft fire, and some searchlight activity. Four aircraft returned safely to base, one landed at Biskia, and 'S-Sugar' touched down on a grassy plain outside the town of Guelma, before returning to base during the day.

Since the 150 Squadron Operational Record Book (ORB) seems to make no further mention of them after 7th May 1943, the fate of the crew of 'S-Sugar' seems to be shrouded in mystery. They are not included in the list of twelve crews detailed for the sortie on either 8th/9th May, against Villacidro and other airfields in Sardinia, nor among the ten crews who took part in an attack on Palermo on 9th/10th May. The ORB further states explicitly that the aircraft detailed for these missions returned safely to base.

Nevertheless, it is a matter of record that Sergeant Donald Rayment, Flying Officer Leslie Goldspink and the rest of the crew of Wellington III DF731 'S-Sugar' are listed as 'Missing, Presumed Killed in Action' on 9th May 1943, and their names are included on the Malta Memorial to those who have no known grave. Perhaps, one day, we shall know what happened to them?

The name of Flying Officer Leslie Newell Whittingham Goldspink, omitted from the stained-glass window in the CRGS Library, has been added to the plaque, also in the Library, which commemorates the sacrifice of those whose names do not appear on the original memorials.

Postscript

From available records and other information, it would appear that Leslie Goldspink's younger brother, Anthony, also joined the RAF. On 24th November 1942, *The London Gazette* reported that 1333503 Anthony Granville GOLDSPINK (130248) had been commissioned as a Pilot Officer in the RAF. Anthony Goldspink appears to have been promoted to Flying Officer in March 1943, to Squadron Leader in September 1944, and to have survived the war.

CONQUERED CHEMISTRY
or " CHESTNUT CORNER "

A collection of useless hints cribbed and edited by the 6th Form Chemedians

ONE student claims to have discovered a Universal Solvent, but fails to realise that it has been stored in the same test-tube for at least six months !

A new element has been discovered by that inquisitive band of scientists the Gestapo ; they call it Nazidum. It has extremely repressive qualities ; in the concentrated form it is known as Kampforated oil. (A full description of Nazidum appears in Mein Kampf.) A disastrous explosion was caused by this element at Munich recently, so, as regards such elements the Fuehrer the better !

Lord Haw-Haw of Zeesen claims that we are suffering through lack of food—actually all we suffer from is lack of materials for the study of chemistry. Rationing has affected the chemist, for he now has to weigh out half an atom of sugar instead of a whole atom, a far more difficult procedure.

EXPERIMENT for the preparation of noise—a sound formula.

Mix in a flask : 50 c.c.s strong alkali (possibly acidum sulphuricum), 1 c.c. water (anhydrous if possible), 50 c.c.s strong acid (possibly ammonium hydrate).

Light blue touch paper, if time, and retire immediately. Return, put all broken glass in the W.P.B., and sign the Breakages Book.

For details of similar experiments we suggest that you refer to " How to be blown up—in three easy parts," by Dinah Might, T.Nt. If there is anything here you do not understand ask your chemistry master—he won't know either.

C. G. Cook,
L. N.W. Goldspink,
Upper 6A.

The Colcestrian, *December 1939*

151

PRACTICALLY PHYSICS

AN EXPERIMENT IN NONSENSE BLOWN UP BY THE 6TH FORM CHEMEDIANS.

How Archimedes Blocked the Drain.

THE first and last of a series of scientific accidents.
Once upon a time there was a very thin man called Archimedes (Double Dutch for " Screwy"), who used to count his money while having his bath. When he was having his daily dip a bee stung him on the bonnet, and he buzzed out of the bath pretty quickly, forgetting all about his half-crowns. When he recovered he dived into the bath and disappeared under the foam shouting " Eureka ! " (Double Dutch for " Yippee.") Since he was very thin he fell down the place where the plug should have been. He was not missed very much, but it was rather a nuisance not being able to empty the bath.

QUESTIONS which will confound your science master.

Was Joule the first man to make synthetic diamonds ?

In his efforts to be the first to make a steam engine was Stephenson 'ampered by Watt, and could he cell his invention?

Does Hooke's Law mean anything to fishermen ?

Was Boyle the brother of Bunyan ?

Was Goering, by reason of his iron crosses, attracted towards the Pole ?

The nth of our series of scientific accidents :—

An Apple for the Master.

One day Newton sat under an apple tree, waiting for an apple to fall. He became impatient and climbed up the tree to get one. His father saw him and took him indoors with a very grave look on his face, and spanked him. In this way Newton discovered the force of his father's gravity.

If this nonsense does not make sense you will sense that it has been senselessly censored by the blue-pencil censor. What's the sense of that, we ask you ?

C. G. Cook,
L. N. W. Goldspink, 6A

The Colcestrian, March 1940

Timothy Everett Cork

Age:	25
Died:	6th June 1943
Service Number:	164837
Rank:	Lieutenant
Service/Regt:	The Suffolk Regiment
Ship/Unit:	4th Battalion
Grave/Memorial:	Thanbyuzayat War Cemetery, Myanmar
Plot/Panel:	Plot B6, Grave F.20

Timothy Everett Cork was the son of a notable Old Colcestrian, Frank Freeman Cork, who had enjoyed great academic success at CRGS, as well as playing a full part in the life of the school, particularly the various drama productions. When Frank left the school, in December 1906, he was a King's Prefect, School Captain and holder of a prize for Mathematics.

Frank joined the Essex & Suffolk Cyclist Battalion in 1909, later transferring to the 15th London Regiment (Civil Service Rifles), where he rose to the rank of Company Quarter Master Sergeant, before being medically discharged in 1919, the result of wounds received during the 1914-18 War, while serving in France.

On 1st January 1915, two months before he left for the frontline in France, Frank married Mabel Dorothy Everett at St Botolph's Church in Colchester. Fourteen months later, after being seriously wounded by a rifle grenade, Frank returned to the UK and spent a further seven weeks being treated at the Royal Victoria Hospital, at Netley, near Southampton.

Timothy was Frank and Mabel's first and only child, being born at Steyning in Sussex on 19th March 1918, and baptised at St Botolph's Church, Colchester on 18th May 1918. He received his early schooling at Hamilton Road Central School, before being admitted to CRGS on 17th September 1926 as a day-scholar, and member of Dugard House.

During his time at the school, Timothy emulated his father in many ways, including regular appearances in school drama productions. In 1929, he was a member of the 'Ladies Chorus' in the G&S production of 'Utopia Limited', and appeared in the Chorus of 'Ruddigore' two years later. He was a member of the school Scout Troop, going on to become a Patrol Leader, and also achieved success in the 1935 Swimming Gala.

Timothy demonstrated his academic ability, by twice winning a Junior Foundation Scholarship prize during his time at CRGS, and achieving Class 1(Honours) in Division II of the Royal Drawing Society examination in 1930. Serving as a School Prefect for his final year, he passed the Cambridge School Certificate examination in July 1934, and left the school on 20th December 1935.

Having also passed the Civil Service Examination (Clerical Class), Timothy joined the Inland Revenue, and was included in the 1939 Civil Service List. He also joined the Old Colcestrian Society, being listed in 1937 as resident at the family home in Shrub End Road, Colchester.

At the start of the war, Timothy Cork again followed in his father's footsteps, by volunteering to serve in the Army. He was selected for officer training and spent five months at an Officer Cadet Training Unit (OCTU), before receiving his commission as a 2nd Lieutenant on 21st December 1940, and joining 'D' Company, 4th Battalion of the Suffolk Regiment.

The 4th and 5th Battalions of the Suffolk Regiment had been created in September 1939 and, together with the 4th Battalion of the Royal Norfolk Regiment (4RNR), formed the 54th Infantry Brigade, within the 18th Infantry Division. The 18th Division, which also included the 53rd and 55th Infantry Brigades, operated as a duplicate of the 54th (East Anglian) Infantry Division, being made up of men from Essex, Norfolk, Suffolk and Cambridgeshire.

In January 1941, having undergone initial training in East Anglia, the 4th Battalion Suffolk Regiment, and the rest of 54 Brigade, moved to Stobs Camp, near Hawick, in Scotland. In April, they moved to the North-West of England, where they assisted with unloading ships in Liverpool docks, and the clearance of debris after the city was 'blitzed'. By mid-summer, the 4th Battalion had moved to Herefordshire, and was considered to be a fully-trained and equipped unit, ready for frontline deployment.

In early October 1941, the troops were informed that they would be going overseas, for service in the Middle East. Issued with khaki drill uniforms, 'topis' etc., the assumption among the ranks was that they were going to Egypt, and on 27th October they entrained for Liverpool Docks. There the 4th Battalion embarked on the SS *Andes*, and set sail across the Atlantic, to Halifax, Nova Scotia.

Having arrived in Canada, the men from Suffolk boarded the USS *Wakefield*, a former luxury liner which had been converted into an American troopship capable of carrying 6,000 men. On 8th November, a heavily-defended troop convoy, including the *Wakefield* and two other large troopships, headed south from Halifax, down the eastern seaboard of America, towards the Caribbean. Replenishing their fuel and stores in Port of Spain, Trinidad, the convoy sailed east, across the Equator, towards South Africa.

On the 9th December, the men of the 4th Battalion were treated to a sight of the Table Mountain on the horizon, before three days' leave in Cape Town, enjoying the glorious warm weather. While in Cape Town they learned of the Japanese pre-emptive strike on Pearl Harbour, and America's entry into the war. However, as they left on 13th December, most of the troops still expected to head north, towards the Suez Canal and the Middle East. There followed wonderful days of sunshine, with cloudless skies and endless horizons, as they sailed across the blue waters of the Indian Ocean.

However, instead of arriving in Egypt, the convoy delivered the 'Suffolks' to Bombay, in India, on 27th December, from where they made an uncomfortable overnight train journey to Ahmednagar, a small market town and former Indian Army barracks. There, they endured two weeks of route marches and strenuous fitness training, as they became acclimatised to the intense heat and mosquitoes.

With the Imperial Japanese Army having already taken Hong Kong, and advancing rapidly through Malaya, the men of the Suffolk Regiment re-embarked on the USS *Wakefield*, and left Bombay on 19th January, with orders to reinforce the garrison on Singapore. The convoy docked in

Singapore on 29th January, and 2nd Lieutenant Timothy Cork, with the rest of the 4th Battalion, took up positions in the north-east of the island, with orders to 'defend the beaches at all costs', although it would be 8th February before all of their equipment was unloaded.

The 'Suffolks' soon came under enemy shell fire, sustaining their first casualties on 5th February. Three days later, the Japanese forces launched their main assault, against the west of the island, where they quickly gained a foothold, and pushed on, towards the heart of the island. Over the next few days, the 4th Battalion struggled with heavily congested roads, inaccurate maps, and conflicting orders as the Allies tried to mount a defence in the confusion.

The 4th Battalion suffered heavy casualties in the fighting that ensued, as the Imperial Japanese Army landed artillery and armoured vehicles unopposed. The Battalion was forced to withdraw, closely followed by the enemy. After a night of almost continual Japanese bombardment, the morning of Sunday 15th February 1942 brought news that the island's water supply had been severed. At 1130 hrs on 15th February 1942, with the Japanese still advancing, a ceasefire was announced and, at 1600 hrs, all Allied troops were ordered to surrender, to save the civilian population from further suffering.

Having spent more than two years in training, and three months spent travelling halfway round the world, the 450 men left in the 4th Battalion Suffolk Regiment had fought with courage and honour for seventeen days, before being ordered to lay down their arms. However, their toughest test was yet to come, as they became prisoners of an enemy which had not signed the Geneva Convention, and had little respect for the men that were now at its mercy.

After the surrender, the Japanese marched some 50,000 British and Australian Prisoners of War (POWs) to the barracks at Changi, where they were allowed three weeks' rest, before being used as forced labour to clean up the debris in the city, help in the construction of an airfield, and build a Shinto shrine to commemorate the fallen Japanese soldiers. Later on, the Japanese started sending groups of soldiers from Changi to other locations, under the pretence that the facilities, food and accommodation, would be far better than was available in Singapore. The reality, however, was that these POWs were being sent to camps where they would be used as slave labour, brutally treated, and starved.

From surviving wartime records, including his Japanese POW record card, it would appear that 2nd Lt. Timothy Cork remained in Singapore for a further fourteen months, during which time his promotion to Lieutenant was published, with effect from 20th June 1942. On 8th April 1943, the Japanese issued orders that, due to a lack of food in Singapore, a further 7,000 POWs, including 3,400 British soldiers, were to prepare for a move to another camp, in a 'pleasant hill location'. There, they would receive good food, enjoy recreational facilities, and receive better medical treatment.

The POWs were told that 'Force F', as it was known, would be organised as twelve groups, each of about 600 men. They would travel most of the way by train, except for a short march at the end of the journey. Lt. Timothy Cork was selected as one of the officers to accompany the men in Group 10, which left Singapore on 27th April. The train journey, in sweltering heat, was made in steel goods wagons, with little ventilation. There were no sanitary facilities in the wagons, with the train only stopping twice a day, so that the men could be fed with a meal of boiled rice and onions.

After travelling for three days and nights, the train arrived the small village of Bampong, near Bangkok, where the POWs were told to dump any kit that they could not carry, and to prepare themselves for a march of 200 miles (320km) to their camp at Sonkrai, where they would be forced to help in the construction of a rail link (later known as the 'Death Railway') between Thailand and Thanbyuzayat, in Burma.

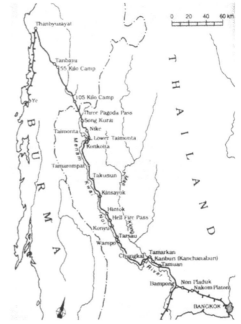

The march would have lasted two to three weeks and been carried out in fifteen stages, with stops at other labour camps along the way. Apart from the first two stages, marching was done at night along a rough jungle track. The men who were fit helped those who were ill or unable to walk unaided, until they too became exhausted and ill. Conditions at the staging camps were awful, with no shelter from the sun or monsoon rain, and little food or water. Although most of the men were suffering from diarrhoea, malaria, dysentery and other tropical diseases, any requests for those too ill to be moved to be left behind would be met with a beating from the Japanese guards, with the result that many died during the march.

Eventually, in mid-May, Group 10 arrived at Sonkrai, where the conditions were the worst of all the camps. All prisoners were expected to undertake hard physical labour for up to fourteen hours a day, often with their bare hands, while they lived on a diet of a little rice, supplemented with whatever they could forage, including any cats, pigs, rats, etc. that wandered into the camp. The men were brutally treated by the guards, who often seemed to take sadistic pleasure in the punishments that were handed out. Medical stores in the camp were almost non-existent, with most treatments having to be improvised from materials that were locally available. Disease and illness were rife, with tropical ulcers, dysentery, diarrhoea, beriberi, cholera and typhus being widespread in the camps. To many prisoners, death often appeared to be the only way of escaping the unrelenting toil and torture.

Lieutenant Timothy Everett Cork died from cholera on 6th June 1943, aged 26 years. In order to lessen the risk of the disease spreading, his remains were cremated, placed in a bamboo casket engraved with his name and service number and buried in the cemetery at Sonkrai.

As soon as the war ended, representatives of a joint British, Australian and Dutch Graves Commission, assisted by small groups of POWs who stayed behind instead of going home, began to search for camp cemeteries along the length of the railway, which contained the remains of thousands of POWs. The graves of those who died during the construction of the 'Death Railway' were transferred to three large war cemeteries, at Kanchanaburi and Chungkai in the south, and Thanbyuzayat, in southern

Burma, where the remains of Lieutenant Timothy Everett Cork were re-interred in December 1945.

More than 12,000 Allied prisoners died during the construction of the railway. Ninety men of the 4th Battalion, The Suffolk Regiment were killed in action in Singapore. 344 died while Prisoners of War, including Timothy Cork. His sacrifice is commemorated on the stained-glass memorial window in the CRGS library.

Linocut.

Howard, 5x

The Colcestrian, December 1942

Peter Pearson Tye

Age:	22
Died:	12th June 1943
Service Number:	1613283
Rank:	Flight Sergeant (Pilot Instructor)
Service/Regt:	RAFVR
Ship/Unit:	No. 34 Elementary Flying Training School
Grave/Memorial:	Mt. Hope Cemetery, Assiniboia, Saskatchewan, Canada
Plot/Panel:	Ref. 8

Peter Pearson Tye was born on 29th September, 1920, the son of Claude Francis 'Dick' Tye, born 24th May 1890 in Colchester, and Flo Lily (née Pearson), born 24th January 1893 in Rowhedge. They married in 1917, and Peter had a sister, Mary, born on 17th February, 1927. Before their marriage, Flo worked as a stationery shop assistant, and from 1914 to 1925 Dick was an engineer in the Merchant Navy. The Pearson family were active members of the community in Rowhedge. Flo's father was a member of the annual Regatta committee and there are numerous newspaper references to her participation in this, as well as winning prizes for flower arrangements, knitting and needlework in the annual East Donyland and Rowhedge Shows. She also sang and acted in a local entertainment troupe, 'The Scarlet Poms'.

Peter entered CRGS in October 1932 from Braintree County High School, receiving a total exemption from fees from Essex LEA. The CRGS Admissions Register gives his father's occupation as 'Ship's Engineer', suggesting that Dick continued with this job, based in Rowhedge, after leaving the Merchant Navy. However, by the time of the 1939 Register he had become a travelling salesman for a wholesale tobacconist. In 1932 their address was 'Quay House', Rowhedge, but by 1939 they were at 'Rockery Cottage' in the High Street.

Peter was an academically able student who achieved his Cambridge School Certificate, including exemption from London matriculation, in July 1936. He also received 'Mr Pepper's prize for English' at the same time. Earlier in his school career he had gained a distinction in the Diocesan Scripture exam. He also excelled at athletics, doing particularly well in sprints, hurdles, high jump and long jump on Sports Days. Outside school he was a member of the East Donyland Church Choir and a keen ornithologist.

Peter left CRGS in November 1936, while still only sixteen. He almost certainly had the ability to go on to university, but his parents probably could not afford this. Instead he got a job as a Laboratory Assistant with Shell-Mex Ltd. at the Shell Haven oil refinery in Thurrock. While he was there, he played rugby for Grays RFC.

Peter joined the RAF Volunteer Reserve in February 1942 and was sent to Canada for training. In January 1943 he got his wings, along with the rank of Flight Sergeant (Instructor) at No. 34 Elementary Flying Training School. It was while training another pilot, Leading Aircraftman (LAC) Norman King, that the accident which caused both their deaths occurred. Peter's aircraft, a Cornell FH953 Mark 1 Trainer, was put into a spin at 2,000 feet. However, the plane developed a problem, failed to pull out of the dive and crashed. The incident took place one mile east and four miles north of Home Airfield, Assiniboia, Saskatchewan. There were three similar crashes involving this type of aircraft during the following month.

Anthony Geoffrey Camille Pissarro

Age:	21
Died:	26th June 1943
Rank:	Sub-Lieutenant
Service/Regt:	Royal Naval Volunteer Reserve
Ship/Unit:	HM Motor Gun Boat (MGB) 644
Grave/Memorial:	Royal Navy Memorial, Portsmouth
Plot/Panel:	Panel 80, Column 1

Anthony ('Tony') Geoffrey Camille Pissarro was born in London on 10th March 1922. As his name might suggest, he was a direct descendant of the great French impressionist artist, (Jacob) Camille Pissarro, who was his great-grandfather. Camille Pissarro (1830-1903) was born on the island of St Thomas, then part of the Danish West Indies (now the US Virgin Islands), where his father, who was of Portuguese-Jewish extraction, owned a general hardware shop. At twelve years of age Camille was sent to France to be educated and he developed an interest in painting which his parents could not shake. On his return, he ran off to Venezuela to pursue his talent, whereupon they finally relented, and in 1855 he left St Thomas for good to work in Paris.

There he married Julie Vellay, a non-Jewish French woman of a lower social class – another cause of concern to his parents. They went on to have seven children. In 1892 their third child, Georges Henri Manzana Pissarro (born 1871), who also became an artist of some renown, married Esther, the daughter of Phineas Isaacson, a London-based West India merchant who owned property on St Thomas. Esther and Georges were half-cousins, who shared a grandmother – the twice-married Rachel Manzana Pomié Petit, mother of Camille Pissarro.

The marriage was short-lived, as Esther soon died, though not before giving birth to a son, Thomas ('Tommy') Clarence Pissarro, Tony's father, on 30th August 1893. In 1897, following his wife's death, Georges Manzana Pissarro became a naturalised British citizen, and he and the young Tommy were living in some grandeur at 1 Colville Square, Bayswater.

However, Georges soon chose to leave Britain, returning to France (he had been born in Louveciennes, a Paris suburb favoured by his father, Camille Pissarro, and other Impressionists) to further his own artistic career. He also remarried - first Amicie Brecy, then Blanche Moriset. They also both predeceased him, though they did bear him five more children between them. Tommy was now brought up in England by his mother's younger sister, Alice Isaacson. At the time of the 1911 census, they were living at 9 Aldridge Road Villas, in Bayswater, along with Alice's father, Phineas Isaacson, who was now 91. Tommy, aged 17, was a junior clerk, working in the City.

By 1921 Tommy had met and married (Mildred) Esmé Oldham, from Windlesham, Surrey. Tony was born in 1922 and another son, Richard Alfred Carl Pissarro, followed in 1925. The family was still living in London, at 11 Christchurch Road, Hampstead, but by the early 1930s they had moved to 'Rose Cottage', Red House Lane, Boxted. The CRGS Admissions Register describes Tony's father as a 'retired clerk in an oil company'.

Having received his early education at Myland Council School, Tony entered CRGS as a day-scholar, on 19th September 1933 with a total exemption from fees from Essex County Council. He was heavily involved in scouts, first as a Patrol Leader and finally becoming overall Troop Leader. He was also prominent in the swimming sports, steeplechases and rugby, eventually captaining the school 1st XV. *The Colcestrian* describes him as a 'fine forward', 'popular and efficient' and a captain who 'intends his orders to be carried out'. He was also a Prefect and passed his Cambridge School Certificate.

He left CRGS at Easter 1940, with the School House report in the July 1940 edition of *The Colcestrian* commenting: 'We were sorry to lose Pissarro at the end of last term; we sadly missed his efforts in the steeplechase and sports'. However, his involvement with the scouts continued and, in June 1941, the magazine reported that: 'the troop was reorganised at the beginning of the Lent term under the leadership of Mr Pissarro, an OC who has kindly come to our aid'.

During the latter part of 1941 Tony joined the Royal Navy, initially as an Ordinary Seaman aboard the mine-layer HMS *Manxman*, where *The Colcestrian* reported his address as 'C/JX27821 Ordinary Seaman AGC Pissarro, 8 Mess, HMS *Manxman*'.

HMS Manxman in 1945

From October 1941 to February 1942, *Manxman* took part in a number of mine-laying operations in the North Sea and the English Channel and, in March 1942, joined the Eastern Fleet in the Indian Ocean. After escort and patrol duties, on 8th October HMS *Manxman* participated in the assault and capture of the island of Nosy Be on the north-west coast of Madagascar, which was occupied by Vichy French forces.

However, naval records indicate that by July 1942, Tony Pissarro had been selected for officer training and, after initial training, was posted to HMS *St. Christopher*, near Fort William in Scotland, which was a Coastal Forces Training Base for the Royal Navy. The recruits, and the base staff of several hundred, were billeted in hotels around the town, or the additional space provided by Nissen huts.

Between 80 and 90 boats, consisting of Motor Torpedo Boats (MTBs), Motor Gun Boats (MGBs), Motor Launches (MLs) and anti-submarine motorboats were based at the site, organised into a number of flotillas.

During their training, which lasted several weeks, the recruits were trained to operate the different types of high-speed, inshore patrol craft used by the Royal Navy, learning the skills needed to sail the boats, as well as activities such as firing torpedoes from MTBs, or live-firing of the guns.

On 24th January 1943, Anthony Geoffrey Camille Pissarro received his commission as a Sub-Lieutenant in the Royal Navy Volunteer Reserve, and continued in his posting at HMS *St. Christopher* until he was sent to command a Royal Navy Motor Gun Boat in the Mediterranean.

MGBs were extremely heavily-armed for vessels of their size and, formed into flotillas alongside MTBs, they helped to sink Italian and German shipping, being used to carry supplies from Italy in support of Axis land forces in North Africa. MGB-644 was a Fairmile Type 'D' boat, built by Tough Brothers of Teddington, and commissioned in December 1942. Over 100 feet in length, and with a displacement of 95 tons, she had a crew of 30 men, and was armed with two 2-pounder guns, four 20mm anti-aircraft guns, four .303" machine guns, as well as being equipped with depth charges, radar and smoke-making equipment.

On the 26th June 1943, as part of the preparations for 'Operation Husky', the invasion of Sicily, which was to take place two weeks later, Sub-Lieutenant Pissarro was on patrol with MGB-644, when it struck a mine off the west coast of Sicily, between Marsala and Mazzara. The explosion killed Anthony Pissarro, and Petty Officer George WW Bird, the boat's motor mechanic. Being severely damaged, MGB-644 was later scuttled by gunfire from another boat in the flotilla.

Anthony's father, Tommy, died in 1980. For his grandfather, Georges Henri (Manzana), the outbreak of WW2 had been a serious threat, as he was of Jewish descent and living in France. It might have been expected that he would take refuge in Britain. He was a naturalised British citizen, and had family there – not only Tommy, but his elder brother and fellow artist, Lucien Pissarro.

However, for reasons which are unclear he rejected this course – maybe he feared that the Nazis would invade Britain successfully too. Instead he took his French family to Casablanca where he saw out the war safely. He returned to France in 1947 to live and paint on the Riviera until his death at Menton, aged 90, in 1961.

Tommy's cousin, Orovida, the daughter of Lucien (who had died in 1944) was also a well-known artist, born in Epping, who lived and worked in London until her death in 1968.

Having no grave but the sea, the sacrifice of Sub-Lieutenant Anthony Pissarro is commemorated on the window in the CRGS library, and on the Naval Memorial at Portsmouth.

Pissarro Family Tree

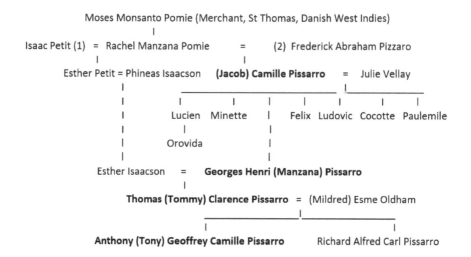

Robert John Cleland Dobbie

Age:	32
Died:	3rd July 1943
Service Number:	785101
Rank:	Leading Aircraftman (AC1)
Service/Regt:	RAF Volunteer Reserve
Grave/Memorial:	Ambon War Cemetery
	(Originally Kario Village, Cape Marakee,
	Haroekoe Island; re-buried 05/02/1947)
Plot/Panel:	Plot 4, Row C, Grave 7

Robert John Cleland Dobbie (known as 'Jack') was born on 1st April 1911, at 'Cross House', Doune, in Scotland, the third child of John Dobbie, a railway clerk, and his wife Edith Florence (née Winter). When Robert was born, his older brother, Alfred Arthur Stanley (later known as 'Bill'), was almost three years of age, while his sister, Edith, was fifteen months.

It seems likely that Robert and his family made their first trip to Ecuador just before the start of the First World War, and that he returned with his mother and brother Alfred on 23rd October 1916, presumably so that the boys could start their education in England. Robert appears to have begun his education at an Ursuline convent school, before joining his brother at Bideford Grammar School in Devon.

Meanwhile, towards the end of 1919, Douglas Cleland Dobbie was born in Ecuador, a third son for John and Edith and, on 14th September 1920, they returned to the UK with their ten-month-old son, initially staying at Appledore, in Devon, and visiting Alfred and Robert. During the trip, John and Edith also arranged for Alfred and Robert to continue their education at CRGS, with the boys being admitted to the School on 24th November, as boarders and members of School House.

In addition, moving the two boys up from Devon, the Dobbie family also visited the lads' maternal aunt, Mrs Emily Susan Adelaide Munday, who lived in Defoe Crescent, Mile End. Unfortunately, while the family were visiting Colchester, Douglas was taken ill, died at the age of eighteen months, and was buried in the graveyard of St Michael's Church, Myland.

The Colcestrian magazine contains many references to Alfred's and Robert's activities during their time at the School, and later, as members of the Old Colcestrian Society (OCS). Many of these focus on their sporting achievements; they both represented School House in a variety of sports, while Alfred seems to have excelled, playing 1st XI Cricket for CRGS, as well as having success at athletics, rugby and football. Alfred also made notable appearances as 'Ko-Ko' in the School production of 'The Mikado', and as 'The Lord Chancellor' in the 1926 Gilbert and Sullivan production of 'Iolanthe'.

In the spring of 1922, the two lads took a trip to South America, to spend the summer with their parents, in Ecuador. The intrepid schoolboys were featured in a report by a British national daily newspaper, with the July edition of *The Colcestrian* including a letter from the two boys, dated 9th May, in which they recounted their 31-day journey, on the SS *Orita*, from Liverpool to Colón, in Panama. Their report described the ship visiting La Rochelle, Corunna, Vigo, Bermuda, Havana and Kingston, Jamaica. They went on to describe how, in Colón, they were met by their father's agent, an American, who escorted them on a further seven-day sea journey aboard a Panamanian boat, passing through the Panama Canal and then travelling down the west coast of South America to Guayaquil in Ecuador.

There they were met by their parents and travelled in John Dobbie's private train to the family home in Huigra. Five months later, the two lads, now aged 14 and 11 years, returned to CRGS on the SS *Haarlem*, again crossing the Atlantic unaccompanied. They arrived back in England on 11th September 1922.

On 16th September 1926 Alfred and Robert again travelled on SS *Orita* to Colón, and thence to Huigra. Scarcely a month after their arrival in Ecuador, on 23rd November 1926, their mother passed away. Returning to the UK, the two lads left CRGS on 23rd July 1927, with Robert going on to further study at St Andrew's School, Larbert, Stirlingshire, and Alfred returning to live in Devon. Two years later, Florence Stanley Winter, Edith's younger sister, became stepmother to her three nephews and niece when she and John Cleland Dobbie were married at the British Consulate in Quito, Ecuador.

In September 1929, Alfred travelled to the Far East, and started working as a planter on the Bertam Estate, in Province Wellesley, part of the Straits Settlements (now part of Malaysia). In June 1934, having returned from Ecuador two months earlier, Robert followed his older brother to the Far East, to work as a planter near Labuan, on the island of Borneo. During the 1930s several editions of *The Colcestrian* contained contributions from a number of OCs who were all working on plantations in the Far East. These included a piece published in the July 1937 issue, entitled 'Life in Lower Burma', written by Alfred Dobbie.

In September 1939, at the outbreak of the Second World War, Robert 'Jack' Dobbie was an Assistant Planter on the Sapong Estate in North Borneo. A big man, standing over six feet tall, and weighing in at nearly fifteen stone, Jack soon became very fluent in the Malay language. He had a great understanding of its culture and people, including different accents.

When, on 7th December 1941, Japanese forces landed at Kota Bharu, in Northern Malaya, Jack immediately left his job, flew to Singapore, and enlisted in the RAF. As a result of the pre-emptive attack on Malaya, and a simultaneous assault on Hong Kong, the UK Government declared war on Japan. At the same time, following the unprovoked attack on the US Pacific Fleet, at anchor in Pearl Harbor, the United States of America also entered the war.

Over the next few weeks, in the face of the Japanese onslaught, the Allies steadily retreated southwards, gradually evacuating the 22 RAF bases in the Malay Peninsula. By 16th January 1942 all RAF aircraft and personnel had been forced back to Singapore. There, amid the chaos, Jack Dobbie helped defend the city, as it was pounded from the air and, ultimately invaded by the Imperial Japanese Army. Eventually, as the RAF withdrew the few remaining aircraft to Palembang, in Sumatra, Jack Dobbie and the remaining ground staff were ordered to evacuate to Java.

By the end of February, a large number of RAF personnel had congregated in Java, including men evacuated from Eastern Sumatra and Singapore, as well as others who had left the UK before war in the Far

East was declared, in order to relieve those who had completed their three-year overseas tour of duty. Just after midnight on 28th February 1942, the Japanese landed on Java and, within a few days, all British personnel had been ordered to move south, towards the last remaining operational RAF base at Tasikmalaya, to await evacuation to Australia.

However, before they could escape, a proclamation by the local Dutch government on 7th March 1942 announced that it had officially surrendered to the Japanese, and that all organised resistance was to cease at noon the following day. Although a few men escaped to safety in Australia, nearly 5,000 RAF personnel, including Leading Aircraftman Jack Dobbie, waited for the Japanese to arrive the following day, and to be taken prisoner.

The first month of captivity was relatively easy, as the Japanese Army consolidated its position on the island, largely leaving the Prisoners-of-War (POWs) under the command of their own officers; the men lived off RAF rations, with the addition of the fruit that was available nearby. However, since the Japanese government had not ratified the 1929 Geneva Convention, it considered that treaty irrelevant and in early 1942 had decreed that no prisoners were to survive long enough to be released when the war ended, but rather should be used as slave labour to further the Japanese war economy.

Therefore, when, in early April, the Japanese turned their attention to the POWs, they started to subject them to hard physical labour, and the harshest military discipline, with brutal treatment meted out to any prisoner unfortunate enough to attract their attention. On May 11th, Jack Dobbie and the rest of the POWs were marched to the railway station at Tasikmalaya, and transported to the city of Surabaya, where the Lyceum School had been turned into a prison camp.

Soaking wet after arriving in a tropical downpour, they were strictly confined in small classrooms, and fed 'pap' - rice cooked in a lot of water - twice a day, with a third 'meal' consisting of dry rice with a thin green soup. For the next three weeks, the POWs were sent to work in the docks at Surabaya, unloading bombs and barrels of fuel from trucks, and loading them on to the ships that delivered the supplies to forward locations.

In early June 1942, Jack was among 300 British and Dutch POWs who were sent to work on the airstrip at Semarang. Despite all their attempts to augment their meagre ration of one and a half cups of rice per day, with snakes and any other wildlife that they could catch, malnutrition steadily took its toll on the health of the POWs; malaria rampaged through the camp, and diseases such as beriberi and dysentery became commonplace.

From early morning until late in the evening, despite their hunger and thirst, the working parties were forced to labour in the tropical heat, while always under the threat of a beating from their captors. On one occasion, a Japanese guard, considering that Jack Dobbie was not working hard enough for the Emperor, berated him for his 'laziness'. When Jack answered back, the guard forced him to the ground, then kicked and beat him mercilessly with his rifle butt.

At 2300 hrs on the 7th February 1943, after eight months at Semarang, the POWs were loaded into two railway carriages, and the following day started the long, hot journey back to Surabaya. Arriving at 2000 hrs that night, the men were marched to another prison camp - this time the former Dutch army barracks at Jaarmarkt, which became the largest POW camp in SE Asia, and the main transit camp to provide slave labour to support the Japanese war effort in the Dutch East Indies (now Indonesia).

Up to 4,000 men were held in the Jaarmarkt camp, with working parties being sent to the docks each day. This provided the POWs with many opportunities to scrounge and pilfer food, medicines, and other items that might make their lives less uncomfortable, although always knowing that getting caught would mean a severe beating, or worse, being handed over to the Kempeitai, the Japanese military police, for torture and almost certain death.

In the spring of 1943, the Japanese began closing down the prison camps in Surabaya and transporting nearly 4,000 British and Dutch POWs to the islands of Ambon, Ceram and Haroekoe (Haruku), to be used as slave labour to create a series of 'unsinkable aircraft carriers' through a programme of airfield construction and expansion. At 0400 hrs on 19th April, a draft of just over 2,000 'fit' men, mainly RAF personnel, was assembled at the Jaarmarkt Camp in Surabaya, issued with a small bag of weevil-infested, uncooked rice as 'emergency rations', and marched down to Tanjung Perak, the docks in Surabaya, where the 5,000 ton coaler, the *Amagi Maru* was tied up.

After waiting for some hours in the burning equatorial sun, they were herded onto the ship and forced to climb down steep ladders into the cargo holds. There, in each hold, up to 400 men endured cramped and unhygienic conditions similar to the 'Black Hole of Calcutta', and were fed a diet of two watery rice meals a day. Despite the urgency with which they had been forced onto the *Amagi Maru*, the ship remained in the docks for three more days, as the rest of the cargo – ammunition, bombs, detonators and high-octane aviation fuel – were loaded on board.

At last the *Amagi Maru* set sail, on the first leg of an 1,100-mile sea journey eastward, through the Flores Sea, past Lombok and Bali, before turning north, towards Celebes (Sulawesi), and eventually arriving at their first stop, the island of Ambon. There, in the pouring rain, and suffering the effects of their starvation diet, Jack Dobbie and the rest of the RAF personnel were forced to help unload the cargo of munitions and drums of aviation fuel. After two days spent unloading the first part of the cargo, the *Amagi Maru* sailed overnight to the island of Ceram, where the next three days were spent repeating the unloading process.

Setting sail again, a few hours later the ship arrived, late in the evening, off the northern coast of the beautiful coral island of Haroekoe (Haruku), in the Moluccas archipelago. At midnight, Jack and the rest of his RAF colleagues were finally told to disembark. Making their way to shore in sampans, they found their way up a narrow footpath to the campsite, only to find that there was no ready accommodation for them. With incessant monsoon rain already turning the ground into a quagmire, many of the POWs were then forced to spend the rest of the night in the open. The following day, with the help of some local natives, the prisoners started to build shelters, called 'atapi', which consisted of a frame and a roof, but no sides, and to construct toilet facilities, which the camp also lacked.

Having already endured many months of starvation, the POWs were soon suffering from the ravages of malnutrition, malaria, tropical ulcers, dysentery, and other serious illnesses such as beriberi and diphtheria. Despite the state of their health, the men were made to turn the coral into an airstrip, from which the Japanese could launch attacks on northern

Australia. During the first three months on Haruku, of the 2,000 'fit' men who paraded at Jaarmarkt in Surabaya, nearly 500 died, with sometimes 30 bodies being buried each day.

In charge of the prisoners at the Haruku camp was the infamous Gunso Mori, who was later tried by the post-war Far East War Crimes Tribunal, found guilty, and hanged in 1946. In addition to being systematically starved, and kept in unhygienic conditions, without proper sanitation, none were safe from his wrath, and his readiness to subject the POWs to severe beatings for the slightest abuse. As a result, while in European POW camps only 4% of prisoners died, under Mori's inhumane treatment the final death rate for RAF prisoners in the Haruku camp was almost 70%, with only one man in three returning to the UK at the end of the war.

On 3rd July 1943, at the age of 32, Leading Aircraftman Robert John Cleland 'Jack' Dobbie died in the Haruku (Haroekoe) POW Camp, as a result of bacillary dysentery. Originally buried on the island, in a graveyard near the beach, just above the shoreline of Cape Marakee, his remains were re-interred after the war in the Ambon War Cemetery, in Indonesia, where his gravestone carries the inscription:

At the going down of the sun, and in the morning, we will
remember him

His sacrifice is to be commemorated by the addition of his name to the memorial plaque in the CRGS Library.

Kenneth Butler Lamonby

Age:	23
Died:	11th July 1943
Service Number:	160965
Rank:	Lieutenant
Service/Regt:	SAS
Ship/Unit:	Special Boat Squadron (S Detachment)
Grave/Memorial:	Suda Bay War Cemetery, Crete
Plot/Panel:	Ref. 13.E.12

Kenneth (Ken) Butler Lamonby was born on 24th October 1919 in Kingston, Surrey, the only child of Harold Lamonby and Dora (née Atkinson). Harold was originally from Kendal, in the Lake District. He trained as PE teacher and worked in Windermere before marrying Dora in Kendal in 1917. They soon moved south, first to Surrey, then arriving in Colchester, where Harold had been appointed 'Organiser of Physical Education for Colchester Education Committee'.

Ken entered the Pre at CRGS in 1927, passing up to the Senior School two years later. In 1929 the family were living at 44 Beaconsfield Road, but later moved to 'Kentmere' (named after the village near Kendal from where they hailed), 38 Victoria Road, Colchester. Ken left CRGS in December 1937.

It would seem fair to say that Ken was not the most academic student, since he contrived to fail his Cambridge School Certificate three times. However, he did excel at sport, presumably taking after his father in this respect. He played 1st XI cricket, as an opening bowler, and 1st XV rugby, as a front-row forward and goal-kicker. *The Colcestrian* describes him as 'a medium pace bowler with an admirable action; can swing the ball, get pace off the pitch and bowls the occasional dangerous ball that goes away.' In 1937 he took 6-40 as the school had a rare victory against the OCs by 45 runs. He was also vice-captain of the team. As a rugby player, the magazine describes him as 'a very hard worker, always up with the ball.'

He won his Colours in both sports and also had success on Sports Days at sprints, middle-distance running, high/long jumps and throwing the

CRGS 1ˢᵗ XV 1937: Ken Lamonby is in the front row, seated, on the far right

cricket ball.

The CRGS Admissions Register does not record his occupation on leaving, but with the advent of war he joined the Royal Artillery, completing his Officer Cadet Training in December 1940. He was then commissioned as a Lieutenant in the Suffolk Regiment. He served with the 8ᵗʰ Army in North Africa until December 1942, taking part in the 'desert push' during the autumn of that year.

In 1943 his war took a radically different course when he was accepted into the Special Boat Squadron, then a newly-formed unit of the SAS, born from the Special Boat Section. In April 1943 the SBS moved to a training base at Athlit in Palestine. There were three Operational Detachments numbering 60 men. Ken Lamonby was allocated to 'S' Detachment, named after Major David Sutherland, one of the founders of the SBS. Ken was one of the more inexperienced of the new SBS officers and was recruited into the unit because he was an expert sailor. He was thus put in charge of instructing 'S' Detachment in sea training. Among its other members was a Dane, Anders (Andy) Lassen, who was to become the only non-Commonwealth serviceman to win a VC in WW2.

In June 1943 'S' Detachment was chosen to take part in 'Operation Albumen', only the second SBS deployment. The first – a raid to disable enemy airfields in Sardinia – had ended in disaster, with most of the participants falling victim to malaria and being captured by the Italians. This new mission, to be led by David Sutherland himself, was another raid on enemy airfields, this time on occupied Crete. What happened has been described by Sutherland himself in *'He Who Dares'*, Gavin Mortimer in *'The SBS in World War II'* and Mike Langley in *'Anders Lassen, V.C, M.C, of the S.A.S'*.

They embarked from Palestine on 22nd June. Sutherland divided his forces into Patrols B and C, with Ken Lamonby commanding Patrol B to attack Heraklion airfield and Patrol C under Andy Lassen to attack the airfield at Kastelli. A third group, Patrol D would arrive four days later to attack Tymbiaki airfield. Sutherland, along with two or three others, formed the HQ party, holed up in caves about 500 metres inshore where they had to maintain wireless contact with all three raiding parties and, above all, remain undiscovered for nearly three weeks. Only Sutherland and Lassen had previous experience of this type of warfare.

They landed at Cape Kokinoxos on the southern shore of Crete, and despite the rough terrain, successfully established Sutherland's wireless base without being seen by any civilians or enemy. Patrols B and C then set off, together for the first two days and nights, after which they split. Eventually Patrol B reached the outskirts of the village of Arkhanes, two miles south of Heraklion. At this point their Cretan guide, Janni, supplied by the Special Operations Executive (SOE), advised that a new objective needed to be found as, due to heavy bombing by the RAF, Heraklion airfield was no longer in use. Fortunately, Janni had an alternative in mind - a fuel depot at Peza just two miles to the west. This held a large quantity of aviation fuel and there was also a bomb dump nearby.

It was decided that Janni, along with a member of the group called Dick Holmes, should deal with the petrol dump, while the others tackled the bomb dump, which was surrounded by wire. Holmes fixed three two-hour fuses underneath the barrels, successfully evading the two guards and their dogs. Meanwhile, Ken had made the decision not to approach the bomb dump because of the sudden arrival of two sentries.

About an hour after their withdrawal from the scene, the bombs in the petrol dump went off. Janni informed them that he had left a Union Jack at the scene so that the Germans would have no doubt who had perpetrated the raid, and, hopefully, not take reprisals on the civilian population. They spent the night in a bat-filled cave. Next morning another guide arrived with the good news that the flames from the explosion had, in fact, engulfed the bomb dump too.

They then left the area for the 30-mile trek across the island to the re-embarkation point, with numerous German patrols scouring the area. Patrol C had been successful too, destroying a number of planes at Kastelli. Patrol D, unfortunately, had found no planes at all at Tymbiaki airfield, but nevertheless had remained undetected. Awaiting their arrival in the cave above the beach, David Sutherland eventually received information that all the patrols were only two hours away. He also learned, ominously, that the Germans had shot 50 local men in reprisal for the raids, and that consequently 25 Cretans had attached themselves to the patrols in an attempt to escape the island.

Sutherland then, with some difficulty as his wireless batteries were by now running low, sent a signal asking for a pick-up boat the following night. By now all the patrols had arrived back. They had to wait in hiding throughout the day until the pick-up boat arrived off the beach at midnight. To celebrate their success, they ate a meal of porridge, cheese, biscuits and sweet tea.

Suddenly, however, they were spotted by two German soldiers on patrol. They immediately confronted the Germans, who surrendered straight away. However, without waiting for orders, the Cretans ran out to search the area themselves. Within minutes a firefight had broken out between them and the other two members of what turned out to be a four-man German patrol.

Sutherland was furious at the Cretans' behaviour and knew that the firing had to be stopped before it reached the ears of even more Germans.

He therefore sent Ken Lamonby and four others to stop the firing and bring back the Cretans, while also trying to ensure that the other two Germans remained trapped on the hillside next to the sea where they had positioned themselves.

It was now less than three hours before midnight, and Sutherland began the task of taking men and equipment to wait beneath the cliffs on the beach. Once this had been completed and there was still no sight of Ken, he sent Andy Lassen and Patrol C to look for him. They spent an hour and a half searching without success before returning to the beach at 2345 hrs.

Just after midnight the motor-launch appeared. Within an hour all the equipment and men, including the other members of Ken's patrol, were on board. Ken Lamonby alone was missing. Sutherland got the launch to sail slowly around Cape Kokinoxos and lay close to the wadi where Ken was last seen. They waited in vain for about 30 minutes before setting sail for Egypt and safety, arriving there on 12th July.

Ken Lamonby was the only casualty of an operation whose

O.C.'s EXPLOITS IN CRETE

The above photograph of O.C. Ken Lamonby and two of his brother officers, Anders Lassen on the extreme left and David Sutherland in the centre, was forwarded to the secretary by his father. The photograph was sent to Mr. Lamonby by the mother of Anders Lassen, and this is what she wrote to explain how it came into her possession : "I found the enclosed photo of our two brave boys in the house of a Greek partisan when I visited Crete recently."

Anders Lassen was killed in April, 1945. He and Ken Lamonby were great friends, and for his last exploit Lassen was posthumously awarded the V.C.

The story of the Crete operations is told in the book The Filibusters, by John Lodwick, in which book Ken Lamonby is mentioned by name. David Sutherland is now Officer Commanding the Black Watch in Germany.

Mr. Lamonby has the opinion that the photograph must have been taken a day or two before Ken was killed and soon after he had blown up a large German petrol dump in Crete.

success was crucial to the prestige of the newly-formed SBS. The participants received a string of awards - Bars to their Military Crosses for both Sutherland and Lassen, and Military Medals for Dick Holmes and three others. In addition to the planes, bombs and fuel which had been destroyed, one of their two German prisoners was carrying a new type of self-loading rifle. Sutherland said: "We were lucky to get hold of this weapon. It was way ahead of its time and provided useful information for the powers in Cairo." The prisoner with the rifle spoke excellent English, and it is said that, before interrogation, he and his partner were taken by Sutherland and Lassen for ice-cream sodas at Groppi's, a popular cafe in Cairo!

Andy Lassen believed that Ken had been wounded and taken away for interrogation. However, his true fate was only discovered after the war was over. It transpired that he had been shot by one of the two Germans he was tracking, and had later died of his wounds in a hospital in Heraklion.

According to *The Colcestrian* (July 1945), the Germans buried Ken Lamonby's body with military honours, 'on the beach'. It goes on to say that, after their withdrawal from Crete in October 1944, the leader of the Greek guerillas on the island took steps to ensure a permanent grave for him. Accordingly, his body was exhumed and re-interred in a monastery, before eventually being transferred to the Suda Bay War Cemetery after the war.

In December 1947 in an article reproduced above, *The Colcestrian* also reported that the mother of Anders Lassen had sent Harold Lamonby a photograph of Ken and Andy, with David Sutherland, in Crete while taking part in this operation. She wrote: 'I found the enclosed photo of our two brave boys in the house of a Greek partisan when I visited Crete recently.' Lassen himself had been killed in April 1945 while leading another SBS operation in Italy – the mission for which he was awarded a posthumous VC.

Gavin Mortimer records that Dick Holmes went to visit Ken's parents in Colchester after the war to give them a 'sanitised' account of the SBS operation and their son's death. He reports Dick as recalling: 'They were nice people. He was an only child.'

Malcolm Huigra Dobbie

Age:	20
Died:	16th August 1943
Service Number:	1292325
Rank:	Sergeant (Wireless Operator/Air Gunner)
Service/Regt:	RAF Volunteer Reserve
Ship/Unit:	1622 (Anti-Aircraft Co-operation) Flight
Grave/Memorial:	Ann's Hill Cemetery, Gosport, Hampshire
Plot/Panel:	Plot 188, Grave 79

Malcolm Huigra Dobbie (known at CRGS as 'Peter') was born on 2nd March 1923, in Huigra, Ecuador where the family was then living, and where his father, John Cleland Dobbie, was employed as general manager of the Ecuadorian State Railway Company.

Malcolm Huigra Dobbie

John Dobbie, then a railway clerk, had married Edith Florence Winter at 'Cross House', Doune in Scotland on 11th March 1908. Their first child, Alfred Arthur Stanley (known as 'Bill') was born in Doune on 10th April 1908, while a daughter, Edith, was born in 1910 and another son, Robert John Cleland (known as 'Jack') born in 1911. A third son, Douglas Cleland Dobbie was born in Ecuador in 1919, but died in Colchester aged eighteen months, and was buried in the graveyard of St Michael's Church, Myland.

The family often visited the UK from Ecuador, with Malcolm making his first transatlantic sea crossing at the age of one. His two older brothers were both educated in England, regularly making the long journey unaccompanied and, on one occasion, featured in a report by a British national daily newspaper. 'Bill' and 'Jack' Dobbie entered CRGS on 24th November 1920, as boarders, and remained at the school until 23rd July 1927.

On 23rd November 1926, while the older boys were in England, and Malcolm was little more than four years old, their mother passed away in Ecuador. Two years later, Florence Stanley Winter, Edith's younger sister, became stepmother to her three nephews and niece when she and John Clelland Dobbie were married at the British Consulate in Quito, Ecuador. In addition to the older boys being educated at CRGS, the Dobbie family had another connection with Colchester in that the lads' maternal aunt, Mrs Emily Susan Adelaide Munday (née Winter), lived in Defoe Crescent, Mile End. When, on 20th September 1937, Malcolm Dobbie followed in his brothers' footsteps, and entered CRGS, it was as a day-scholar rather than as a boarder, with his aunt being named as his guardian in the school Admissions Register. There is little information regarding his two-year stay at CRGS, before he left on 29th July 1939, to become a clerk in a firm of electrical engineers.

It appears that during 1941, having reached the age of eighteen, Malcolm Dobbie enlisted in the RAF. After initial training, he was selected for flight crew training, emerging as a Wireless Operator/Air Gunner with the rank of Sergeant. It appears likely that Sergeant MH Dobbie was posted to 1622 Flight (No. 2 Anti-Aircraft Co-operation Flight) at RAF Gosport in the spring of 1943. There he met with an American, Flight Sergeant Wilbur James ('Bill') Shaver, who originated from Lansing, Michigan.

On 21st November 1941, Shaver had enlisted in the Royal Canadian Air Force at Windsor, Ontario, having crossed Lake Huron from the United States. A year later, after completing his training, he was posted to the UK, arriving at 1622 Flight in April 1943. On 16th August 1943, Shaver and Dobbie took off in a Boulton & Paul Defiant aircraft, an old obsolete night fighter, used at RAF Gosport for target towing. The flight in Defiant DR896, from Gosport to the Anti-Aircraft Range off Eastney, Portsmouth, was trouble-free. However, during the exercise, the aircraft suddenly nose-dived into the sea from a height of about 200 feet, killing the pilot, 'Bill' Shaver, and winchman, Malcolm Dobbie, instantly. An operation was launched to recover the bodies and wreckage of the aircraft.

Sergeant Malcolm Dobbie RAFVR and Flight Sergeant Wilbur James Shaver RCAF were buried adjacent to each other, in the War Grave Section of the Ann's Hill Cemetery, in Gosport, Hampshire. Malcolm Dobbie's gravestone carries the inscription:

There Are Many Doors That Open Into Paradise,
But None So Lit With Glory As The Door Of Sacrifice

He is also commemorated in the stained-glass window of the CRGS library.

Postscript

Of the three Dobbie sons, only 'Bill' Dobbie survived the war, serving as a Captain in the Indian Army, before returning to his occupation as a Rubber Planter in Malaya. A 'larger-than-life' character, 'Bill' became recognised as the leader of the European community in the Pahang area, and was appointed a Justice of the Peace in 1953.

In 1955, he had the distinction of hosting two local Sultans to a party on the estate which he managed, and was further honoured by the Sultan of Pahang two years later, when he was awarded the local equivalent of a knighthood, or life peerage. In 1958, he was awarded an MBE for services to the British community in Malaya. He died in 1964.

Alec Joseph Ruffle

Age:	20
Died:	28th August 1943
Service Number:	1392212
Rank:	Sergeant (Pilot)
Service/Regt:	RAF Volunteer Reserve
Ship/Unit:	No. 9 (Observers) Advanced Flying Unit
Grave/Memorial:	Colchester Borough Cemetery
Plot/Panel:	Section X, Division 14, Grave 32

Alec Joseph Ruffle was born on 29th April 1923, the son of Harold George and Eva Ruffle (née Sage). He was the eldest of three sons, his brothers, Norman and Warwick, being born in 1924 and 1927 respectively. The family lived at 11 Lion Walk, Colchester, where his father worked as the caretaker of Lion Walk Baptist Church, later becoming a Senior ARP Warden when war started.

Alec attended St John's Green Primary School before coming to CRGS as a day-scholar, and member of Harsnett's, in September 1934 on a scholarship from Essex County Council. While at CRGS, he played rugby for the school 1st XV, cricket for the 2nd XI, and was also a good swimmer. Alec left the school in July 1939, after passing his Cambridge School Certificate, and found employment in the Telephone Engineering Department of the General Post Office (GPO). During his work, Alec experienced the blitzes in both London and Birmingham, which prompted him to volunteer for the RAF in 1941. After flying training in Canada, Alec Ruffle returned to England as a Sergeant Pilot, and was posted to No. 9 OAFU (Observers Advanced Flying Unit) at RAF Llandwrog, near Caernarfon, in North Wales.

While at the unit, Alec flew twin-engine Anson Mk1 aircraft on sorties, to provide advanced training for Wireless Operators, Gunners, Air Bombers and Navigators. Unfortunately, while piloting Anson EF952 for a training flight on 28th August 1943, the aircraft crashed on the approach to land back at the base.

Of the crew of five, Alec and a trainee Air Bomber were killed, while a trainee Navigator and two Wireless Operators/Air Gunners, one of whom was under training, were injured.

The Operational Record Book (ORB) for No.9 (O)AFU records the flight crew of EF952 as:

1392212	Sgt. Ruffle A.J.	Pilot	Killed
1396214	Sgt. Melvin G.	Air Bomber (u/t)	Killed
1395440	Sgt. Benton W.A.	Navigator (u/t)	Seriously Injured
1579922	Sgt. Richards A.J.	Wireless Operator/Air Gunner	Multiple Injuries
1579680	Sgt. Carmel G.H.	Wireless Operator/Air Gunner (u/t)	Slightly Injured

Alec's body was brought back to Colchester, and was buried in the Borough Cemetery, where his grave carries the inscription: *Faithful Unto Death, A Crown of Life.*

His younger brother, Norman, also served in the RAF, but survived the war, and died in 1996. Alec's youngest brother, Warwick, died in 2001, having served in the Home Guard during the war.

Alphabet League.

It was impossible for each team to play every other team, but the results show that " F " and " J " teams are the best. " F " won all six matches.

5 points are awarded for a win, none for a loss, 2 for a draw.

	A	B	C	D	E	F	G	H	I	J	K	L	M	N
A	..	o	5	5	o	o	o			5				
B	5	..		o	5	o								
C	o		..	o	o		o	5						2
D	o	5	5	..			o		5			5		
E	5	o	5		..	o		5						
F	5	5			5	..	5					5	5	
G			5	5		o	..	5			o			
H			o		o		o	..	o		o			
I			o					5	..			5	o	
J							5	o		..	5	5	5	5
K	o							o			..	5	5	5
L						5	5		o	o		..	o	5
M			o		o			o	o	o	5		..	
N			2			o			5	o	o	o		..

The following represented F team :—

K. C. Davis (captain)	H. R. Leete
D. J. Allen	K. S. Moss
T. R. Bax	E. L. Page
J. C. Barton	H. G. Rudlin
R. O. Clarke	A. J. Ruffle
P. B. Colleer	M. T. Walker
D. T. King	R. E. Wightman

Account of Alec and his other "F" team members' success in the Alphabet League, in July 1937

185

Reginald Edward Cox

Age:	42
Died:	17th September 1943
Rank:	Civilian
Grave/Memorial:	Commemorated in Westminster Abbey, London
Plot/Panel:	Civilian War Dead Roll of Honour

Reginald Edward Cox was born in Colchester on 14th October 1901, the son of Reginald Arthur & Nellie (née North) Cox of Old Heath Road. His father was a schoolmaster and, after receiving his early education at Barrack Street Council School, Reginald entered Form III of CRGS on 7th May 1912, as a day-scholar and member of Harsnett's House.

The Colcestrian records many of Reginald's achievements during his time at the school, including representing his House at cricket, soccer, shooting and athletics, and performances in several school drama productions.

As well as rising to the rank of Quartermaster Sergeant in the school Cadet Corps, Reginald, known as 'Jim' to his school friends, was selected as a School Prefect, and awarded School Colours for both cricket and soccer.

He was also successful academically, winning prizes for Latin and Science, passing the Cambridge Junior Local Certificate each year from 1915 to 1917, and achieving the Cambridge Senior Certificate in 1917. Reginald went on to pass both the London matriculation, and the Chartered Accountants' Preliminary Examination, before he left CRGS on 26th July 1919, and was articled to Longcroft, Smith & Co. in London.

On leaving the school, he joined the Old Colcestrians, and played hockey and soccer for the OCs, becoming Honorary Secretary for both sections in 1922, and an OC committee member in May 1924.

In December 1924, his mother having passed away three years earlier, Reginald was listed by *The Colcestrian* as living at 'Derwa Lodge', New

Town Road, Colchester. In April of the following year, he passed his final chartered accountancy exam, and in December 1925, *The Colcestrian* reported that: 'Mr RE Cox is now with a firm of Chartered Accountants in the Straits Settlements', although correspondence was still being directed to his address in Colchester.

On 18th July 1929 Reginald married Edith Iris Cox (née Squire) at All Saints' Church, Colchester, sailing two months later from London to Singapore, travelling first-class on-board SS *Gleniffer* via Genoa, the Suez Canal and Penang. From Singapore, Reginald and Edith travelled on to the Federated Malay States, where he took up a post in Kuala Lumpur with the Co-operative Societies Department.

The April 1938 edition of *The Colcestrian* reported on a number of OCs working in the Far East, including 'Jim Leach, Alf Dobbie, Blackburn ('Navvy'), Blackburn 'mi', Cox and Rob Leach'. Two years later, on Wednesday, 18th September, 1940, Edith gave birth to their son, Simon James in Kuala Lumpur, Malaysia.

In early December 1941, almost simultaneously with a pre-emptive surprise air attack against the US Navy at anchor in Pearl Harbor, the Imperial Japanese Army launched a land assault on Thailand and the Malay Peninsula, and opened the Far East theatre of the Second World War.

At the start of the war in Europe, British civilians running businesses in Malay States, particularly the rubber and tin industries had been asked to stay in country, to support the war effort. However, despite plans for women and children to be evacuated to Australia, the speed of the Japanese progress through the jungle caught the Allies by surprise, and many civilians were forced to flee to Singapore for refuge.

It is unclear how, or when, Edith and her young son were able to escape to Australia, but wartime records show that they both survived the Japanese onslaught, and were able to return to the UK, sailing from Adelaide on the TSS *Narbada* on 14th October 1943. They arrived in Avonmouth three months later, and returned to Essex, where they set up home in West Mersea.

Meanwhile, Reginald had remained in Singapore, surviving the aerial bombardment and shelling of the city, until the surrender to the Japanese, on 15th February 1942. Two days later, all British civilians of European descent were required to report to the occupying forces, to be interned. After being held for two weeks in temporary accommodation, they were marched to Changi Prison, a grim concrete building to the east of the island.

The civilian prison, which had been built by the British administration in 1936, and was designed to house 600 inmates, eventually held some 3,500 civilians, including women and children. Internees were separated by gender, with no contact allowed between husbands and wives.

Together with the other prisoners held in Changi, Reginald endured shortages of food and brutal treatment from the Japanese until, on 17th September 1943, he died from kidney failure, and was buried in the local cemetery.

In February 1962, during preparations for the redevelopment of the area, the remains of thousands of civilian victims of the Japanese occupation were unearthed in the area around Changi, and a decision was taken to create a memorial in the centre of the city.

The project was started in the spring of 1963, and in November 1966 over 600 urns, containing the remains of thousands of unknown civilians, were interred on either side of the memorial podium (pictured on the next page). Each year, on 15th February, a memorial service is held at the Civilian War Memorial to remember the victims of the war.

Having survived the war, Edith Cox continued to live for many years in West Mersea, until her death in 1973. Simon Cox studied at Christ's Hospital and St Thomas' Medical School, graduating in 1965, and going on to obtain his FRICS in 1970. He became a highly respected consultant surgeon in Watford, before retiring to Scotland in 2003, where he died on 11th November 2009.

189

Cyril Herbert Cleveland

Age:	31
Died:	2nd October 1943
Service Number:	112739
Rank:	Flight Lieutenant
Service/Regt:	RAF Volunteer Reserve
Ship/Unit:	61 Squadron
Grave/Memorial:	Durnbach (Bad Tolz) War Cemetery
Plot/Panel:	Plot IX 9.A.20

Cyril Herbert Cleveland was born on 16th October 1911, in Colchester, the son of John Charles Cleveland and his wife, Ida Beatrice (née Goate). Having been educated previously at Hamilton Road Central School, in Colchester, Cyril was admitted to CRGS Form Upper VA on 14th September 1928, as a day-scholar, and member of Parr House.

In his brief time at the school, Cyril appears to have shown an aptitude for sport, particularly at cricket and athletics, and to be academically bright, gaining exam passes in six subjects as well as Spoken French.

When he left CRGS 26th July 1929, having passed the Cambridge School Certificate, Cyril trained as a teacher. In the 1939 Register, he was recorded as living in Lewisham, London, where he worked as a schoolmaster. Early in 1941, Cyril married Winifred Olney, a Post Office clerk, who had lodged at the same address in Lewisham.

On 29th September 1941, following the completion of his flying training, Cyril was commissioned as a Pilot Officer in the RAF and, a year later, was promoted to Flying Officer.

In April 1943, Cyril was posted to 617 squadron, which was then being formed for the famous 'Dams' raid. However, his stay with the new squadron was brief and, on 25th April 1943, he received another posting, this time to 61 Squadron, which was also part of 5 Group, based at RAF Syerston, in Nottinghamshire.

Between May and September 1943, Cyril Herbert flew seventeen missions with 61 Squadron over enemy territory, including attacks on the cities of Dortmund, Duisburg, Düsseldorf, Wuppertal, Bochum, Oberhausen, Cologne, Berlin and Hannover.

With the squadron, Cyril also took part in attacks on the Skoda works in Pilsen, the Krupp steel works in Essen, and the famous RAF raid on 17th/18th August, on the German V1 and V2 rocket development site at Peenemunde.

On 29th September 1943, Cyril was again promoted, to Flight Lieutenant. Three days later, in Lancaster ED718 'QR-P', he took off from RAF Syerston at 1832 hrs, as part of a force of nearly 300 aircraft, in a raid against the German city of Munich.

At about 2300 hrs, whilst flying at about 20,000 feet, to the south of the city, the Lancaster came under a sustained attack from a night-fighter, probably the twin-engine Messerschmitt Bf 110 flown by Oberfeldwebel Hans Kreutzberg of 5./NJG101.

As the Lancaster took evasion action, and dived in an attempt to get away, there was an explosion at approximately 6,000ft, which catapulted Squadron Leader Cousens and Sergeant Dunn out of the aircraft.

The two men parachuted to safety, but were soon captured, and taken as prisoners-of-war. Squadron Leader Cousens was held in the local village jail for some hours, before being interned until after the war in the notorious Stalag Luft III, of 'Great Escape' fame, while Sergeant Dunn was taken to Stalag Luft IVB, about 30 miles north of Dresden.

The rest of the crew of ED718 were killed, with the wreckage of the plane being found scattered over an area of six square kilometres. Those who died were buried in Klein Trautshofen Cemetery. However, after the war, their remains were re-interred by the Commonwealth Graves Commission, in Durnbach War Cemetery, on 26th May 1948.

Flight Lieutenant Cyril Herbert Cleveland's gravestone, pictured below, carries the following inscription:

Greater love hath no man than this, that a man lay down his
life for his friends

Arthur Vincent Gowers

Age:	30
Died:	24th October 1943
Service Number:	41066
Rank:	Squadron Leader
Service/Regt:	RAF Volunteer Reserve
Ship/Unit:	183 Squadron
Grave/Memorial:	Runnymede Memorial
Plot/Panel:	Panel 118

With kind permission of www.bbm.org.uk

Arthur Vincent 'Gus' Gowers was born in Chelmsford on 18th June 1913, the second child of Henry Herbert and Hilda Mary Gowers (née Bedingfield). Arthur's siblings were an older brother, Lawrence George Albert, born 17th August 1910, and a younger sister, Mary Louise, born 15th February 1916. Their father was the clerk to Chelmsford Rural District Council, and when Arthur entered CRGS as a day-scholar, on 4th May 1923, the family were living in Clacton, where he had previously been educated at St Clare's College.

Reports which appeared in the *The Colcestrian* during his time at the School indicate that Arthur had an aptitude for art, passing the Examination of The Royal Drawing Society for four years in succession, and culminating in the award of a Division IV Honours Certificate. Arthur left the School on 18th December 1928, and was employed for a short time at the Marconi factory in Chelmsford, before going to work as a junior clerk in the Rates Department of Clacton Urban District Council, and later at Kalamazoo Business Systems.

Arthur's association with military service began in June 1932, when he joined the Honourable Artillery Company (HAC) as a private. However, he discharged himself a year later, enlisting in the Territorial Army as a member of the Royal Army Service Corps (RASC), and receiving a commission as a 2nd Lieutenant in March 1934. Two years later, Arthur resigned both his commission and his job, and worked for a time as a car salesman in Clacton. He obviously had a great affinity with cars and, judging by his regular appearances in the magistrates' court, enjoyed driving them fast!

On 5th July 1937, Arthur Gowers joined the RAFVR, having been provisionally accepted for a Short Service Commission in the RAF. He successfully completed his ab initio flying training at No. 13 Elementary Flying Training School (EFTS) at White Waltham, near Maidenhead, in Berkshire. After making his first solo flight, Arthur wrote in a letter: 'It's a grand feeling, being up there all on your own, swearing into the telephones at an imaginary instructor! I had an irresistible desire to 'shoot up' the neighbouring village, but was checked by the thought that low flying is the quickest way out of the Service.'

Commissioned into the RAF on 24th October, Acting Pilot Officer Arthur Gowers continued his training at No. 5 FTS, at RAF Sealand, in North Wales, receiving his 'wings' on February 18th 1938. On 4th June, having completed his flying training, he was posted to No. 26 Maintenance Unit, at Cardington, in Bedfordshire, for flying duties. Little more than two months later, on 10th August 1938, he joined 85 Squadron, recently re-formed as a fighter squadron at Debden, in Essex, and soon to be re-equipped with the new Hawker Hurricane Mk1 single-wing fighter. There the squadron started to prepare in earnest for the coming conflict, which now seemed inevitable.

In the spring of 1939, with the threat of war continuing to grow, Arthur married Joan Renée Church at Newmarket. Their daughter, Gloria, was born in the October of that year. In the meantime, with war having been declared in Europe, September 1939 saw the squadron move from Debden to Normandy, as part of 60 Fighter Wing of the British Expeditionary Force, to help in the defence of France. However, a few months later, suffering badly from jaundice, and unable to fly, Arthur Gowers was repatriated to hospital in England.

When he returned to 85 Squadron on June 21st 1940, having fully recovered from his illness, the squadron had returned to Debden, having lost all but three aircraft during the 'Battle of France'. It was now commanded by Squadron Leader Peter Townsend DFC, whose own accomplishments during the 'Battle of Britain' in the summer of 1940 would lead to him becoming an equerry to George VI, and, after the war, to a relationship with Princess Margaret which would have led to marriage, had he not been a divorcee.

By mid-July 1940, Arthur had returned to operational flying with 'B' Flight, carrying out North Sea convoy patrols by day, and defensive sorties over East Anglia by night. In early August the squadron scored its first victories against the Luftwaffe over England, while continuing to provide air cover for Allied shipping. In the evening of 18th August, having been ordered to patrol over Canterbury, the squadron spotted an enemy raid of some 200 aircraft several miles to the east of Chelmsford, over the Essex coast. In the dogfight which followed, Gus Gowers, got his first 'kill', shooting down a German Ju 87 'Stuka' aircraft over Foulness Island, while the squadron tally included ten enemy aircraft destroyed, four more being claimed as 'probables', and six damaged.

The following day the squadron moved to Croydon, exchanging duties with 111 Squadron. On 28th August they engaged another large enemy formation over Dungeness, which resulted in Gowers being credited with damaging a Messerschmitt Bf 110. Two days later, he destroyed another Bf 110 over Bethersden. During the morning of 31st August, the squadron was again engaged in combat over southern England, with Gowers being credited with the 'probable kill' of a Bf 109 fighter near Biggin Hill. In the evening of the same day, he was involved in another dogfight with a Bf 109 fighter, this time over Folkestone. Firing two short bursts from his eight machine guns, and seeing bits of the enemy aircraft fly off, he eventually saw it go down in flames.

On 1st September, while again in combat over Oxted, in Surrey, with a number of Messerschmitt Bf 109s, Gowers' Hurricane was badly damaged by enemy cannon fire. Wounded in the foot, and with severe burns to his hands and face, Gus was unable to bale out of his aircraft. Fortunately, as the Hurricane rolled over, he was tipped out of the cockpit, and was able to deploy his parachute. Descending from 15,000 feet, and protected from enemy fighters by another Hurricane circling round him, Gus landed safely and was taken to Caterham Mental Hospital for medical treatment, where he was later visited by his Commanding Officer. In his book *Duel of Eagles*, Squadron Leader Peter Townsend describes his visit to the hospital, and how, despite his agony, the 'irrepressible 'Gus' Gowers, to whom life was a huge joke was amused by the thought that he had ended up in a 'loony-bin'. Two days later Gowers' promotion to Flying Officer was confirmed.

After nearly four months of treatment and convalescence, Gus returned to 85 Squadron on 28th December 1940, by which time the RAF had effectively won the 'Battle of Britain'. The squadron had, by now, moved to a new base at Gravesend, in Kent, and was carrying out night patrols against Luftwaffe bomber raids on London. Six months later, on 1st July 1941, *The London Gazette* reported that Flying Officer Arthur Vincent Gowers had been awarded the Distinguished Flying Cross for 'gallantry and devotion to duty in the execution of air operations.'

Having completed his tour of duty, Gus was attached to RAF Kenley, where he undertook Control Room duties. On 3rd September 1941, he was promoted to Flight Lieutenant and three weeks later received a 'Mention in Despatches'. After being posted to 56 Operational Training Unit (OTU), RAF Sutton Bridge, for refresher training, he joined 504 Squadron in November 1941, as a Flight Commander at RAF Ballyhalbert, in Northern Ireland. A posting to Air HQ Far East followed three months later, but the hot climate so badly affected his burned hands that, after spending a month in hospital in Delhi, Gus was forced to return to the UK in May 1942.

He was then sent to 53 OTU, at RAF Llandow, in South Wales, to learn to fly the new Hawker Typhoon fighter-bomber. After completing the training, Gus joined 56 Squadron at Snailwell on 8th August 1942, but less than three weeks later, the engine of his Typhoon over-revved, causing him to crash land in a field at Oulton in Norfolk. The aircraft bounced over a hedge, and across a road, with the starboard wing hitting a tree along the way, and the engine falling off, before the wrecked fighter finally came to a halt. Although the aircraft was written off, Gus escaped with only slight injuries and, after being treated for a couple of days at Norwich Hospital, he was transferred to the Sick Quarters at RAF Coltishall.

On November 20th 1942, Arthur Gowers received a further promotion, to Squadron Leader, and was posted to RAF Church Fenton, to take command of the newly-formed 183 Squadron, equipped with the Type 1B bomber version of the Hawker Typhoon. Poor weather, and teething problems with the aircraft, initially hampered flying training. Finally, during March 1943, the squadron was able to fly operational sorties against dummy targets several times a day, and it was eventually declared operational on 5th April 1943.

183 Squadron, December 1942 – Squadron Leader Gowers is seated in the centre of the photo
(Photo: John & Susan Rowe, via A. Goodrum)

On 19th April 1943, and led by Squadron Leader Gus Gowers, 183 Squadron took part in its first raid on France, bombing the Yainville Power Station. Various ground targets were also attacked on the return journey and all the squadron's aircraft returned safely, although the starboard aileron of the CO's plane was hit by enemy fire.

Over the next few months, the squadron had a somewhat nomadic existence, moving from one airfield to another, and living under canvas, despite occasionally inclement weather. During this period, the local press in Essex reported, with no small amount of pride, that Gus had accepted an invitation to take the salute at a 'March Past' as part of a 'Wings for Victory Week' Parade in Chelmsford.

During June, the squadron began making regular attacks on enemy airfields and shipping, which were to continue throughout the summer of 1943. Meanwhile, Gus attended a course on 'Combined Operations', before returning to lead an armed shipping reconnaissance sortie on 2nd July. In September 1943, the squadron moved to Cornwall, first to Perranporth, and then Predannack, from where it escorted Mosquitos on operations over the Brest peninsula, as well as continuing to attack enemy shipping and airfields.

In the early evening of Sunday, 24th October, flying Typhoon 1b JP396, Squadron Leader Arthur 'Gus' Gowers led an attack at zero feet on the MS *Münsterland*, which was believed to be carrying rare metals for the production of V1 and V2 missiles, and was moored in the heavily-defended docks at Cherbourg. Unfortunately, following an earlier attack by 263 Squadron, escorted by Hurricanes of 257 Squadron, the dock defences were on high alert.

As a result, the 183 Squadron Operational Record Book notes that: 'The Squadron had to fly through the fiercest concentration of flak yet encountered, *(yet)* the attack was made with great courage and daring. Two bombs were thought to have made direct hits, while others were very near.' The CO's aircraft was seen to go down in flames, just outside the mole, while two other Typhoons were brought down by the flak, and a fourth had to make a 'wheels-up' landing back at base.

Having no known grave, the sacrifice of Squadron Leader Arthur Vincent 'Gus' Gowers DFC is remembered on Panel 118 of the Runnymede Memorial. However, in the cemetery at Cherbourg, there lies the grave of an unnamed senior RAF officer, who died on the 24th October 1943, and is marked by a stone with the inscription *'Known Unto God'*. Recent research has unearthed strong evidence to suggest that this may, after all, be the final resting place of Gus Gowers.

Arthur John Berry

Age:	22
Died:	4th November 1943
Service Number:	136184
Rank:	Flying Officer
Service/Regt:	RAF Volunteer Reserve
Ship/Unit:	RAF Belvedere, Flight Training School
Grave/Memorial:	Harare (Pioneer) Cemetery, Zimbabwe
Plot/Panel:	Europe Plot, Grave 116

Arthur John Newton Berry was born on 14th June 1921, in Bromley, Kent, the only son of Walter James Berry, a music salesman, and his wife, Alice Mabel (née Newton).

Arthur John Newton Berry

John Berry (as he was known) and his family were living in Trinity Street, Colchester, when he was admitted to CRGS on 16th September 1932, as a day-scholar and member of Parr's House, having previously attended St John's Green School, in Colchester, and Bromley National School, in Kent.

During his time at CRGS, John Berry demonstrated great all-round prowess at sport, playing soccer, representing the school at swimming and cricket, and showing himself to be a fine athlete, equalling the school record for the 220-yard sprint.

However, it was as a rugby player that he excelled, playing for the school 1st XV, and winning full colours as a member of the team that created a record for the number of matches won in a season, scoring over 300 points, while conceding only 108. He was also selected to play for the Eastern Counties Public Schools XV against his native county, Kent Public Schools, at Blackheath.

Early in his playing career, *The Colcestrian* described his play at stand-off half as promising: 'He is powerful and fast, and has scored two or three good tries in the matches, but his passing is uncertain, and his tackling poor. He will never do much if his tackling does not improve.' A year later, it reported that he was 'very fast in attack, and quick to find an opening.'

His success continued into the early part of the following year, with the April 1937 issue of the *The Colcestrian* relating further stories of CRGS wins with John Berry among the backs to score, including two matches in which he ran in a hat-trick of tries.

John Berry left the school on 7th March 1938, returned to Bromley with his family, and joined Southern Railways as a junior clerk in the London Eastern Divisional Superintendent's Office. There he became a regular member of the company's rugby XV and was selected to play for the English Railways against their Irish counterparts, in Ireland, scoring twice in the match.

Shortly after the outbreak of war, John Berry volunteered to serve in the RAF, and was called up in June 1940. He initially trained as a Wireless Operator, before he was selected for pilot training, and sent to No. 25 EFTS (Elementary Flying Training School) at Belvedere, near Salisbury in Southern Rhodesia (now Zimbabwe).

Initially, pupil pilots spent six weeks at Hillside Camp, on an Initial Training Wing (ITW) course lasting six weeks, before progressing to the Elementary Flying Training Scheme (EFTS), for a further six-week course, where they received 50 hours of basic aviation instruction on simple trainer aircraft such as the de Havilland Tiger Moth, and tuition in a variety of ground subjects.

Those pilot cadets who showed promise, progressed to No. 20 SFTS (Service Flying Training School), and received intermediate and advanced training, either as fighter or multi-engine pilots, using aircraft such the North American Harvard and Airspeed Oxford. The complete pilot's course initially lasted six months, with each trainee having to fly at least 150 hours to qualify.

Having graduated from the SFTS course, and been awarded his 'wings', John Berry was commissioned as a Pilot Officer on 16th January

1943. He then continued, to take an instructor's course, before being posted back to 25 EFTS to teach further trainee pilots.

During his time in Rhodesia, John wrote many letters home, describing his situation in that country, where, inevitably, he played for the station rugby XV. Two of his letters were printed in *The Colcestrian*, while in another John wrote of his thrill at seeing his first pupil receive his 'wings'.

Having been promoted to Flying Officer with effect from 16th July 1943, John Berry had completed almost 1000 hours of flying time, when he took off from Belvedere on 4th November 1943, for a solo flight in Tiger Moth T7480. Unfortunately, about two miles from Pendennis, south-east of Bulawayo, his aircraft was involved in a mid-air collision with another Tiger Moth (DE270), and both aircraft crashed to the ground.

Miraculously, the crew of the other aircraft survived, but Flying Officer Arthur John Newton Berry was killed in the crash, and was laid to rest in the Salisbury (now Harare) Pioneer Military Cemetery.

136184 P/O Berry,
R.A.F., Belvedere,
S. Rhodesia.
29, Sept.

Dear Mum and Dad,

I suppose it's about time I wrote to you again. Really there's nothing very interesting to write about. The rugger season has ended out here and the rag game that I told you about last time did not come off. I expect later on we shall have a rugger supper and invite all the other people to come along

Two weekends ago I went to a place called Mazoe with the tennis team. I did not play myself but thought it would make quite a nice day out. One of the chaps has a car so we went out in this. The journey out was quite pleasant except for one rather unfortunate occurrence. About half-way there we had a puncture. With several of us there to help we soon had the wheel off and the spare one fixed. I suppose it took us about three minutes to fix. When we arrived there we were not quite sure of the way, so we stopped and asked someone who told us one way and then somebody told us another way, so we didn't quite know which way to go. However we finally arrived there quite safely and found the opposing team waiting for us. There was also a bowling green as well as the tennis courts and one of the people there asked those of us who were not playing tennis if we would like to play bowls. Well I've never played bowls before in my life so I thought I'd like to try. So we were given four "woods" as they are called and told how to set about it. There are all sorts of queer expressions that are peculiar to bowls and we found it rather amusing to try and learn some of them. I rather enjoyed my first game of bowls. The day was quite a success all round because the tennis team won their match and those of us who weren't playing tennis learnt how to play bowls.

I hope you can read this typing. Please excuse any mistakes as this is the first time I have tried typing. I think this is the best way of writing these things as you can get far more in the small space you have.

Love,
John.

Letter from John to his parents, from Southern Rhodesia, December 1943

Eric Ralph Pearson

Age:	23
Died:	12th December 1943
Service Number:	61977
Rank:	Flight Lieutenant
Service/Regt:	RAFVR
Ship/Unit:	72 Sq.
Grave/Memorial:	Rome War Cemetery
Plot/Panel:	Ref. I. E. 6

Jack Pearson
(courtesy of
Richard Lucking)

Eric Ralph Pearson, known as 'Jack', was born on 11th April 1920, the only son of Sydney Walter Pearson, an Elementary Schoolteacher at Lexden Council School, and Florence Ethel (née Berry). Eric had two sisters, Sybil who was five years his senior, and Doreen, known as Dawn, five years younger. Sydney originally hailed from Nottinghamshire and had served in WW1, enlisting in 1915 just a year after getting married. The family lived at 44 Mersea Road, Colchester, but later moved to 18 Gladwin Road.

Jack came to CRGS in September 1930 from Canterbury Road Council School and left in July 1939. He received total exemption from fees from Essex LEA and passed his Cambridge School Certificate in 1935. He was particularly proficient at rugby and in his final year, 1938-39 was 1st XV captain, as well as being a Prefect and Head Boy. *The Colcestrian* describes him as 'a good bustling (prop) forward' though adding 'his height makes it difficult for him to fit in comfortably and he seems to find it rather a long way to his opponents' knees'. Perhaps unsurprisingly he was 'most conspicuous in line-outs'. As for his leadership, he was 'an able and popular captain'. He also represented the school at water-polo, and, after leaving, he played rugby for the OCS Rugby Club, turning out against the school in 1940 and 1941.

Jack did not get a job immediately after leaving CRGS – the 1939 Register describes him as 'not yet employed, seeking work'. In fact, he had decided to take the Civil Service entrance exams. By May 1940, and now awaiting admission, he chose instead to enlist, joining the RAFVR.

In July 1940 Jack began his training at No. 1 Recovery Wing at Babbacombe, Devon, before moving on to No. 8 Flight Training School at RAF Montrose from November 1940 to April 1941. He then went to RAF Coltishall in Norfolk, followed by Sutton Bridge, Lincolnshire, in September 1941. The Imperial War Museum Archive holds fourteen letters which he wrote to his sister, and which provide useful historical detail on RAF training, flying solo for the first time and the quality (or otherwise) of RAF accommodation, as well as recording Jack's frustration at being unable to fly in times of bad weather.

Jack began his active service with 504 Squadron based at RAF Ibsley in Hampshire from March 1942 to March 1943, as a Flight Lieutenant, flying a mixture of defensive and offensive missions, including taking part in sweeps across France. He was then transferred to 72 Squadron, also known as Basutoland Spitfire Squadron because a number of its planes were donated by the government of Basutoland (now Lesotho) in Southern Africa. The squadron was involved in supporting the Allied invasion of Sicily and Italy. *The Colcestrian* of December 1943 reports that it claimed its 200th enemy aircraft in Italy when Jack Pearson shot down an FW190.

However, on 9th December 1943 Jack was one a group of six Spitfires which took off from Capodichino, Naples, to strafe enemy transport just north of Pescina, 75 miles east of Rome. A POW who was one of a group of escapees witnessed what happened next. He described one of the Spitfires as firing on a truck, which was believed to contain dynamite, from a very low altitude. The plane was caught in the blast from the explosion and crashed within 25 yards of the POWs.

Jack Pearson, the pilot, was killed instantly in the explosion. He was buried in Montelibretti Civil Cemetery by Italian priests, and later transferred to Rome Military Cemetery. He was 23 years old.

John Scales

Age:	30
Died:	20th December 1943
Service Number:	120525
Rank:	Flying Officer
Service/Regt:	Royal Air Force
Ship/Unit:	466 (RAAF) Squadron
Grave/Memorial:	Rheinberg War Cemetery
Plot/Panel:	Plot 18, Row E
Additional Notes:	Collective Grave 19-25

John Scales was the eldest child of Edward Herbert Athol Scales and Victoria Maud (née Arnold), of Harvey's Farm at Peldon in Essex. Edward Scales, who originated from near Wellington, New Zealand, had served as a First Mate in the Merchant Navy, and then joined the Royal Navy during the First World War, before settling in the UK. In 1951, leaving George Scales to run the farm, Edward, Victoria and Maude emigrated to New Zealand aboard the SS *Rangitata*.

John Scales

Edward initially made his home in London, where John was born on 3rd June 1920. John had two younger brothers, George and Arthur (also known as 'Joe'), and a sister, Maude, who were also born in London. In the mid-1920s, the family moved out of London, to Merrick's Farm near Vange, in Essex, before moving to Peldon in 1933.

Having previously attended Pitsea Council School, and Palmer's School at Grays, John was admitted to CRGS on 16th October 1933, joining Dugard House as a day-scholar. While at the school, John did well at athletics, particularly the steeplechase and other long-distance events, as did his brother, George, who also attended the school. Neither, however, was particularly academic. John left the school on 27th July 1938 to work with his father on the family dairy farm.

John Scales joined the RAF in late 1941 and, having passed through the Initial Training Wing, learned to fly at No. 22 Flight Training School. He was commissioned as a pilot on 29th April 1942 and promoted to Flying Officer with effect from 29th October 1942. During August 1943 he was posted to 466 Squadron, a Royal Australian Air Force (RAAF) Squadron, operating under RAF command as part of No. 4 Group. For most of the war it formed part of the main Bomber Command force.

At this time the squadron was transitioning from the two-engine Vickers Wellington bomber to the new, four-engine Handley–Page Halifax Mark II aircraft. This involved a three-month period of training on the new aircraft, and 466 were the first non-Pathfinder squadron to be equipped with H2S, a revolutionary airborne, ground scanning radar system.

The squadron resumed combat operations on December 1st, when twelve aircraft laid mines off Terschelling Island. However, the squadron's first real test came on the night of December 20th/21st, when sixteen of the squadron's Halifaxes were part of a force of 650 aircraft which attacked Frankfurt. The attack was largely unsuccessful, with two of the squadron's aircraft lost, and another returning to England badly damaged.

One of the two aircraft that failed to return was Halifax III 'HX236 HD-J', piloted by John Scales, which had taken off at 1703 hrs, and is believed to have crashed in the vicinity of Wiesbaden. All of the crew were killed. They were originally buried in Winzenheim, but were re-interred after the war in Rheinberg War Cemetery.

The headstone on John Scales' grave, pictured on the next page, bears the inscription:

O Valiant Heart
Tranquil you lie
Your memory hallowed in the land you loved

Postscript:

John's brother, George, served in the Royal Navy in WW2. In 1945 he was awarded the Croix de Guerre by the Provisional French Government in for his bravery on D-Day – unloading 400 tons of ammunition on 'Juno' beach under heavy fire – though he did not actually receive the medal until 2007. After the war, he increasingly took on the responsibility for running his parents' farm - they finally decided to emigrate back to New Zealand in 1951. Having worked hard to turn a profit, he sold Harvey's Farm in 1955, buying another, ultimately more profitable farm at Abbess Roding, near Chelmsford.

Following his success in this, George became well-known for his farming expertise. By 2007 he had had 41 letters published in The Times, even more in the farming press, and dozens read out on Radio 4. He also lectured in agricultural colleges, schools and to NFU groups. His farm was consistently the top of the agricultural 'league tables' compiled by Cambridge University, and his success featured in several radio and TV programmes. His life was also made the subject of a biography by Ian Baird. He died in 2013, aged 92.

Robert Carmichael Purkis

Age:	20
Died:	13th January 1944
Service Number:	258690
Rank:	Lieutenant
Service/Regt:	Essex Regiment
Ship/Unit:	2nd Battalion
Grave/Memorial:	Rangoon Memorial, Myanmar
Plot/Panel:	Ref. Face 15

Robert Carmichael Purkis, known as 'Michael', was born on 13th March 1923, in Lewisham. He was the elder son of Dr George Samuel Purkis and Marjorie Carmichael Purkis (née Craig). He had a younger brother, Ian Edward, born in 1925. Dr Purkis taught Modern Languages at CRGS from September 1927 until his retirement in 1954, eventually becoming Second Master (Deputy Head) in 1950. He had served in the Middle East with the Royal Artillery in WW1 and helped to run the school Cadet Corps. He taught mainly French but was also proficient in Italian and had compiled an English-Italian dictionary.

Michael was at the CRGS Senior School from April 1932 to July 1940, having previously attended the Pre from 1929. The family initially lived at 151 Maldon Road, Colchester, but soon moved to 'Holwood', Alexandra Avenue, West Mersea. Michael passed his Cambridge School Certificate in July 1939. He was a good swimmer, achieving considerable success at the school swimming sports, and also enjoyed rugby. He was a committee member of the stamp club, and in July 1940 he was on a list of CRGS students engaged in some form of National Service as a 'Messenger' at West Mersea, where his father was an officer in the local Home Guard.

Soon after leaving CRGS, Michael enlisted in the forces, joining the 70th Battalion of the Essex Regiment. *The Colcestrian* of June 1941 records him as the Lance-Corporal of D Company. His commission as a 2nd Lieutenant in the Essex Regiment was published on 9th March 1943.

Robert's memorial also indicates service with the Coldstream Guards at some stage in his military career.

According to his obituary notice in the Essex County Standard Michael appears to have been transferred, at some point, to the 1st Battalion of the Sierra Leone Regiment. This Regiment served in Burma and was involved in heavy fighting against the Japanese in the Arakan campaigns, which aimed to push the Japanese out of the north-west of the country. The first Arakan campaign had been a failure, but, after months of training, re-arming and resupplying, a second offensive was begun in late December 1943. At the beginning of 1944, the leading formations came up against the Japanese defence lines running from the port of Maungdaw to Buthidaung. For nearly a week a series of bitter battles was fought north of Maungdaw.

On 9th January 1944 forces of the 5th Indian Division finally took the port, finding that during the previous night the Japanese defenders had slipped away. Preparations then began to capture two railway tunnels linking Maungdaw with the Kalapanzin valley, but the Japanese struck back first. A strong force from the Japanese 55th Division infiltrated Allied lines to attack the 7th Indian Infantry Division from the rear, overrunning the divisional HQ and cutting both Divisions' supply routes.

Michael is recorded as having died on January 13th, 1944 on active service on the India Command, so it seems probable that it was during this campaign. He is commemorated on The Rangoon Memorial which honours nearly 27,000 land forces of the British Empire who died during the campaigns in Burma and who have no known grave.

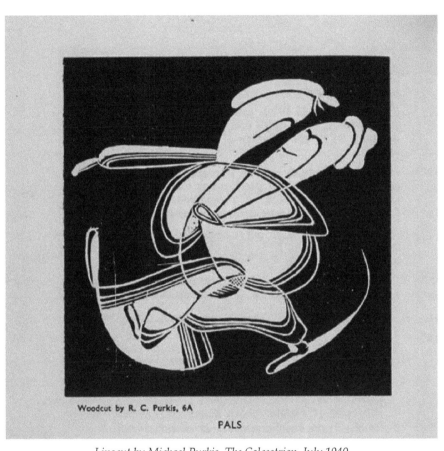

Woodcut by R. C. Purkis, 6A

PALS

Linocut by Michael Purkis, The Colcestrian, July 1940

Guy Currie Bevington

Age:	27
Died:	16th February 1944
Service Number:	289940
Rank:	2nd Lieutenant
Service/Regt:	Dorsetshire Regiment
Grave/Memorial:	Beachhead War Cemetery, Anzio, Italy
Plot/Panel:	Plot XXII Grave D.12

The life of Guy Currey Bevington, and the circumstances of his death on active service, are something of a mystery, due to the limited information about him that is available.

It is known that he was born on 18th January 1917 in Edmonton, North London, the youngest of three sons of John Currey Bevington and his wife Hilda Mary (née Burton). Guy's eldest brother, John Rex Bevington, had been born in June 1911, while his second brother, Timothy Burton Bevington was born in July 1913.

It would appear that Guy's family were fairly affluent, since his father, a stockbroker, had attended Harrow School as a boy. During the mid-1920s, the family moved away from London, to live in 'Woodham Lodge', a 17th century house at Bicknacre in Essex. Having previously been educated at Eversley School, at Southwold, in Suffolk, Guy followed his older brothers to CRGS, where he was admitted, as a boarder, on 23rd September 1927.

His time at the school was brief, as he left CRGS at the beginning of April 1929, apparently for reasons of ill health, and moved to Maldon Hall Preparatory School. However, in July 1929, *The Colcestrian* reported on the performance of TB Bevington in the Chorus for the school production of Gilbert & Sullivan's 'Utopia Limited', while GC Bevington was noted as playing timpani in the school orchestra.

Although Guy's father died in June 1933, the family continued to live at 'Woodham Lodge', although by the time that WW2 began, John Rex

Bevington, having married in September 1937, was living in Kent, where he was an Assistant Inspector of Weights and Measures. However, Timothy Bevington, who was employed by the Electric Supply Company as a transport officer, continued to live at home with his mother until his marriage in November 1939.

While neither of his brothers appears to have a wartime service record for the armed forces, a notice in *The London Gazette Supplement*, published on 2nd November 1943, stated that Cadet Guy Currey Bevington had been commissioned as a 2nd Lieutenant in The Dorsetshire Regiment with effect from 28th August 1943. It would seem that not long afterwards, Guy was sent overseas, to take part in the Allied campaign to liberate Italy.

Towards the end of 1943, with Allied forces making slow progress in their advance from southern Italy towards Rome, Winston Churchill ordered British commanders to devise a plan to speed up the advance, by launching a two-division amphibious assault behind the German defensive lines, known as the 'Gustav' line.

Code-named 'Operation Shingle', the landings at the Agro Pontino, an area of reclaimed marshland near Anzio, started on 22nd January 1944. The assault by a combined British and US force achieved complete surprise, putting 36,000 men and over 3,000 vehicles ashore on the first day, and succeeded in establishing a beachhead against minimal opposition, and with few Allied casualties.

However, instead of capitalising on the element of surprise, by advancing towards Rome in order to force the Germans to divert troops from defending the Gustav Line, or turning south, to attack the German defences from the rear, the Allied commander chose instead to consolidate the beachhead against a possible counter-attack. This hesitation was to cost the Allied forces dearly.

The delay in moving out from the beachhead allowed the German commander, Field Marshal Albert Kesselring, to respond to the attack by rushing troops to block all of the roads leading from Anzio, and then to reinforce their position with over 40,000 men. A few days later, in early February 1944, the Germans began their first attack, which was followed by several days of heavy artillery exchanges between the two opposing forces.

211

An Allied counter-attack on 11th February was repulsed by the Germans, who had intercepted US and British radio communications, and thus had been prepared for the assault. Five days later, the Germans launched 'Operation Fischfang', which succeeded in pushing the Allies dangerously close to the beach, until a carefully timed counter-attack by Allied reserves halted the German advance.

However, during these four days of fighting at Anzio the Allies suffered 3,500 casualties and the Germans 5,400. Two days later, the Allied commander, Major General John P Lucas was relieved of his command. It was on 16th February 1944, during the first day of the German assault, that 2nd Lieutenant Guy Currey Bevington was killed at Anzio, and was buried in the Beach Head War Cemetery.

The situation at Anzio then developed into a stalemate, with both sides bringing reinforcements into the area, until the Allies had amassed 150,000 men in the Anzio beachhead. On 23rd May, five British and two US divisions broke through the German blockade and headed towards Rome. Twelve days later, they marched into the Italian capital.

Ivor Meirion Carter

Age: 36
Died: 1st March 1944
Rank: Sub-Lieutenant
Service/Regt: Royal Naval Volunteer Reserve
Ship/Unit: HMS *Gould*
Grave/Memorial: Plymouth Naval Memorial
Plot/Panel: Panel 93, Column 1

Ivor Meirion Carter was born on 8th March 1907, the eldest son of Charles and Elizabeth Margaret Carter (née Adams), of Errington Road, Colchester, Essex. Two siblings having previously died, Ivor had two surviving older sisters, Gwladys and Olwen, a younger brother, Idris, and a younger sister, Bronwen. In the 1911 census, his father described his occupation as 'House Decorator's Foreman', but by the time Ivor started attending CRGS, Charles had become the manager of the plumbing and decorating business.

Ivor Meirion Carter

Having been educated at the Wesleyan School, Ivor was admitted to CRGS on 17th September 1918, as a day-scholar and member of Dugard House. He left the school on 7th February 1925, having passed his Cambridge School Certificate examination the previous year, and went to work in London at the Sun Fire Office, where he remained for seventeen years, and becoming an Insurance Inspector.

During his time at CRGS, Ivor Carter became the only boy to be given his Full Colours in four different sports: rugby, soccer, cricket and hockey.

He was the first rugby captain in the school, and later captain of the Old Colcestrian team. He also played rugby for Upper Clapton and cricket for Chelmsford Cricket Club.

The December 1923 edition of *The Colcestrian* reported his selection as a School Prefect, and his election to the committee of the CRGS 'Tudor Society'. It commented that, as a footballer, he was: 'A much improved player, good ball control, very hard working, the makings of a good back', and had been awarded his school First XI Colours.

The following year he was awarded School Colours for cricket, represented CRGS in the school's first game of rugby football, and was noted to be 'One of the best House Captains that Dugard's have had'.

Having left the school, Ivor joined the Old Colcestrian Society, playing rugby and cricket for them, and becoming a member of the OCS committee. He was described as 'one of our keenest OCs, and perhaps one of the best all-round (cricket) players we have produced'.

Ivor Carter entered the Chatham Division of the Royal Navy on 11th May 1942, as an Ordinary Seaman. On completion of his three months 'New Entry' training, at HMS *Ganges*, in Shotley in Suffolk, Ivor Carter was posted to HMS *Porcupine* (G93), a newly commissioned P-class destroyer.

In September 1942, having completed her sea trials, *Porcupine* sailed to Scapa Flow, to join the Home Fleet. However, her time in the Orkneys was brief, and she was soon on her way to Gibraltar, to join Force 'H', and other P-class ships, as part of the 3rd Destroyer Flotilla.

On her arrival in the Mediterranean, HMS *Porcupine* was used to escort military convoys. On 11th November, she helped rescue 241 men from the *Nieuw Zeeland*, a Dutch troop transport that had been torpedoed by U-380 about 80 miles east of Gibraltar. *Porcupine* was also part of the destroyer screen for Royal Navy battleships engaged in 'Operation Torch', the Allied invasion of French North Africa, and carried out anti-submarine patrols in the days following the landings.

On 8th December, *Porcupine* was deployed, with four other destroyers, to escort two troopships and a depot ship from Gibraltar to Oran, in Algeria. During the passage, the convoy came under attack from submarine U-602, and HMS *Porcupine* was hit by a torpedo, killing seven men, and nearly splitting the ship in two. However, though critical, the damage was localised, and after most of her crew had been taken off by HMS *Vanoc*, *Porcupine* was towed into the Algerian port of Arzeu.

Later, having been towed to the port of Oran, she was declared a total loss, stripped of her armament, stores etc., cut into two halves, and towed back to the UK. In Portsmouth, the two halves were used as accommodation, with the fore part of the ship being known informally as HMS *Pork*, while the rear was known as HMS *Pine*! Meanwhile, the surviving members of her crew were eventually brought back to the UK, where they arrived at the beginning of the New Year.

During his service on HMS *Porcupine*, Ivor's abilities had obviously been noticed, and he found himself selected for officer training. He arrived at HMS *King Alfred*, the RNVR Training Establishment on Whale Island, in Portsmouth, on 21st January 1943, and three months later was promoted to Acting Sub-Lieutenant. While at HMS *King Alfred*, the following comment was placed in Ivor's Service Record:

> 'A very sound type of older officer. He is athletic for his
> age (36) and could be relied upon to see any job through.
> Has also a useful brain.'

Four months' further training followed, at the Royal Naval College, Greenwich and at the Royal Navy Gunnery Training Schools (HMS *Wildfire*, HMS *Wembury* and HMS *Excellent*).

In July 1943, as Ivor came to the end of his training, he became engaged to be married to Mary Arnold, of Tiptree. However, a month later, Ivor found himself on the other side of the Atlantic, having been posted overseas, to help supervise the commissioning and sea trials of HMS *Gould* (K476).

HMS *Gould* was a Royal Navy Captain-class Frigate, originally constructed as the US Navy Evarts-class Escort Destroyer USS *Lovering* (DE-272). Under the command of Lieutenant Daniel William Ungoed RN, she was commissioned into service in the Royal Navy on 18th September 1943, and started sea trials off the eastern seaboard of the United States.

HMS Gould during sea trials. Photo: Paul Shaw

On 9th October 1943, Ivor was confirmed in the rank of Sub-Lieutenant, and on 1st December HMS *Gould* conducted her first operation, by helping to escort the 52 ships of Convoy HX 268 across the Atlantic, from New York. She left the convoy when it arrived in UK waters ten days later, and joined the 1st Escort Group, based in Belfast, and consisting of nine Captain-class Frigates. Such Groups were a Royal Navy tactical response to the threat of the Kriegsmarine's U-Boat 'wolfpacks'. They were well-organised, and rigorously trained in anti-submarine tactics, using teamwork as an effective means to defend shipping convoys in the Battle of the Atlantic.

The Group's first operational patrol took them into the North Atlantic and, on 25th February 1944, having got a sonar contact, HMS *Gore* made an initial depth charge attack, without producing any result. She was then joined by HMS *Affleck*, which guided HMS *Gore* and HMS *Gould* in a 'creeping attack', which damaged U-91 so badly that it had to surface, where the gunners on the *Affleck* finished it off. Sixteen survivors were picked up and taken prisoner, but 38 of the U-Boat crew lost their lives.

The 1st Escort Group were next directed to a position near the Azores. There, on 29th February, HMS *Garlies* detected a German submarine, but her 'Hedgehog' anti-submarine mortar failed to operate when she tried to attack the U-Boat. HMS *Affleck*, HMS *Gore*, and HMS *Gould* then joined the attack, which continued through the night, with the four frigates dropping more than a hundred depth charges between them.

Needing to refuel, HMS *Gore* and *Garlies* were forced to head for Gibraltar, but HMS *Affleck* and *Gould* continued with the attack, despite worsening weather. During the afternoon of 1st March, U-358 was forced to the surface, but succeeded in firing two acoustic torpedoes, known to the Allies as 'GNATs', which were designed to home in on the propeller of escort ships.

One torpedo missed, but the second struck the *Gould*, destroying the stern section. Without power the crew were unable to fight the fire, and having lost most of the 'Carley' life-rafts in the stern section, the crew of the *Gould* were forced to abandon ship at position 45°46'N 23°16'W. HMS *Affleck* continued to press home the attack on U-358, eventually sinking it. However, 124 members of the crew of HMS *Gould* died in the sinking, with only fourteen of her crew surviving.

Sub-Lieutenant Ivor Meirion Carter was among those who perished with the loss of HMS *Gould*, leaving his parents, and his fiancée, to mourn his passing. In July 1944 *The Colcestrian* reported that: 'Sub-Lieutenant Ivor Carter of 'Gwynfa', 23 Errington Road, Colchester, has been officially posted as missing, presumed killed'. After the war, in the December 1948 edition, a correspondent also recollected his 'bland impishness, singing comic songs, during school sing-songs'.

Having no grave, but the sea, Ivor Meirion Carter is commemorated on the Plymouth Naval Memorial, and on the stained-glass window in the CRGS library.

Philip Edward John Weatherly

Age:	23
Died:	19th March 1944
Service Number:	112978
Rank:	Captain
Service/Regt:	Queen's Own Royal West Kent Regiment
Ship/Unit:	6th Battalion
Grave/Memorial:	Cassino War Cemetery, Italy
Plot/Panel:	Ref. VIII.F.5

Philip Edward John Hugh Weatherly was born on 30th April 1921. His father, Rev. Alfred William Moore Weatherly (1858-1943) was Rector of St Andrew's Church, Weeley, a post he held for 23 years, before becoming Rural Dean of St Osyth towards the end of his life. His mother, Florence, (née Yates), was born in 1885. Philip had two sisters, Julia (1913-2002) and Alice (1915-1935), and a brother, Frederick (1914-2004), who also attended CRGS, before going on to St John's, Leatherhead. His uncle, also named Frederick Weatherly, was a barrister and lyricist who composed over 3,000 songs in his lifetime. He is famous for writing the words to 'Danny Boy' and 'Roses in Picardy'.

Philip entered CRGS in May 1930 from St Mary's School in Colchester. He was in the Pre before moving up to the Senior School in 1932, when he was granted total exemption from fees by the Governors. He was a keen sportsman who played rugby for the 1st XV as a wing-forward ('his tackling and falling are exceptionally good' – *The Colcestrian*), but cricket was his main love. *The Colcestrian* describes him as 'a batsman with a thoroughly sound defence and good scoring strokes all around the wicket.' He captained the 1st XI in 1938, when he was School Captain as well. He also played cricket for Colchester and East Essex, Frinton and Tendring. Just a few years later, in his letters home from the war he would recall past matches, as well as looking forward to playing again in the future.

Philip left CRGS in December 1938, determined on a career in the army, and in August 1939 began his officer training at Sandhurst. When war broke out just a few weeks later, he was immediately drafted into the Royal Army Service Corps and promoted to acting Captain. He was then granted a transfer to the Essex Regiment, but in 1942 and at the age of just 21, he was attached to the 6th Battalion Queen's Own Royal West Kent Regiment as acting Captain and Adjutant.

Towards the end of 1942 the 6th Royal West Kents landed in North Africa as part of 'Operation Torch' and were subsequently involved in the 'Run for Tunis'. The battalion fought throughout the Tunisian Campaign, notably helping to capture Longstop Hill in April 1943. Philip himself was wounded at this time. The campaign ended in mid-May 1943, with the capture of Tunis and over 238,000 Axis soldiers surrendering. Philip received the Military Cross for his bravery. His brother, Fred, also served in North Africa in the Royal Artillery and fought at the Battle of El Alamein.

The 6th West Kents then took part in the Allied invasion of Sicily from July to August 1943 before landing in Italy on 24th September 1943. There Philip met up with Fred, who had been in action on the beaches at Salerno. For this he too was awarded a Military Cross. The 6th then saw action in the Moro River Campaign as the advance towards Rome began.

On 9th March 1944, however, Philip was killed as the Allies ran into difficulties around the stronghold of Monte Cassino. Fred describes the situation in a letter to Harry Cape, written on 27th April 1944 and published in *The Colcestrian*:

> 'I had seen Philip a few days before and he was in the best of spirits, having recently taken over the command of a Company. At the time he was having a Company party in a small village just behind the lines at Cassino. What impressed me most was that at the age of 22 he seemed to have complete confidence in himself to tackle any situation. Actually, he was killed while making a reconnaissance of the area allotted to his Company. After his death the Company put up a magnificent performance

when they were heavily attacked by German paratroopers fighting as infantry. They held their ground, inflicting many casualties and taking prisoners.'

My dear Mr. Eves,

Thank you very much for your letter and enquiries about Philip's progress.

He got into Sandhurst in August, 1939, with a satisfactory place in a large number—April 30th was his 18th birthday. As soon as war broke out in September he with the rest of the Cadets was drafted into the R.A.S.C. in the ranks without losing his cadetship. On receiving his commission he remained in the R.A.S.C. and did well—it was not long before he was promoted until he became acting captain. He asked for a transfer and was allowed to join the Essex Regiment, reverting to lieutenant. Again he did well and became acting captain again.

Then came another change. It came about through direct or indirect volunteering for special tasks—he was "attached" to the Royal West Kent and just recently he was confirmed in his captaincy and was appointed adjutant—not bad for just 21. His cricket has followed him, and he has generally been told off to look after games. The position that was given him as captain at cricket when he was quite young has with his "straight bat" been a good service to him. In his last letter he was looking forward to a cricket match.

His elder brother Fred, who was at the Grammar School before he went to Leatherhead, was a footballer always on the ball in the scrum. He had just qualified as A.C.A. before he was mobilised. After rather a dull time as a gunner he was chosen for a commission in the Lancashire Fusiliers, now drastically mechanised. With all good wishes.

Yours very sincerely,

A. W. M. Weatherly.

Weeley Rectory,
Clacton-on-Sea.
June 3rd, 1942.

Letter from Philip's father to FJ Eves, OCS Honorary Secretary and Acting Treasurer, The Colcestrian, July 1941

Stanley Ernest Rayner

Age:	23
Died:	25th March 1944
Service Number:	1394183
Rank:	Sergeant
Service/Regt:	RAF Volunteer Reserve
Ship/Unit:	640 Squadron
Grave/Memorial:	Reichswald Forest War Cemetery
Plot/Panel:	Plot 7, Row B, Grave 3

Stanley Ernest Rayner was born on 3rd February 1921, the son of John Henry Rayner, a clerk, and his wife, Ethel Selina (née King), of Drury Road, Colchester. He was initially educated at St. John's Green School, before entering Form Upper IIIA of CRGS, as a day-scholar, on 16th September 1932.

Stanley Ernest Rayner

The Colcestrian reports that Stanley was known for a genial disposition that won him a wide circle of friends. During his time at CRGS, and later as an OC, he performed as a soloist in a number of school drama productions. As a Patrol Leader, he was one of the school party which attended the World Scout Jamboree in the summer of 1937, at Eindhoven in the Netherlands. In 1939, he was a member of the party of CRGS scouts on a tour to Switzerland which had to be abandoned a week before war broke out, and he also appeared in many gang shows.

His love of performance also extended to more serious theatre. In the 1937 CRGS opera 'HMS Pinafore' he played Captain Corcoran, and he had roles in other plays, including 'Lawyer Quince', 'Box and Cox' and an open-air production of 'MacBeth'. In the 1939 CRGS opera 'The

Mikado', where the principal roles were allocated to recent old boys, he took the part of Ko-Ko, the Lord High Executioner. By all accounts he was an accomplished soloist.

Stanley Rayner had left Form V^A at the school on 18th December 1937, having been unsuccessful in his Cambridge School Examination. He became a member of the technical staff at Mitcham Work Ltd., and later a member of the Institute of Electrical Engineers. Although he was in a 'reserved' occupation, sometime after the start of the war, Stanley volunteered for flying duties with the RAF, and was sent to train as a navigator.

On completion of his training, in 1943, he was promoted to Sergeant and, after being posted, firstly to an Operational Training Unit (OTU), to train as part of a bomber crew, and then to a Heavy Conversion Unit (HCU), for the crew to learn to fly the Halifax aircraft, he arrived at No. 466 Squadron at RAF Leconfield in Yorkshire.

The squadron had initially been formed, in October 1942, flying the twin-engine Vickers Wellington bomber, manned by RAF personnel and others from air forces of British Commonwealth countries excluding Australia. However, the flight crews and ground staff were gradually replaced by Australians and, in late 1943, 466 Squadron converted to the four-engine Handley Page Halifax heavy bomber.

Having flown three missions with 466 Squadron, Stanley Rayner and the rest of the Hodgson crew were transferred to 640 Squadron, as part of the original 'B' Flight, when the squadron was formed at RAF Leconfield on 7th January 1944.

As the navigator on his aircraft, Stanley Rayner would have worked closely with the Squadron Navigation Leader, and fellow Old Colcestrian, Flight Lieutenant Benjamin Robinson.

Although 'B' Flight wasn't officially considered operational until the end of the month, the Hodgson crew flew their first mission for their new squadron, in an attack on Berlin, on 29th January 1944.

During the next two months, Stanley Rayner flew six further missions, against targets in Berlin, Versailles, Leipzig, Le Mans, and twice to Frankfurt. On 24th March 1944, Halifax III MZ510 'Q-Queenie' took off from RAF Leconfield at 1922 hrs, as part of a force of over 800 aircraft sent to attack Berlin, in what would be the last major raid on the city. The trip should have taken approximately seven and a half hours, with the aircraft due to be over the target between 2239 and 2245 hrs.

However, a strong northerly jet stream disrupted the bomber stream at every stage of the flight, and the aircraft became very scattered, particularly on the homeward flight. With clear skies over Berlin assisting enemy searchlights, the crews risked an intense flak barrage, and a strong force of Luftwaffe night-fighters, to press home the attack on the German capital.

Halifax MZ510 'Q-Queenie' crashed at Dinslaken, about twelve miles NW of Essen in Germany. The cause of the crash was never established, and the only survivor, Flying Officer AH Bunster, became a prisoner of war.

The rest of the crew were killed in the crash, and buried in the Düsseldorf North Cemetery. On 16th October 1946, their remains were re-interred by the Commonwealth Graves Commission in Reichswald Forest War Cemetery.

On Remembrance Sunday, 9th November 1947, Stanley Rayner's wartime sacrifice was commemorated in Stockwell Congregational Church, in a ceremony attended by a large congregation, which included CRGS staff, pupils, scouts and OCs.

An oak plaque was unveiled by former Headmaster Mr HJ Cape, who described Stanley as a leader of complete trustworthiness, with a high sense of honour and ideals, whose integrity had a marked influence on the members of the Scout Patrol of which he was leader.

The plaque, like the headstone on Sergeant Stanley Rayner's grave, carries the inscription:

He Loved Chivalry, Truth and Honour, Freedom and Courtesy

Henry Ernest Parsloe

Age:	23
Died:	1st April 1944
Service Number:	1271920
Rank:	Warrant Officer
Service/Regt:	RAFVR
Ship/Unit:	500 Sq.
Grave/Memorial:	Malta Memorial
Plot/Panel:	Panel 13 Column 2

Malta Memorial

Henry Ernest Parsloe was born on 13th July 1922, the son of Stanley Heath Parsloe and his wife, Dorothy Ethel (née McEwen). Henry had an older brother, John, born in 1920. Stanley Parsloe was a bank manager for Lloyds Bank and consequently moved around the country quite frequently. Henry and his brother were both born in Nottinghamshire, and both sides of the family were originally from Devon, Stanley's father being a surgeon in Plymouth.

At the time of Henry's admission to CRGS in October 1931 the family were living at 'Somerford' on Lexden Road, in Colchester. Henry had previously been a pupil at Lindisfarne College, a private school in Westcliff-on-Sea. He was a highly academic student who won numerous school prizes and was awarded a Junior Foundation Scholarship by the Governors from September 1934. In July 1938 he passed his Cambridge School Certificate. In the report of his death in *The Colcestrian*, Henry was described as 'one of the most brilliant of the many able boys that the Royal Grammar School has trained.'

Henry left CRGS in the summer of 1939, after which his parents moved again – this time to East Grinstead in Sussex. The following year Henry enlisted in the RAF Volunteer Reserve. He trained as a Wireless Operator/Air Gunner and joined 500 (County of Kent) Squadron, becoming a Warrant Officer. He was engaged in operations over Germany and other occupied countries, before being sent to North Africa in 1942. A letter to *The Colcestrian* from ER Pearson mentions meeting 'the younger Parsloe' in Algiers and states that he was a member of one of the crews in the North Africa campaign when a whole squadron of light bombers were shot down. This is a reference to Henry's remarkable escape during the course a daylight raid on Bizerta, Tunisia, in November 1942. Henry's plane crashed into a hill and burst into flames, yet he and all the crew survived. He subsequently spent seven months in hospital.

Eventually Henry returned to his squadron which was now involved in operations supporting of the invasions of Sicily and Italy. His luck, however, finally ran out in April 1944 and ironically it was 'friendly fire' which caused his death. After taking off from La Sénia airfield at Oran, Algeria on 1st April for a routine convoy patrol in the Mediterranean, Henry's Lockheed PV-1 Ventura failed to return and was reported missing three days later. It was discovered that the plane had been shot down in error by an Allied Beaufighter. All five crew members, including Henry Parsloe, were killed.

Jack Wright OC laying a cross at the base of the Malta Memorial

David Glasse

Age:	26
Died:	4th May 1944
Service Number:	148869
Rank:	Captain
Service/Regt:	Royal Norfolk Regiment
Ship/Unit:	2nd Battalion
Grave/Memorial:	Kohima War Cemetery, India
	(Originally buried in Norfolk Hill Cemetery;
	re-interred 29th August 1944)
Plot/Panel:	Plot 2, Row A, Grave 17

David Glasse was born in Colchester on 28th May 1917, and baptised at St Botolph's Church, in Colchester on 22nd September 1917. The younger son of Arthur Edwin Glasse and his wife Emily Mary (née Wagstaff), his parents had married on 26th May 1910, at St Nicholas' Church, in Colchester, and his father had gone on to serve in the Army during the Great War, before taking up employment as a cattle food salesman.

David's older brother, Hubert, who had been born on 18th June 1911, also attended CRGS, joined the Old Colcestrian Society, and later served in the Royal Artillery during World War Two. He survived the

David Glasse

war, concluding his service as a sergeant. The family was living in

Pownall Crescent, Colchester when David transferred from the CRGS Junior School to the Main School on 23rd September 1927, as a day-scholar and member of Parr's House.

Reports in *The Colcestrian* show David's progress through the school, and indicate an aptitude for drawing, for which he was awarded a prize by the Royal Drawing Society in late 1932. He also took leading roles in two of the annual School Gilbert & Sullivan drama productions, giving 'A very good performance, in a very difficult part' as 'Robin Oakapple' in 'Ruddigore' in the spring of 1931, before appearing two years later as 'Nanki-Poo' in 'The Mikado'.

David also showed considerable ability at swimming, on one occasion winning three races in the School Gala and breaking the school swimming record in two of them, in each case by more than two seconds. In 1933, he was one of three pupils awarded the Royal Life Saving Society Award of Merit, a first for the school, and he was also awarded the OCS Gold Medal for Best Swimmer.

He was also a useful athlete, both in sprint races, and the steeplechase, and was described as being a 'very robust' rugby forward. Advised to 'learn not to waste his energy by tackling high', and noted as being 'very effective in the line out', David played for the school 1st XV at rugby in 1932, and was awarded his Full Colours the following year, having played for the 1st XV throughout the season.

He was active in the school Scout Troop, first becoming a Patrol Leader, then qualifying as a King's Scout, before going on to lead the Troop. Finally, at the start of the 1933-34 academic year, David was selected as a School Prefect. On 10th April 1934, he left the School when his parents left the district, with the Admissions Register noting that he went on to gain employment in a 'commercial clerkship'.

In December 1934, the OC Membership Directory gave his address as Gilbert Road, Cambridge, but five years later, in the 1939 Register, David Glasse was listed as lodging in London; his occupation was described as 'Brass Foundry and Ironmongery Salesman'. A few months later, he enlisted in the Army, and after five months training at an Officer Cadet Training Unit, received his commission, as a 2nd Lieutenant in the Royal Norfolk Regiment, on 14th September 1940.

When David joined the 2nd Battalion of the Royal Norfolks (2 R NORFOLK), it had just moved to the village of Hessle, situated on the River Humber, on the opposite bank to Hull, where it occupied a number of requisitioned houses. The battalion had been re-formed during the summer, not long after the evacuation from Dunkirk. During the retreat to the French coast, amidst heavy fighting, the battalion was reduced to less than a quarter of its fighting strength, with only 134 eventually making it back to Britain. Almost a hundred men had been captured by the Waffen SS during the last days of the fighting in France. Although they had surrendered, the Norfolk men were marched away, lined up against the wall of a nearby farm building, and machine-gunned in cold blood; only two survived. After the war Hauptsturmführer Fritz Knoechlein, the commander of the SS Company responsible for the massacre at Le Paradis Farm, was hanged for the crime, with the two Royal Norfolk survivors testifying at his trial.

In January 1941, the battalion was sent to HMS *Glenearn*, based at Loch Fyne, to try out new types of landing craft, and take part in combined operations training, as part of long-term planning for the invasion of Europe. 2nd Lt. Glasse had been assigned to the 'Carrier Platoon' – carriers were used to test the Landing Ship Tanks (LSTs), with the officer's 'Bren Gun Carrier' leading the way off the ship. On one occasion, there was a surprise for all on board as the carrier entered the water, and a fountain shot into the air, soaking everybody – someone had left the 'plug' out of the hole in the bottom of the vehicle!

The battalion returned to Hessle, and continued an intense fitness programme, involving the troops in frequent, long distance route marches. However, the men and officers also had the opportunity to mix socially with the locals in the pubs and bars in the area, and many friendships and relationships developed. One result was that David became acquainted with a young lady and, on 21st October 1941, having two months earlier been best man at the wedding of his future brother-in-law, he married Louise Lacey of Hessle, East Yorkshire at All Saints', the local parish church. 2nd Lieutenant Peter Edrupt was his best man, while Louise was attended by her sister, Alice, for whom she had been bridesmaid a few weeks previously.

Less than two months later, 2 R NORFOLK left Hessle, moving to Fairford in Gloucestershire. Rumours of postings abroad were rife among the men, and after inspections by King George VI and Winston Churchill, everyone was prepared for the inevitable news. On 15th April 1942, after travelling up to Glasgow, the Norfolks boarded the SS *Orbita* as part of the British Army 2nd Division, and sailed as part of the largest convoy that had ever left the UK, surrounded by a large fleet of Royal Navy ships, including a battleship and a couple of aircraft carriers.

After a brief stop at Freetown, the convoy sailed on to Cape Town, where the battalion went ashore, and was billeted just outside the city. On 19th May, the men of 2 R NORFOLK left South Africa, and soon received news that their destination was India. They arrived in Bombay on 10th June, and immediately entrained to Chinchwad Camp, near Poona (Pune) where they started the process of acclimatising to the heat and the monsoon rains which greeted them!

Learning to march and fight during the middle of the day was part of acclimatisation, and they were soon marching up to 25 miles a day in the searing heat, while contending with illnesses caused by the local conditions, such as dysentery and 'prickly heat'. After a month at Poona, the battalion moved 75 miles north-east, to Ahmednagar, where it would be based for the rest of its time in India.

There, despite living in buildings constructed from wattle and daub, and contending with the local insects (and other creatures) they were nevertheless able to enjoy some of the benefits, such as the 'dhobi wallah', who came round once a week, and would do their laundry wonderfully. During the next few weeks, 2 R NORFOLK also became involved in maintaining law and order in Bombay, treading a fine line to keep the peace without recourse to force, as the Indian independence movement flexed its muscles.

2 R NORFOLK spent most of the next eighteen months training, taking part in specialised combined operations exercises and, with the Imperial Japanese Army advancing through Burma, towards India, there was great emphasis on honing their jungle warfare skills in preparation for the anticipated fighting. In January 1944, the battalion was addressed by the Supreme Allied Commander in South East Asia, Admiral Lord

Louis Mountbatten, who told them that the time was soon coming when they would be called upon to put all of their training into practice. The Norfolks did not have long to wait.

Kohima and Imphal stood at the gateway between Burma and India. Behind them lay the vital military railhead and logistic base of Dimapur, with its series of supply dumps covering eleven square miles of the plains of north-east India. As the capital of Nagaland, Kohima's strategic importance arose from its position on the main supply route between Dimapur and Imphal, at the summit of the pass offering the best route from Burma into India.

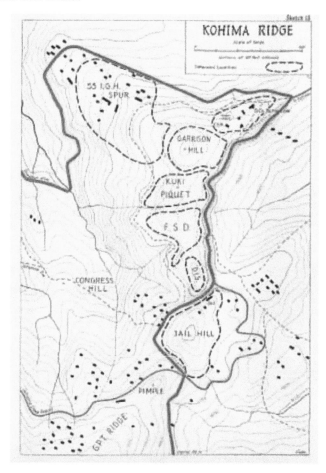

When, on 15th March 1944, Japan launched 'Operation U-Go', the invasion of India, the Allies soon recognised that the capture of Dimapur would be disastrous, and moved quickly to support Imphal, which was soon besieged by the main body of the Japanese 15th Army. At Kohima, the small garrison was reinforced by elements of the British 2nd Division, including 2 R NORFOLK, and a contingent of Indian Army troops.

Often referred to as the 'Stalingrad of the East', the Battle of Kohima is, with the Battle of Imphal, considered to be the turning point in the war with Japan and, for many, 'Britain's Greatest Battle'. The battle, which was fought in three stages from 4th April to 22nd June, centred on the Japanese attempt to capture the Kohima Ridge, a small range of hills running from north to south, and dominating the road from Dimapur to Imphal.

Japanese forces entered the area on the evening of 3rd April, and by 6th April controlled GPT (General Purpose Transport) Ridge and Jail Hill. Soon, they occupied Kuki Picquet, DIS (Detail Issue Store) Ridge and FSD (Field Supply Depot) Hill.

All that remained in Allied hands were Garrison Hill, the area around the District Commissioner's bungalow, the adjoining tennis court, and the IGH (Indian General Hospital) Spur. Here, some of the heaviest fighting was to take place, with opposing trenches so close together that troops could throw grenades at one another.

Meanwhile 2 R NORFOLK was resting in Bangalore, South India, having just completed another period of jungle training. They were quickly recalled from leave, moved rapidly by rail to Calcutta, and then flown by RAF Dakota transport aircraft to Dimapur, where they arrived on 10th April, to be immediately tasked with supporting the Allied troops still clinging on to Garrison Hill.

Over the next two weeks, the Kohima garrison defended desperately, inflicting heavy casualties on the Japanese. This eventually caused them to change strategy, defending their existing positions to prevent the Allies from moving south along the road to Imphal and relieving the siege there. With the British now holding the initiative, but recognising that a frontal assault on prepared positions would be suicidal, it was decided to attempt to outflank the Japanese by cutting through the thick, mountainous jungle, in order to break the enemy lines of communication and launch an attack from the rear.

Code-named 'Operation Strident', 2 R NORFOLK set off on 25th April, just as it started to get dark, with local Naga tribesmen as porters, and everyone heavily loaded with supplies and ammunition. Gradually, the Norfolks climbed higher and higher, faced by impenetrable jungle, mountainous terrain, and drenched by torrential rain. As they went, Mortar Platoon commander, Captain David Glasse, and 4th Brigade Intelligence Officer, Captain John Howard, wondered about what lay in store for them, realising that not everyone would survive the coming battle, and chatted about David's wife, Louise, at home in Hessle.

At last, on the 2nd May, the Norfolks crossed the Aradura Valley, and climbed to a vantage point overlooking the GPT Ridge, and the Japanese positions below. The following day was spent in reconnaissance, and recovering from the exertions of the march. Then, just before dawn on the 4th May, they started moving down the hill, through the thick undergrowth, towards the Japanese. As they descended, they came under fire from enemy snipers, before coming into contact with Japanese troops in hidden bunkers.

Eventually, they reached the edge of the jungle, where the battalion regrouped in preparation for the attack on the lower ridge. The CO, Colonel Bob Scott, realising the need to maintain their momentum, immediately led his men into the attack, rather than wait for artillery support. The attack caught the Japanese by surprise, and the Norfolks drove forward to within 100 yards of the end of the ridge, gaining their objective. With dogged determination, they quickly dug in on the top of GPT Ridge. In capturing the position, the battalion had lost 22 men killed, and 55 wounded, but the battle was not yet over.

Beyond them, on a hillock at the far end of GPT Ridge lay an interlocking series of Japanese bunkers. These overlooked the track to Jotsoma, which meant that the battalion could only be supplied by parachute drops. With the Royal Scots covering the high ground to their rear, it was crucial that 2 R NORFOLK try to remove this thorn in their side while the Japanese garrison was still disorganised by the loss of most of GPT Ridge. Many more would die trying to capture what became known as 'Norfolk Bunker'.

Despite the lack of artillery support, Captain David Glasse was immediately ordered to lead his Carrier Platoon, in a dangerous, improvised attack on the enemy positions. Feeling that he would not survive, David gave his watch to close friend Lt. Sam Hornor, saying, "Take that and write to Louise, won't you, and see that she gets this." In the attack which followed, the Norfolks overran the enemy, but came under fire from other bunkers below, and were unable to hold on. Later, with the attack having been suspended, Captain 'Dickie' Davies went out, with his batman, to recover some of the dead and wounded still scattered across the ground. Seeing David Glasse's body, they picked him up, to find that he had died literally cut in two by machine-gun fire.

The Norfolks went on to take the rest of GPT Ridge, at the cost of 120 men killed or wounded. The casualties included Captain John Randle, who, despite an earlier knee wound, led his men in an attack on a Japanese bunker. Mortally wounded by machine gun fire, Randle threw grenades into the bunker, before sealing it by laying his body across the firing slit, thus ensuring the destruction of the enemy position. His action resulted in the posthumous award of a Victoria Cross, Britain's highest award for gallantry.

Captain David Glasse was buried in the Norfolk Hill Cemetery, on top of what will be forever known as 'Norfolk Ridge'. A few months later, his remains were re-interred in the Kohima War Cemetery. The inscription on his gravestone, *'Loved by all'*, is a reflection of the opinion, voiced by his Platoon Sergeant, Ben Macrae, that David "was a nice bloke, a grand chap really".

The Kohima Memorial to the 2nd Division is inscribed with a familiar message:

When you go home,
Tell them of us and say,
For your tomorrow,
We gave our today

Among those who gave their today at Kohima were Captain David Glasse OC, six other officers and 79 soldiers of the Royal Norfolk Regiment.

Postscript:
By early June, with his forces under incessant attack throughout the area and their food supply failing, the Japanese commander decided to withdraw from Kohima. British and Indian troops pursued the retreating Japanese and, on 22nd June, forces from Kohima and Imphal met at Milestone 109, thus lifting the siege of Imphal. It also brought the Battle for Kohima to an end, after 64 days of some of the fiercest fighting of the war. The Imperial Japanese Army left behind some 7,000 dead, while the defending British & Indian Armies suffered about 4,000 casualties.

David Glasse, pictured at top

(Both photographs courtesy of David Coppin)

Walter Thomas Olyott

Age:	21
Died:	4th June 1944
Service Number:	151238
Rank:	Flying Officer
Service/Regt:	RAF Volunteer Reserve
Ship/Unit:	635 Squadron
Grave/Memorial:	Downham Market Cemetery, Norfolk
Plot/Panel:	Row 6 Grave 5

Walter Thomas Olyott was born on 16th October 1922, the elder son of Thomas and Maude Annie Olyott (née Purser), of 'Runnymede', Bourne Road, Colchester. Thomas Olyott was a Detective Sergeant, later an Inspector, in the Colchester Police Force. He had begun his working life as a Telegraph Operator and served in the Royal Navy during WW1.

Walter had a younger brother, Leonard Eric (1926-2005) who also attended CRGS (1939-44). After serving in the Royal Navy Volunteer Reserve at the end of WW2, Leonard took his BA in London, before training for the Church at Westcott House in Cambridge. Following a number of appointments around the country, he became Archdeacon of Taunton in 1977 until his retirement in 1992.

Walter attended CRGS from September 1933 to December 1939, coming from Canterbury Road Council School. He received a partial exemption from fees from Essex County Council. He was a good swimmer and a strong all-around athlete, winning both the Under-13 and Under-15 Victor Ludorum. He played cricket for the 2nd XI and rugby for the 1st XV as a wing-forward who was 'tireless in attack and defence' (*The Colcestrian*). He won his full colours for rugby and, upon leaving CRGS, played for the OCS Rugby Club. He was also a member of the 9th Colchester Scout Group.

After CRGS Walter found employment as an apprentice at the Colchester engineering firm, Davey, Paxman & Co, before joining the RAF in early 1942. On completion of his basic training, Walter was selected as an aircrew candidate, and sent to the USA and Canada for further training as an 'Air Bomber'.

The 'Air Bomber' (more usually known as the 'Bomb Aimer'), who was often a commissioned officer, would man the front gun turret of a heavy bomber for most of a mission, as well as providing assistance to the navigator. As the aircraft approached the target, the bomb aimer would crawl into his position in the lower part of the aircraft nose. Using the bomb sight, the bomb aimer would give instructions to the pilot, to guide the aircraft to the target. At the right time, the bomb aimer would press a button to release the bombs and activate a flash photograph of the target below.

In a letter, published in the December 1942 issue of *The Colcestrian*, fellow OC KS Moss mentions meeting Walter as they travelled across the Atlantic for training. There, in relative safety, pilots received elementary flying training, while navigators and bomb aimers attended specialist 'Air Navigation' or 'Bombing and Gunnery' Schools. On successful completion of their training, aircrew received their flying badges at a graduation ceremony, and were either commissioned as officers, or given sergeant's stripes.

After receiving his commission as a Pilot Officer on 19th February 1943, Walter returned to the UK, to continue his training at an Operational Training Unit (OTU). There, large groups of air-crew would be left to mingle in a large hall, and sort themselves into crews. Very often one or two men, who knew each other from training school, would agree to fly together, and then seek others in the room to make up a crew.

Each crew would then spend several weeks on night flying, cross-country navigation, bombing, air gunnery and fighter affiliation practice operations, often being taught by men who had already completed an operational tour of thirty missions and were being 'rested'. However, the training was not without risks, the RAF suffered over 8,000 casualties from crashes due to the inexperience of those under instruction.

By the middle of the war, Wellingtons, and other twin-engine bomber aircraft, were often used by OTUs for training, after which each new crew would go on to a Heavy Conversion Unit (HCU), where they would be joined by a flight engineer, and learn to fly four-engine heavy bomber aircraft, such as the Handley Page Halifax or Avro Lancaster, which they would fly on operational missions.

Six months after receiving his commission, Walter was promoted to Flying Officer and, on 17th October 1943, was posted from 1658 HCU at Marston Moor, in Yorkshire, to 158 Squadron, equipped with Halifax aircraft, and based at RAF Lissett, near Bridlington on the Yorkshire east coast.

Flying Officer Walter Olyott flew on three missions with 158 Squadron, to Düsseldorf on 3rd November, Mannheim on 18th November, and Frankfurt on 20th December, before being posted to 'B' Flight of 640 Squadron, when it was formed on 7th January 1944.

Less than a month later, with 'B' Flight still deemed 'non-operational', Walter was posted again, as part of the crew led by Flying Officer George Ambrose Young, to 35 Squadron. Based at RAF Graveley in Huntingdonshire, they became part of the RAF's Path Finder Force (PFF), which had been created by Bomber Command to improve the accuracy of bombing. Elite aircrews would fly ahead of the main bomber force, and drop marker flares, known as 'Target Indicators' (TIs), directly on to the target, which would be used as an aiming point by the less experienced crews following them.

From its inception, until the end of the war, PFF crews, who wore special gilt metal 'Pathfinder' wings on their uniforms to denote their status, led the main bomber forces to targets all over Europe. Due to their operational methods, and the gallantry of the crews, losses among the PFF were heavier than that of other front-line squadrons.

The 'Young' crew flew only one mission with 'C' Flight of 35 Squadron, to Stuttgart on 1st March 1944, before they were again posted, this time joining 635 'Pathfinder' Squadron on 20th March 1944, when it was formed at RAF Downham Market in Norfolk.

The squadron was equipped with Lancaster Mk III aircraft, which could carry up to 14,000 pounds of bombs and target indicators, and were fitted with the most up-to-date radar equipment. The squadron's first mission was flown on 22nd March 1944, against targets in the city of Frankfurt.

Over the next few weeks, Walter and the rest of the 'Young' crew flew eight further Pathfinder missions with 635 Squadron, against targets in Germany such as Berlin, Karlsruhe, Essen and Aachen, as well as attacking targets at Lille and Rouen, in France. In addition to operations, the crew took part in an intensive regime of almost daily training flights, honing their skills in flying, navigation, bombing and gunnery.

At 0027 hrs on 4th June 1944, Lancaster bomber ND841, with the call-sign 'D-Dog', took off from RAF Downham Market, to bomb the coastal batteries around Calais. The mission was part of the plan to convince the Germans that the imminent Allied invasion, which had been postponed to 6th June due to bad weather, was to take place in the Pas de Calais, rather than in Normandy.

As the plane took off, it suddenly swung to starboard, clipped the top of one of the hangars, and crashed just outside the airfield, near to Brookhill Farm. As it did so, one of the large bombs on board exploded, and all seven crew were killed instantly. Flying Officer Walter Olyott was buried in the cemetery the Downham Market parish church of St Edmund's.

The inscription on his grave reads:

Peace, Perfect Peace

Herbert James Broom

Age:	28
Died:	11th June 1944
Service Number:	899874
Rank:	Warrant Officer II (Battery Sergeant Major)
Service/Regt:	147th Field Regiment (Essex Yeomanry), Royal Artillery
Ship/Unit:	413 Battery
Grave/Memorial:	Tilly-sur-Seulles War Cemetery, France (Originally buried at Le Haut D'Audrieu)
Plot/Panel:	Plot I. Grave J. 8

Herbert James Broom was born on 27th September 1915, the youngest child of William Arthur and Florence Annie Broom (née Digby) of Barrington Road, Colchester. Herbert had an older brother, Geoffrey, who died in 1924 at the age of 19, and two older sisters, Doris and Violet, born in 1910 and 1912 respectively.

Herbert, whose father was chief clerk for a firm of house furnishers and removal contractors, entered CRGS on 17th September 1926, having previously attended Canterbury Road Council School. Academically able, he passed his Cambridge School Certificate in July 1931, with matriculation and pre-exemption.

Herbert left the school in December of that year, uncertain as to his future career. The CRGS Admissions Register indicates that he was seeking some form of commercial clerkship, and eventually found a position with a firm of auctioneers.

At the outbreak of war in 1939, Herbert joined the Royal Artillery and, in January 1941, married Joan Frances Richer, setting up home on Hythe Quay, in Colchester. Herbert eventually became a Sergeant-Major (Warrant Officer Class II) in 147th (Essex Yeomanry) Field Regiment, Royal Horse Artillery, which was formed at the outbreak of WW2.

The regiment was headquartered at Chelmsford, with 413 Battery based at Colchester, and 414 Battery based at Harlow. It was reclassified as a Field Regiment in 1941, and was eventually equipped with Sexton self-propelled guns, which had been developed by fitting British 25-pounder guns to a Sherman tank chassis.

The regiment remained in England, training with their new equipment until D-Day, 6th June 1944, when they were among the first wave of troops to land in France, arriving little more than an hour after the first infantry had gone ashore. Even as they were running in to land on 'Gold' beach, the gunners were firing their 25-pounder guns from the landing craft. Once ashore, fighting as part of the British 8th Armoured Brigade as a spearhead unit, the regiment struck south from the beachhead towards the town of Bayeux, which was captured during the afternoon of 7th June.

Meanwhile, since the enemy had retreated to a defensive line around the city of Caen, General Montgomery ordered the immediate launch of 'Operation Perch', to encircle and seize the city, while the 8th Armoured Brigade, including 147th (Essex Yeomanry) Field Regiment, pushed south from Bayeux, in an attempt to capture the town of Tilly-sur-Seulles, and cut a vital line of communication for the German Army between Caen and its forces in the Cotentin Peninsular and Brittany.

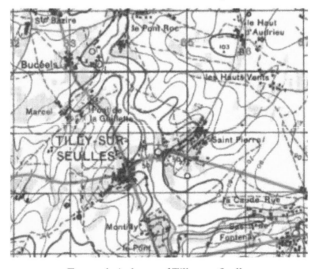

Topograhpical map of Tilly-sur-Seulles

Determined not to allow any of the main east-to-west roads fall into British hands, the Germans moved two powerful armoured units to defend important road junctions along the Tilly road. On the night of 8th/9th June 1944, the first elements of the elite Panzer Lehr Division, which consisted of more than 14,500 men and nearly 100 Panther and Tiger tanks, positioned themselves in the area of Tilly-sur-Seulles. Further east, another armoured division, the 12th SS (Hitler Youth), completed the defensive line.

The 147th RHA Regimental War Diary entry for 8th June records that Major GJ Sidgwick was wounded near the commune of Putot-en-Bessin (about half-way between Bayeux and Caen), and that Captain ECB Edwards had assumed command of 413 Battery.

On 9th June the Diary reported:

> 8th Armoured Brigade advance from Rucqueville area to Point 103 Square 8570. RHQ established at 854707 – all vehicles arrived safely. Regiment now two miles further into France than any other Allied unit. Heavy and bitter fighting at St Pierre. St Pierre held by us at last light. Enemy holding Tilly-sur-Seulles. Dividing line between troops being approximately River Seulle (approximately 1km from the centre of Tilly).

The following day, the 1st Battalion of Panzer Lehr Regiment 901 attacked Tilly from the west and succeeded in occupying the village. Tilly-sur-Seulles then became the centre of a furious duel, lasting ten days, with each side seizing control of the village, only to be repulsed by opposing forces.

A report in the 147th War Diary indicates that, between midnight and one o'clock in the morning of 11th June, the 413 Battery position came under short range mortar fire, with the rest of the regiment coming under fire later in the day. It would seem likely that Battery Sergeant Major Herbert Broom, and Gunner Albert Nevitt, were killed as a result of the mortar fire that fell on 413 Battery, with both men being laid to rest at Le

Haut d'Audrieu, and later re-interred after the war in the War Cemetery at Tilly-sur-Seulles.

Tilly-sur-Seulles War Cemetery

In July 1944, former Headmaster, Harry Cape, wrote in *The Colcestrian* that he

> 'treasured the memory of a happy day in Colchester, (January 24th) when I had the good fortune to meet Sergeant-Major HJ Broom of the Essex Yeomanry, who told me how well CRGS is represented in the Sergeants' Mess – himself, Sergeant-Major JV Brown, Sergeant-Major SS Tatam, Sergeant Ronald Edmunds and Sergeant DM Taylor. My last memory of Herbert Broom is typical – praise for others, none for himself!'

The following December, *The Colcestrian* published a letter from Sergeant-Major Arthur Parsonson, also of the Essex Yeomanry, describing Herbert Broom as 'a fine soldier who died through his ardent devotion to duty'.

The grave of Sergeant Major Herbert J Broom, pictured below, carries the inscription:

"God his watch is keeping tho' none else be nigh"
Decus et tutamen (An ornament and a safeguard)

Benjamin Reginald Robinson

Age:	29
Died:	17th June 1944
Service Number:	132863
Rank:	Flight Lieutenant
Service/Regt:	RAF
Ship/Unit:	640 Squadron
Grave/Memorial:	Herwen-en-Aerdt (Tolkamer)
Plot/Panel:	General Cemetery Plot A.15

Benjamin Reginald Robinson was born in North London on 6th July 1914, the only son of Benjamin William Robinson, a bootmaker, and his wife Charlotte (née Atkinson). Ben had two sisters, 'Kay' (Kathleen b. 1912) and 'Connie' (Constance b. 1921).

Benjamin Reginald Robinson

The family later moved to Clacton-on-Sea, where Benjamin attended St Osyth Road School, before being admitted to Form Upper IIIC at CRGS on 15th September 1925, as a day-scholar.

During his time at the school, Benjamin was a keen player of cricket and rugby football, as well as being academically very gifted. While a member of the Sixth Form, he penned the following poem:

To CRGS

The path of countless ages has been trod
By many a scholar now forgotten, save
For the inscribed tombstone of his grave

244

(If not already sunken 'neath the sod).
And if these men be now mere names or less,
They've done their share to keep the School alive,
And uphold that tradition we derive
From those men in the days of Good Queen Bess;
And we must let our fame be ne'er outshone,
Holding aloft the school's honour and name,
That she may continue to rise in fame,
Surpassing heights attained in years now gone.
However, this our work cannot be done
Unless a share is taken by each one.

In due course, Benjamin passed his Cambridge School Certificate with Honours, and left the school on 19th December 1930, entering the Civil Service at the start of the following year. Shortly afterwards, he moved to Hayes, Middlesex, where he was employed at Uxbridge County Court for some years. On May 3rd 1941, Benjamin married Bettina Joan Allitt, at the Uxbridge Registry Office, and later that month, joined the RAF, and was sent for training in the USA and Canada.

Having passed through Initial Training School, Elementary Flying Training School (EFTS), and Service Training School, Benjamin Robinson received his 'wings' on 23rd October 1942, and was commissioned as a Pilot Officer in the RAF.

Further training followed, including time spent at No. 10 Operational Training Unit in St Eval, flying as part of a five-man crew of a Whitley bomber, captained by New Zealander Flight Sergeant Colin Penfold. The crew were then sent to the 1652 Heavy Conversion Unit (HCU) at RAF Marston Moor, in North Yorkshire, where they were joined by two air gunners, and were taught to fly the four-engine Handley Page Halifax bomber.

On 11th August 1943, the crew was posted to 158 Squadron at RAF Lissett, near Bridlington in East Yorkshire. During their time with the squadron, the crew flew about fifteen missions over enemy territory, including raids on Düsseldorf, Frankfurt, Hannover, Kassel, Munich, Berlin, Nuremberg, Mannheim and, perhaps most notably, the raid on the

German V1/V2 rocket development site at Peenemunde on 17th/18th August 1943.

Like many others from 158 Squadron, Flight Lieutenant Benjamin Robinson was transferred to 640 Squadron when it was formed at RAF Leconfield, near Beverley in East Yorkshire on 7th January 1944.

The Penfold crew, with whom he flew on 158 Squadron, also joined 640 Squadron, albeit with a new navigator, and flew nine operations before being shot down on a mission to Düsseldorf on 23rd April 1944.

Having been promoted to Flight Lieutenant, and appointed as the Squadron's first Navigation Leader, Benjamin Robinson was not assigned to a specific crew, but was responsible for managing the squadron's navigators.

Although Bomber Command orders limited the number of operations flown by any of the squadron's command team, he would occasionally fly as a substitute navigator when required, and flew a total of eight operations between his arrival at the squadron in January, and his death on 17th June 1944.

On 1st/2nd March, Flight Lieutenant Robinson flew with the Penfold crew in a raid on Stuttgart, from which they returned early, due to hydraulic problems, having jettisoned their bombs. Five days later, he again joined his former crew, this time leading a raid on the railway yards at Trappes, SW of Paris. The following night, flying with the Sirel crew, he led a similar mission to bomb the railway yards at Le Mans, and on 15th/16th March, again joined the Penfold crew in an attack on Stuttgart.

After standing down throughout April, Flight Lieutenant Robinson resumed operations on 6th/7th May, flying with the crew of Wing Commander Carter, in a raid on the railway yards at Mantes, halfway between Paris and Rouen. He again flew as part of the Carter crew in the raid, on the 12th/13th May, to bomb the marshalling yards at Hasselt, but on this occasion the aircraft had to return early, when the pilot was taken ill soon after the plane took off.

On 12th/13th June, Flight Lieutenant Robinson flew as part of the Cameron crew, in place of their regular navigator, to attack the railway yards at Amiens. Four days later, despite a poor weather forecast, the Cameron crew, again with Benjamin Robinson as navigator, took off from

RAF Leconfield at 2307 hrs, as part a force of over 300 aircraft, to bomb the synthetic oil plant at Sterkrade, a few miles NW of Essen, in northern Germany.

Unfortunately, the route of the bomber stream passed close to a German night-fighter beacon at Bocholt, only 30 miles from Sterkrade, which had been chosen as the holding point for the local night-fighters. Based on the information available, it seems likely that Halifax LW463 was attacked at about 0140 hrs on 17th June 1944, by a Luftwaffe Junkers 88 night-fighter, flown by Feldwebel Heinz Misch of Nachtjagdgeschwader 2 (NJG 2), based at Volkel airfield.

During the attack, the Halifax exploded, with most of the wreckage falling in the area between the villages of Spijk and Tolkamer, on the north side of the River Waal, about fifteen miles SE of Arnhem. It would seem that the German aircraft was also damaged in the encounter, with Misch being forced to make an emergency landing 35 minutes later, at the nearby Twente (Enschede) airfield.

All seven members of the crew of Halifax III LW463 'A-Able' were killed in the incident, and were buried in the local Tolkamer cemetery at Herwen en Aerdt.

BELIEVED KILLED

F/Lt. B. R. Robinson of the R.A.F. was reported missing from air operations over Germany in June, 1944. In September his wife heard that he was believed killed, but so far there has been no official confirmation of this fact. It is understood, however, that in accordance with the usual practice, he will be presumed killed this month if no further news is received of him.

F/Lt. Robinson was trained in the U.S.A. and in Canada and as a Navigator in Bomber Command he had been on several sorties.

After the war, *The London Gazette*, dated 21st December 1945, published the following citation on the award of the Distinguished Flying Cross, with effect from 16th June 1944:

> 'Acting Flight Lieutenant Benjamin Reginald Robinson (132863), Royal Air Force Volunteer Reserve, No. 640 Squadron:
>
> On his first tour of operational duties, F/Lt. Robinson has completed many attacks against very heavily defended targets in Germany, including Berlin. In October 1943, he was navigator of an aircraft detailed to attack a target in Germany. Shortly after leaving this country, the navigational equipment became unserviceable. F/Lt. Robinson successfully navigated the aircraft through difficult weather to the target, and back again to this country.
>
> On another occasion, his pilot was taken ill in the air, and it was largely due to the steadfastness of this officer, that the aircraft landed safely at base. His technical skill and great enthusiasm for operational flying have made him an invaluable officer to his squadron.'

The inscription on the gravestone of Flight Lieutenant Benjamin R. Robinson, pictured on the next page, reads:

In Proud and Loving Memory of Our Dear Son and Brother -
Mother, Kay and Connie

Edward Dalgleish

Age:	25
Died:	16th July 1944
Service Number:	177620 (formerly 1397356)
Rank:	Flying Officer (Pilot)
Service/Regt:	RAF Volunteer Reserve
Ship/Unit:	207 Squadron
Grave/Memorial:	Lignieres-de-Touraine Communal Cemetery, France
Plot/Panel:	Row B, Grave 5

Edward Dalgleish

Born on 14th January 1919 in Leith, Scotland, Edward Dalgleish was the youngest son of Edward Dalgleish and Catherine Agnes Webster (née Hanley); his older brother, John, was born in August 1908, and his middle brother, Norman, five years later.

Edward Dalgleish received his early education at Canterbury Road Council School, in Colchester, and was admitted to CRGS on 18th September 1930 as a day-scholar. Edward's father, having served with the Cameron Highlanders and in the Labour Corps during the Great War, was employed as a 'printer's overseer', but died, at the age of 44, a year after his son entered the school.

During his time at CRGS, Edward demonstrated a great flair for the arts, appearing regularly in the school productions of Gilbert & Sullivan opera, which included playing the part of 'a terrifying' Katisha in the April 1933 production of 'The Mikado'. He was also a gifted singer, regularly performing in school concerts, and on other occasions, including the 1932 production of 'Iolanthe', when Edward was described as having 'a very charming voice'.

In April 1934, *The Colcestrian* reported that he had been awarded the Sixth Form prize for Spanish and, on 25th July 1935, Edward left CRGS and joined a local company as an apprentice Engineers Draughtsman.

In late summer of 1942 Edward Dalgleish married Margaret Emily Maude (née Moore), in Colchester. It would seem likely that shortly after their marriage Edward joined the RAF and, after initial training, was selected for flying training, probably in the United States, or Canada. There, his training would have begun at an Elementary Flying Training School (EFTS), learning basic flying skills in a Tiger Moth, or similar aircraft.

After successfully completing his EFTS training, Edward progressed to a Service Flying Training School (SFTS) where he flew a more advanced aircraft, such as the North American Harvard T-6 trainer skills. On finishing his SFTS training, Edward received his Pilot's Wings, and was selected to train as a bomber pilot.

About fifteen months after joining the RAF, in February 1944, Edward was posted to No. 17 Operational Training Unit (OTU) at RAF Silverstone, about ten miles north-west of Bletchley, where Pilots, Navigators, Bomb Aimers, Wireless Operators and Air Gunners learned to fly as the five-man crew of a twin-engine Vickers Wellington bomber, and prepare for front-line duties.

After OTU, Edward and his crew moved on to 1661 Heavy Conversion Unit (HCU) at Winthorpe, near Newark, where they were joined by two more crew members, and progressed to flying four-engine Short Stirling aircraft. Finally, the Dalgleish crew were posted to the nearby No. 5 Lancaster Finishing School (LFS), at RAF Syerston, to be given familiarisation training on Avro Lancaster heavy bombers.

On 9th July 1944, Sergeant Edward Dalgleish, and his crew, joined 207 Squadron, part of RAF Bomber Command's No. 5 Group, and the first occupants of the recently-opened RAF Spilsby bomber station, in Lincolnshire.

Six days later, having received news of his commission with effect from 21st May 1944, Flying Officer Edward Dalgleish took part in his first operational sortie, joining the crew of Flight Lieutenant GL Jones for a 'familiarisation ride', as 'second dickie' (2nd pilot), in an attack on the railway yards at Nevers, 130 miles south of Paris.

The Bomber Command plan called for a force of 222 Lancasters and seven Mosquitoes to launch simultaneous raids on railway marshalling yards in Northern France, with the force splitting over the French coast, with half the aircraft attacking Nevers, while the other half headed to Châlons-sur-Marne, 90 miles to the east.

Flight Lieutenant Jones, his regular crew, and their 'passenger' in Lancaster III ME807, were one of six crews from Spilsby assigned to the raid, taking off from their base at 2214 hrs. Five minutes later, also as part of the raid, Flight Lieutenant Murphy and his crew took off from the 467 Squadron (RAAF) base at Waddington, in Lancaster ME851.

At 0130 hrs, on July 16th 1944, the two Lancaster aircraft collided in mid-air over Marnay, in the commune of Ligniéres, and exploded in flames. Accounts from the inhabitants of Ligniéres-de-Touraine reported people being awoken by terrible explosions, and seeing fireballs falling from the sky. They recovered fifteen English, Canadian and Australian airmen from the wreckage of the two aircraft and buried them in the old town cemetery at the local church. Every year since the crash, the town has conducted a ceremony on 16th July to honour the memory of the brave airmen.

Poignantly, the December 1944 edition of *The Colcestrian* included the birth announcement of a son, Ian Edward, for Edward and Margaret Dalgleish, born on August 9th 1944, at 76 Irvine Road, Colchester.

George Dyer Nott

Age:	32
Died:	16th July 1944
Service Number:	193416
Rank:	Captain
Service/Regt:	Royal Armoured Corps
Ship/Unit:	153rd Regiment
Grave/Memorial:	Banneville-la-Campagne War Cemetery
Plot/Panel:	Ref. XII.B.8

George Dyer Nott was born on 19th October 1911, the youngest of the four sons and one daughter of Frank and Emily Nott (née Dyer). Frank Nott was a prosperous farmer who lived and farmed at 'The Hall', Wickham St Paul, near Halstead.

George came to CRGS as a boarder from Ascham College, Clacton in September 1924, joining his brother, (Edward) Stacey, at the school. He was an academically successful student, recorded in *The Colcestrian* as receiving numerous prizes. He was also a member of the school Scout Troop. He left CRGS, with his Cambridge School Certificate, in July 1928.

George decided to make his career in the law and was first articled to Mr JO Steel of Messrs Steel & Steel, of Long Melford and Sudbury. In 1934 he passed the final examination of the Law Society with honours, joining the Midlands practice of Mr Leslie Hale, in charge of the Burton-on-Trent office. In 1937 he returned to Essex to become a partner in the firm of Messrs WA Smith, Morton and Son, of Halstead. In the same year he joined the committee of the OCS. *The Colcestrian* describes him as a well-known, popular and highly respected figure. He also became Honorary Secretary of Halstead Hospital and, when war broke out in 1939, helped with air-raid precautions and gave numerous talks on anti-gas measures.

He joined the army in July 1940 and after a year was sent for officer training. On completing this successfully, he was commissioned as a Captain in the 153rd (8th Battalion Essex Regiment) Royal Armoured

Corps. In September 1941 he had married Margaret Julietta Richardson, only daughter of Mr & Mrs Cedric Richardson, of 'Prospect Cottage', Earls Colne. The wedding took place at The Friends Meeting House in Coggeshall. A son, Michael Richardson Nott, was born in October 1942.

153 RAC was transported to Normandy from 2nd to 4th July 1944, and on 9th July were ordered to prepare for an attack on Caen. However, the fall of the city meant that they finally went into action on 16th July in support of an attack in the Esquay–Évrecy area to the west. The object of the operation was to divert the enemy to that front while preparations for the next breakthrough were actually being made to the east of Caen.

The attack began at 0530 hrs on 16th July, and the final objective was reached by 1025 hrs, but there were still enemy troops in the nearby woods, and at 1450 hrs the Germans counter-attacked. The regimental war diary refers to 'a slogging match' throughout the rest of the day. The casualties included Captain George Dyer Nott, killed by a sniper's bullet at the age of 32. He left not only a widow and his young son, Michael, but also a second son, Cedric, born to him posthumously in October 1944.

On 20th November 1945, in a happy twist, George's brother, Stacey, married Margaret, George's widow. This wedding also took place in Coggeshall. After CRGS, Stacey had attended Chadacre Agricultural College, and eventually took over Hall Farm from his father, Frank, who died in 1973 at the age of 101. Stacey is recorded in *The Colcestrian* as contributing to the CRGS WW2 memorial window which names his brother. He died in 1980.

There is also a memorial in honour of Capt. George Dyer Nott inside Wickham St. Paul Church.

Banneville-la-Campagne War Cemetery(also on the next page)

CAPTAIN
G.D. NOTT
ROYAL ARMOURED CORPS
16TH JULY 1944   AGE 32

I WILL GO WITH THEE
AND BE THY GUIDE
IN THY MOST NEED
TO GO BY THY SIDE

Charles Alexander Whyatt

Age:	23
Died:	28th July 1944
Service Number:	127154
Rank:	Flight Lieutenant
Service/Regt:	RAFVR
Ship/Unit:	252 Sq.
Grave/Memorial:	Alamein Memorial, Egypt
Plot/Panel:	Ref. Column 279

Charles Alexander Ian Whyatt, known as Ian, was born on 21st April 1921. He was the son of Leo Arthur Whyatt (1893-1955), a Mercantile Marine Chief Engineer who was born and worked in the port of Harwich, and Agnes, née Ironside (1896-1984), from Canning Town. The family lived at 'St Clare', St George's Avenue, Dovercourt.

Ian attended Dovercourt County High School before coming to CRGS in September 1933, on a partial scholarship from Essex County Council. He left in July 1940. He was a Prefect and played rugby for the 1st XV as 'a lively scrum-half'. He was also a very strong swimmer, with many successes in the Swimming Sports, and represented the school in the swimming and water polo teams.

On leaving CRGS he volunteered for the RAF straight away, only to be turned down because of hammer toes on both feet. He then went to Liverpool to work for the Admiralty on the de-gaussing of ships. While he was still occupied with this, the RAF wrote to him saying that hammer toes were no longer considered a disability and that as long as he passed their tests, they would take him.

He therefore joined the RAF on 3rd May 1941. After his initial Training Wing course at Paignton in Devon, he was sent, via Canada, to the USA as one of the first draft of RAF personnel to train as pilots at Pensacola, Florida, on the Gulf of Mexico. Following a six-week ground school course, he began flying in September 1941. He received his commission as a Flight Lieutenant on 25ᵗʰ March 1942 and returned to England in the July of that year by piloting a brand-new bomber straight from the factory across the Atlantic via Bermuda and Montreal.

Ian was stationed at various RAF bases in Britain, before flying operations from Gibraltar in Wellingtons. He then returned to England to learn to pilot a Bristol Beaufighter, joining 252 Squadron in North Africa in October 1943 for operations against Axis shipping in the Mediterranean.

In early July 1944 he was awarded the DFC for attacking and sinking a valuable enemy ship in convoy. The citation states:

> 'FL Whyatt has consistently displayed enterprise, determination and courage of a high order in all his operational undertakings. He has participated in many attacks on enemy shipping, on which numerous vessels have been hit. One night in July 1944 FL Whyatt attacked a small merchantman which was heavily escorted. In spite of a fierce barrage, he pressed home his attack. He obtained hits which set the vessel on fire.'

Very soon after this, on 28ᵗʰ July 1944, Ian attacked another enemy convoy in the Aegean. He was hit by flak and went down into the sea with one engine on fire. Both Ian himself and his navigator were killed. He was 23 years old.

PENSACOLA

I THOUGHT that I would give you some idea of my life since joining the R.A.F., so here goes.

After being called up in May I went through the usual Initial Training Wing course at Paignton, completing it towards the end of June. Returning from forty-eight hours' leave, most of which was spent in the train, I found I had been posted abroad for flying training, probably to America. Shortly afterwards we sailed in a medium-sized convoy accompanied by —— and ——, and after a voyage broken only by the dropping of a few stray depth charges we were landed at a northern Canadian port. During the voyage I was one of a party of U/T pilots detailed to man the ship's light ack ack, and our four on and eight off watches helped to pass the time on an otherwise monotonous voyage, as the only planes we saw were definitely ours. From the port we travelled for two days by train to a city near the border, where we spent a few

257

days by train to a city near the border, where we spent a few hectic days while our papers were prepared. The scenery during the train journey was particularly fine. As we were passing through well-wooded country following the river valleys, the views at sunset were really grand. As soon as we reached our transit camp, as they are called, we were told that we were going to the U.S. Navy's crack training station at Pensacola on the Gulf of Mexico. We were naturally excited about this, especially as we were the first draft of R.A.F. personnel to be accepted by the U.S. Navy, so we passed another train journey through America in a cloud of conjectures and rumours. To many people the name Pensacola only recalls the scene of one of Mr. Robert Taylor's efforts, but to Americans it is the password to the best aviation training obtainable.

The station is built on an island protected from the open gulf by a long sandy island which provides sheltered water for landing flying boats and seaplanes. We are housed in one of the very comfortable aviation cadets' buildings and have our own mess complete with corn on the cob and coloured waiters. There is one land 'drome on the station, which is now used by the instrument flying squadron, and on the mainland there are three main 'dromes and about twenty outlying fields used by the primary squadrons. On arrival here we spent six weeks doing another ground school course, finally starting flying the second week in September. Though two hurricanes in the Gulf kept us on the ground for several days we have all " soloed " now with very few failures. As for the town of Pensacola, it is rather small, too small to accommodate us all during the week-ends, but we are within easy reach of Mobile and New Orleans, so always find somewhere to go.

Hoping that this isn't too long-winded and that it will give you some idea of my life in the R.A.F., despite the rather vague references to places and times.

With best wishes,

C. A. WHYATT.

British Flight Battalion,
U.S. Naval Air Station,
Pensacola, Florida.

Ian writing to The Colcestrian about his life in the RAF, December 1942

Leslie Frost

Age:	32
Died:	19th August 1944
Rank:	Second Radio Officer
Service/Regt:	Merchant Navy
Ship/Unit:	SS *Wayfarer* (Liverpool)
Grave/Memorial:	Tower Hill Memorial
Plot/Panel:	Panel 117

Leslie Frost was born in Brightlingsea, on 20th October 1911, the only son of Charles Daniel Frost and his wife, Grace Mary (née Smith), of New Street, Brightlingsea. Leslie, who had an older sister, Edna, was baptised at All Saints' Church, Great Oakley on 30th June 1912, and received his early education at Brightlingsea Church of England Primary School. His father was a cook on a private yacht.

He was admitted to CRGS on 14th September 1923, as a day-scholar, joining Lower Form IVB. There are several references in *The Colcestrian* to Leslie's academic successes during his time at the

Leslie Frost

school, indicating that he was a bright scholar. He later contributed articles to the magazine, describing 'Oyster Dredging at Brightlingsea', and a trip that he had undertaken to the West Indies, carrying thorough-bred horses. Leslie passed his Cambridge School Certificate examination in July 1928. He left CRGS in December of the same year, to join the Merchant Navy, and undertook his first voyage, as a cadet, in April 1929.

Some ten years later, on 6th May 1939, Leslie Frost sailed from Liverpool, as Third Officer on board the British steamer SS *Huntsman*, destined for Calcutta, in India. On the return journey, just after the war started, the ship was instructed to return to Durban. While heading for Freetown, on 10th October 1939, she was captured by the German pocket battleship *Admiral Graf Spee*, which had initially approached the *Huntsman* under a French ensign, before running up a Nazi flag.

Just prior to the break of the Second World War, the German Navy had sent the *Graf Spee* to patrol the South Atlantic merchant sea lanes. Operating under instructions to stop and search ships, and to evacuate the crews before sinking them, the *Graf Spee* sank nine merchant ships in four months, between September and December 1939.

The crew of the *Huntsman* dumped secret papers over the side, in a weighted bag, and were boarded by a German lieutenant, who informed them that the ship was being taken as a prize, and that resistance would result in the ship being sunk.

Since the *Graf Spee* was unable to accommodate the crew of the *Huntsman*, a prize crew was put on board, and the ship sailed alongside the battleship for two days, to a pre-arranged location, where the *Graf Spee* rendezvoused with her supply ship, the *Altmark*. After refuelling, and transferring her prisoners to the *Altmark*, the *Graf Spee* scuttled the *Huntsman* on 17th October.

After remaining in the area for some weeks, while the *Graf Spee* intercepted more merchantmen, and gathered more prisoners, the *Altmark* eventually set off on her return journey to Germany, leaving the *Graf Spee* to continue her patrols, while the Royal Navy conducted a strenuous search of the South Atlantic for her.

Eventually on 13th December, the *Graf Spee* was engaged by three British cruisers in the 'Battle of the River Plate'. Although the Royal Navy ships suffered heavy damage, they also inflicted sufficient damage on the *Graf Spee*, to force her to put into Montevideo harbour for repairs, and to evacuate the wounded crew.

Under the Hague Convention, the *Graf Spee* was required to leave the port within 72 hours. Her captain, knowing that if she was interned, the neutral Uruguayan government would allow British intelligence officers access to the ship, and convinced by false reports of superior British naval forces awaiting his ship in the Atlantic Ocean, evacuated the ship, and scuttled her in the outer reaches of the harbour.

Meanwhile, the *Altmark* attempted to steam around the north of Great Britain, before heading south along the Norwegian coast, in order to gain access to the Baltic Sea. On 14th February 1940, the steamer was discovered by three aircraft from RAF Thornaby, and pursued into Jøssingfjord by a flotilla of British destroyers, led by HMS *Cossack*.

There, the British seamen tried to sound the alarm, by shouting and singing, but were threatened by the Germans. Leslie Frost found a whistle, and proceeded to blow SOS on it loudly, but without any apparent success. However, late on 16th February 1940, the seamen heard the crushing sound of ice against the hull of the boat, and a sudden bump, as German ship was run aground.

The *Altmark* was then boarded by a party from HMS *Cossack*, who set about freeing the prisoners. Below decks, the seamen heard a shout, saying, 'Any British down there?' and, on receiving an affirmative reply, shouted, 'We'll have you out in no time.' Unfortunately, during the skirmish, eight German seamen were killed, and a further ten wounded, while a British and a Norwegian sailor were also seriously wounded.

Leaving the rest of the German crew behind, and with the released prisoners on board, HMS *Cossack* reversed away from the *Altmark* and sailed 400 miles back to the port of Leith, in Scotland. After hospital checks, the British seamen were soon able to depart on the last stage of their journey, back to their homes and loved ones.

Having been previously reported as an internee in German camp, on Thursday, 22nd February 1940, Leslie Frost returned home to an enthusiastic welcome and civic reception in his hometown of Brightlingsea. On the Monday following, he visited CRGS, and spoke to the boys of his experience as a prisoner on board the *Altmark*. In his speech, Leslie Frost paid tribute to the generosity of his employers, the Harrison Line, and expressed the desire to sit for his Master's ticket, and get back to sea as soon as possible.

Four years later, Leslie Frost was to be found sailing as Third Officer on the Harrison Line merchant steamship SS *Wayfarer*, skippered by Captain John Wales. In March 1944, the 5,068-ton *Wayfarer* had started her journey from Liverpool, and sailed to Bombay (now Mumbai), on the west coast of India.

SS Wayfarer; Photo: Allen Collection

From, there she had continued south, to Colombo in Ceylon (now Sri Lanka), and then across the Indian Ocean, to the port of Beira, in Mozambique. On 16th August 1944, the *Wayfarer* left Beira, unescorted, and laden with 3000 tons of copper and 2000 tons of coal, intending to sail north, through the Suez Canal, and via the Mediterranean Sea, back to the UK.

The *Wayfarer* had been at sea for three days, when she came in contact with the German submarine U-862, commanded by Korvettenkapitän Heinrich Timm, which had sailed from Germany the previous May, and was making her way to join the 33rd U-boat Flotilla, code-named 'Gruppe Monsun', based at Penang, in Japanese-controlled Malaya.

The U-862 was patrolling the area just south of the Comoros Islands, at the northern end of the Mozambique Channel between Madagascar and Portuguese East Africa, where she had torpedoed three of her four victims in the last five days, and in her first attack on the *Wayfarer*, the U-862 had fired a spread of two torpedoes, which missed well ahead, and detonated at the end of their run.

Ninety minutes later, despite continuing to sail a zig-zag course, the *Wayfarer* was hit on her port side, between No. 4 and 5 holds, by a single torpedo, and sank about 150 miles east of Mozambique. Of the 62 people on board, the master, 44 crew members, five gunners and one passenger were lost. Eleven days later, the remaining nine members of the crew, and two gunners, made landfall on an uninhabited island in the Mozambique Channel, from where they were rescued, and brought to safety in Portuguese East Africa.

Leslie Frost was among those lost at sea from the sinking of the SS *Wayfarer*. His sacrifice is commemorated on the Merchant Navy War Memorial at Tower Hill, in London (pictured below), and on the memorial window in the CRGS library.

Ralph Campbell Chopping

Age:	29
Died:	26th August 1944
Service Number:	70126
Rank:	Squadron Leader
Service/Regt:	RAF Volunteer Reserve
Ship/Unit:	7 Squadron
Grave/Memorial:	Runnymede Memorial, Surrey
Plot/Panel:	Panel 200

Ralph Chopping

Ralph Campbell 'Pin' Chopping was born in Colchester on 12th September 1914, the eldest son of Wasey Chopping, and his wife Amy Mina (née Dodd). Ralph's father, a master miller, served as a JP and was Mayor of Colchester in 1922. There were further additions to the family on 14th April 1917, when Ralph was joined by twin younger brothers, Richard (Dickie) and Alan.

Unfortunately, Alan died not long after his first birthday, succumbing to the Spanish flu epidemic which swept through Europe the following year. Dickie, however, went on to become an acclaimed artist and book illustrator, and achieved fame for his creation of first edition dust jacket covers for the early 'James Bond' novels, thus helping turn Ian Fleming's spy into a global phenomenon.

Ralph, meanwhile, having received his early education at the County High Preparatory School, was admitted to CRGS on 16th September 1924, with the Admissions Register listing the family home address as Queens Road, in Colchester. During his time at the school, Ralph demonstrated academic ability in Mathematics, Science, and also in Drawing, passing several Royal Drawing Society Schools Exams, and regularly being placed in the top three for form prizes.

Ralph left CRGS in July 1928, continuing his education at Charterhouse School, before entering Queen's College, Oxford in 1933, as an Open Exhibitioner in History, from where he graduated in 1936, with a First Class Honours degree in Jurisprudence.

While at Oxford, Ralph was Treasurer of the Taberdars' Committee, Secretary of the Moot Club and gained his hockey colours. He was also a member of the Oxford University Air Squadron, receiving his commission as a Pilot Officer in the RAF Reserve on 22nd June 1937, and being transferred to the newly-formed RAF Volunteer Reserve (RAFVR) on 1st January 1938.

After leaving Oxford, Ralph entered the Colonial Administrative Service, and spent some time at the Colonial Office in London, before being sent to Nigeria in 1938, as an Assistant District Officer.

When war was declared, as a member of the RAFVR, Ralph was called up, and sent on a refresher course at No. 4 Flying Training School (FTS), at Habbaniyah in Iraq, followed by navigation training at Abu Sueir in Egypt. In February 1940, Pilot Officer Ralph Chopping was posted to 223 Squadron at Khartoum, where he flew Vickers Wellesley medium bomber aircraft.

In June 1940, with the squadron now based at Summit in Sudan, Ralph Chopping became Squadron Adjutant. He was promoted to Flying Officer on 3rd September that year and remained with the Squadron when it returned to Egypt in April 1941, to become an Operational Training Unit (OTU).

In September 1941, Ralph Chopping was promoted to Flight Lieutenant, and two months later returned to flying duties, with 216 Squadron, based at Khanka, near Cairo. The squadron, which was part of Transport Command, was engaged in supply and casualty evacuation duties. During his time with the squadron, Ralph flew Bristol Bombay aircraft, qualifying as an aircraft captain in March 1942, and assuming command of 'A' Flight in July that year.

In March 1943, Ralph was posted back to the UK, initially employed in a staff capacity at Transport Command HQ. In September of that year, he transferred to Bomber Command in order to return to flying duties, subsequently training at 1536 Beam Approach Training Flight at

Spitalgate, near Grantham and No. 26 OTU, RAF Wing, in Buckinghamshire, before being sent to 1651 Heavy Conversion Unit (HCU), at Wratting Common, where he learned to fly the four-engined Short Stirling bomber.

As 1944 opened, Ralph Chopping was learning to fly the radial-engined, Avro Lancaster II at 1678 HCU, based at Stradishall in Suffolk. At the end of January, he was posted to 514 Squadron, at Waterbeach in Cambridgeshire, and two weeks later flew in his first sortie with the squadron, as second pilot, in an attack on Berlin. Further missions during February 1944 included Stuttgart on 21st, Schweinfurt on 24th and Augsburg on 25th.

Ralph Chopping proved to be an exceptional Lancaster pilot, and was promoted to Squadron Leader in May 1944, after completing fourteen operational sorties with the squadron. Shortly after, he received the Distinguished Flying Cross for bravery, when his Lancaster was caught in bad weather at the start of a bombing raid. He ordered his crew to bale out, while he remained at his post, eventually regaining control of the aircraft, jettisoning his bombs and landing the aircraft safely.

The citation for the award of the Distinguished Flying Cross was published in *The London Gazette* on 21st July 1944. Referring to his flying ability, it stated:

> 'This officer has completed very many sorties as pilot and captain of aircraft. He has displayed a high standard of skill and his determination to achieve success has been most commendable. Squadron Leader RC Chopping has successfully completed twenty-four bombing sorties as the pilot and captain of Lancaster aircraft. He is a most experienced captain, keen and enthusiastic, and the photographs he has obtained bear out the excellence of his work.'

> On the night of 24th February, when returning from an attack on Schweinfurt he was attacked by an enemy fighter, which he outmanoeuvred and which his gunners

claim to have damaged. The following night he had three combats with night fighters during a raid on Augsberg. Each attack was broken and two of the enemy fighters were damaged by the air gunners.

At Stuttgart, on the 2nd March, Squadron Leader Chopping's aircraft received a direct hit and he had to return on three engines, while on the 19th May, his aircraft was again badly damaged by anti-aircraft fire when crossing the French coast. On this occasion the port wing was badly holed and the Wireless Operator was knocked unconscious, but despite this Squadron Leader Chopping continued to the target at Le Mans, and bombed it successfully.'

Meanwhile, reports from the Air Ministry News Service and *The Essex Telegraph* provide a graphic description of the heroic action which resulted in the immediate award of the DFC:

'On the night of 22nd May, Squadron Leader Chopping took off in 'S-Sugar' to attack Dortmund. The weather was deteriorating, and by the time the aircraft had reached seven hundred feet the Lancaster was coated with ice. It was imperative to get above the dense clouds, but the icing became worse and, by the time the Lancaster reached 10,000 feet, the speed had dropped and it began losing height.

Chunks of ice, flying off the propellers, beat a ceaseless tattoo on the wings and fuselage, smashing the perspex windows, tearing away the aerials, putting two turrets out of action, and causing the aircraft to vibrate violently. Finally, the ice became so heavy that the Lancaster fell towards ground at an alarming rate, as it was forced down out of control.

Ralph Chopping decided that the only thing to do was to jettison his load of an 8,000-pound bomb and incendiaries, but because he feared the damage that might be caused if it fell in this country, Chopping ordered his crew to abandon the aircraft, while he remained in the aircraft hoping to regain control.

The crew wanted to stay with him, but Chopping had made up his mind to go alone, and ordered the others to bale out over Norwich. A minute later he was alone, and flew his aircraft out to sea to drop his bomb load. Not until the aircraft broke cloud at 2,500 feet, was he able to regain control, fly out over the North Sea, and jettison the bombs. The Lancaster then ran the gauntlet of British anti-aircraft fire, before making an emergency landing at Woodbridge.

Squadron Leader Chopping was quoted as saying: "It was as though somebody was continually pushing the Lancaster down with a giant's hand. The cloud was so thick that I couldn't see a thing. The whole thing was like a nightmare. The black-out curtain between the cockpit and the navigator's table light was flapping; the ice was rattling all over the fuselage. I couldn't climb, or increase the power of the engines. All I could do was try and hold the Lancaster on course and hope for the best. At last, when the aircraft was down to 2,000 feet, the cloud began to break, and I managed to regain control. I flew well out to sea before I dropped the bombs. When I released the 8,000-pounder the Lancaster jumped 300 feet in the air, and I thought it might have been damaged. But it was all right; I got it back to the English coast. I ran into our own anti-aircraft fire then, and I had to alter course and make for the nearest airfield."'

Following the abortive raid on Dortmund, Ralph Chopping completed seven more successful bombing operations, and was involved in a further fighter attack, claiming one more enemy fighter damaged. Finally, after 28 operational flights over Germany and France with Bomber Command, he flew his last sortie with 514 Squadron in July of the same year and was posted to join the Pathfinder Force. He joined 7 Squadron (Lancasters), Oakington, in August 1944.

At 2224 hrs on the night of 25th August 1944, piloting Lancaster III NE123 'MG-J', Ralph Chopping took off from RAF Oakington, as part of a force of 334 aircraft sent to attack eight coastal batteries, near Brest in France. Unfortunately, that night, Lancaster 'MG-J' was lost without trace; it was the only aircraft from 7 Squadron not to return safely.

Sq/Ldr. Ralph Campbell Chopping DFC
70126 RAFVR Age 29. Missing - believed killed

Use of photo with kind permission of the Chopping family and from Aircrew Remembered (aircrewremembered.com)

Charles Patrick Hickey

Age:	21
Died:	15th September 1944
Service Number:	314202
Rank:	2nd Lieutenant
Service/Regt:	Border Regiment
	(King's Own Scottish Borderers)
Ship/Unit:	5th Battalion
Grave/Memorial:	Geel War Cemetery
Plot/Panel:	Grave II.A.3

Charles Patrick Hickey

Charles Patrick ('Pat') Hickey was born in Boxted on 29th July 1923, the eldest son of John Hickey, and his wife Caroline (née Bowler). Pat also had a sister, Georgina who was born in October 1925, and a brother, Michael who was born in April 1931. In the late 1920s, the family moved to a staff cottage on the Severalls Estate, Mile End, Colchester, where his father worked as an attendant at Severalls Mental Hospital.

Following his early education at St James' School, Priory Street, Colchester, Pat entered Form Upper IIIA at CRGS on 18th September 1934, as a day-scholar in Harsnett's House.

Reports in *The Colcestrian* indicate that, as well as being academically successful, he was a good swimmer, playing water polo for the school, and being awarded a Bar to his Royal Life Saving Society Bronze Medallion award in 1939. After a 'shaky start', Pat Hickey also became a very competent rugby forward, winning Half Colours for the school, and then going on to play regularly for the Old Colcestrians.

In July 1940, his name appeared among those selected as 'Prefects-Designate' for the following school year, his last at CRGS. On leaving school in 1941, he entered the service of the LNER (London & North-Eastern Railway) as a member of the office staff. Reports in *The Colcestrian* indicate that he was an active member of the Railway Workers' Union, and the Workers' Education Committee.

In 1942, Pat Hickey volunteered for military service, enlisting as a trooper in the Royal Armoured Corps (RAC), and later being attached to the Green Howards, where he captained the regimental rugby team. In December that year, *The Colcestrian* printed a letter from Pat, in which he described his current situation. He indicated that he was coming towards the end of the six months training, and that he was being 'taught every aspect of tank warfare, driving every type of vehicle, and maintaining them. To this is added a dash of wireless, gunnery and a vague thing called 'collective training', which constitutes a resumé of everything we do'.

On completion of his tank warfare training, Pat Hickey was recommended for a commission, and sent for officer training. During this time, on November 24th 1943, at St James-the-Less Roman Catholic Church, Colchester, he married his boyhood sweetheart, Jean Kathleen Heath, of Mill Road, Mile End.

On 1st April 1944, Pat Hickey was commissioned as a 2nd Lieutenant in the 5th Battalion of The Border Regiment, a training unit which provided personnel to other regiments. The records suggest that, during the summer of 1944, 2nd Lt. CP Hickey was transferred to the 6th Battalion, King's Own Scottish Borderers (KOSB). Lt. Hickey landed in Normandy on 1st August 1944, joined his new regiment, and was immediately involved in the heavy fighting around Caen, as part of 44th Brigade in the 15th (Scottish) Division.

After Caen had been liberated, the 6th Battalion KOSB was involved in heavy fighting for Mont Pinçon, before it advanced through the Falaise Gap, crossed the River Seine, and on into Belgium, where it was to take part in the battle at the Geel (Gheel) bridgehead.

After Antwerp had fallen, the German Army regrouped along the waterways of the Belgian/Dutch border, and prepared to make a stand.

At Geel, on the Albert Canal, there was a fierce battle between the advancing British troops, and the beleaguered German infantry which lasted from 7th to 13th September, when the Germans retreated to the northern bank of the Maas-Scheldt Canal, and the 15th Division occupied the town, meeting little resistance.

The Scots then pushed on to the town of Ten Aard, about three miles north of Geel, and were involved in heavy fighting, sometimes hand-to-hand, before they were able to establish a bridgehead across the Escaut Canal, and eventually force the Germans to withdraw.

It would seem likely that Lieutenant Charles Patrick Hickey was killed in action during the establishing of the bridgehead across the Escaut Canal, and died in the area around Ten Aard on 14th September 1944. He was originally buried near Geel Mental Hospital, but after the war the Commonwealth Graves Commission re-interred his remains in Geel War Cemetery on 24th May 1945.

His gravestone carries the inscription:

I Have Glorified Thee On The Earth: I Have Finished The
Work Which Thou Gavest Me To Do

On hearing the news of Pat's death, his wife Jean suffered a miscarriage, losing their daughter.

TPR. C. P. HICKEY WRITES FROM ENGLAND.

I must apologise for this rather belated acknowledgment of *The Colcestrian.* Time flies so quickly here, however, that I have not really noticed so many weeks have elapsed since receiving it.

Our training here is very intensive, and generally interesting, though details are not permitted to be divulged. I am allowed to state, however, that it consists of six months, during which we are taught every aspect of tank warfare, driving every type of vehicle and maintaining them. To this is added a dash of wireless, gunnery and a vague thing called collective training, which sonstitutes a resume of everything we do. The latter is the last stage and is occupying my time now.

The object of the course is to provide officers and N.C.O.s for the R.A.C. Whether I provide the material for either of these remains to be seen.

At the moment I am in an agony of suspense as we are due for leave in a fortnight and I have contracted a slight attack of a prevalent skin infection. This necessitates my going about with delicate shades of blue on my face, very detrimental to my personal beauty.

The School is very sparsely represented here ; so far I have only met one Old Colcestrian. Apparently the R.A.F. had a particular lure for the C.R.G.S. Perhaps it is the uniform, though personally I think the black beret is quite as good.

Taking things as a whole the life is not too bad, though I must confess the moves of the Army sometimes mystify me. I have been informed that they have mystified greater men than I, and will continue to do so ; therefore I must persevere and hope some day I shall become enlightened.

The news has arrived that the N.A.A.F.I. has opened, so I'll away now to bury my rrows in watery tea !

Letter to The Colcestrian from Pat about his army training, December 1942

Aubrey Arthur Barker

Age:	22
Died:	22nd September 1944
Service number:	261644
Rank:	Lieutenant
Service/Regt:	Somerset Light Infantry
Ship/Unit:	4th Battalion
Grave/Memorial:	Groesbeek Canadian War Cemetery, Netherlands
Plot/Panel:	Grave XIX. E. 3

Aubrey Barker was born near Ipswich on 27th March 1922, the only son of Mr Arthur Christopher Walter & Mrs Hilda Alice Barker. Aubrey was admitted to CRGS Form II on 15th January 1932, having come up from the CRGS Junior School, where he had been a pupil since the autumn of 1928.

For the first four years he attended the Senior School as a boarder, but became a day-scholar from September 1936, following the death of his father earlier in the year.

Aubrey Barker was an exceptionally clever linguist, gaining medals for French, and highest honours in Italian and Spanish. He was also

Aubrey Arthur Barker

good at athletics, being one of the School House hopes for success in the steeplechase.

In December 1938, *The Colcestrian* reported that Aubrey Barker had passed his Cambridge School Certificate examination, and had been the winner of a special prize in the 'Société Nationale des Professeurs de Français, Grand Concours en Angleterre'.

The December 1940 issue of *The Colcestrian* published his poem:

"Bombs fell in open country"...
The sirens blew, but there was no sound
to make us fear the dull grey clouds
that made the road seem long and dreary.
The breeze that stirred the grass and leaves
grew deeper and mechanical.
Then, clear and unmistakable, we heard
the distant chorus of a drove
of bombing planes.
We were ignorant and not afraid;
a frightened woman seeking shelter
just surprised us.
The noise increased; within the clouds
blind malice fled from more machines.
In the cave beneath the clouds
the threatened air in echo trembled,
then shrieked at being so defiled
by thrown-up clods and burning steel.
The thud of the explosion raised no echo
in the plain, until the air was rent
again, by the prosaic tubes of metal.
Blind, not knowing, still less caring,
the planes flew on and left the field in peace.

Aubrey was an active member of the CRGS Scout Troop, becoming a Patrol Leader, and also of the school Stamp Club. In June 1941, he was listed as a Prefect Designate, and congratulated on gaining a scholarship to King's College London, where he studied in the Faculty of Arts, and worked in connection with Basque refugees, before joining the Army in 1942.

Aubrey Barker was commissioned as a Second Lieutenant in the Somerset Light Infantry (SLI) on 30th January 1943, and assigned to the 4th Battalion SLI, which was one of four Territorial battalions of the Regiment.

As part of the 129th Brigade, alongside the 4th and 5th Battalions of The Wiltshire Regiment, the 4th Battalion SLI served throughout WW2 within the 43rd (Wessex) Infantry Division.

For most of its existence, the 4th Battalion was based in Kent under XII Corps of Southern Command, but on D-Day, 6th June 1944, it was ordered to 'stand-to' at Dymchurch, in Kent, although it wasn't until a week later that it received orders to move into the Sussex marshalling camps, in preparation for the crossing to France.

On 18th June, the 4th Battalion vehicles embarked at the Victoria Docks in London's East End, while the rest of the troops boarded transport ships in Newhaven, arriving off the coast of France in the evening of the following day. However, due to one of the worst Channel storms in living memory, the ships were unable to dock at the 'Mulberry' temporary harbours, and it was 23rd June before all of the vehicles and men had been off-loaded on to the beach at Arromanches, and gathered in the assembly area at Ryes.

In the 4th Somerset Light Infantry (SLI) Order of Battle, dated 24th June 1944, Lt. AA Barker is shown as one of the 'C' Company Platoon Commanders. Two days later, the 4th SLI moved towards the front line, travelling through the ripening harvest in the French countryside on a variety of transport, including Bren Gun Carriers, tanks and bicycles, as well their own vehicles, before halting near Brécy for the night.

The following day, the Battalion struggled through the rain, and muddy roads, to St Mavieux, where they replaced a Scottish unit in the reserves, and came under enemy shell fire for the first time. As they fought through late June and early July in the battle for Caen, particularly during the unsuccessful attack on Hill 112, the Battalion was involved in trench warfare, like that of WW1.

The 4th SLI suffered 556 casualties out of an initial strength of 845. In consequence, between 26th June and 14th July, the Battalion received nearly 500 officers and other ranks as replacements.

At the end of July, with 43rd Division now under the command of General Brian Horrocks' 30th Corps, the 4th SLI headed south through the Normandy countryside, to Mont Pinçon. There, in the first week of August, the Battalion faced stiff opposition, as it attacked uphill under very heavy machine gun and mortar fire. Eventually, however, the Germans were driven off, and the British troops were able to secure their position.

After fighting their way through to the Falaise Gap, in late August, the 43rd Division was ordered to the town of Vernon, to mount an assault crossing of the River Seine, where it faced stiff opposition from the 49th German Infantry Division.

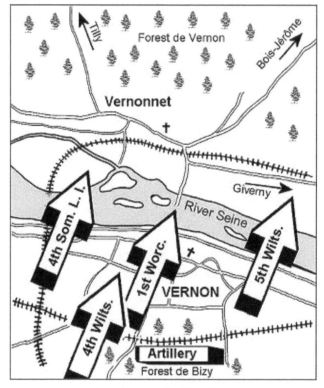

Assault across the River Seine

At Vernon two temporary bridges were built across the river by the engineers, at the cost of 80 lives. The 4th SLI was involved in heavy fighting to secure a foothold on the far bank and capture the village of Bois-Jérôme.

Having become the first British formation to cross the River Seine, the 43rd Division pushed on, across northern France and into Belgium, where Brussels and Antwerp were liberated on 4th September 1944.

On 29th August, the 4th SLI moved into the village of Le Mesnil Milon, where they were billeted for two weeks, resting and recovering. Initially, the welcome from the local population was not as cordial as it might have been, due to British artillery shelling the village during recent fighting. However, by the end of their fortnight there, the attitude of the villagers had changed, and 'Entente Cordiale' had been restored.

During the 4th SLI's period of rest, British troops had made tremendous progress, advancing through Belgium, and allowing the government in exile to return to Brussels. On 14th September, the 4th SLI received orders to move forward rapidly, to catch up with other ground forces preparing for 'Operation Market Garden'.

The objective of this combined airborne and ground assault was to thrust deep into enemy territory and gain a foothold over the River Rhine at Arnhem, to create an Allied invasion route into northern Germany. The plan required the capture of nine bridges by airborne forces ('Operation Market'), with land forces swiftly supporting them ('Operation Garden') by advancing over the bridges.

As the 4th SLI raced through northern France and Belgium as part of an endless column of troops, the joyous population turned out to greet the 'Tommies', lavishing them with fruit, wine and other carefully hoarded provisions, while the soldiers reciprocated with cigarettes and chocolate.

As they passed along the route, the soldiers could also see the widespread devastation caused by RAF fighter aircraft strafing enemy tanks and transport vehicles. 30 hours later, on 15th September, the 4th SLI reached the town of Linkhout, about 25 miles NE of Brussels, where they learned of the ambitious Allied plan to move swiftly to the Rhine.

On the morning of 21st September, having seen an apparently endless armada of aircraft pass overhead, carrying airborne troops to their drop zones, 4th SLI moved off again, crossing into Holland a couple of hours later. Travelling all of that day, and with a hectic drive through the night, the Battalion arrived outside the town of Grave, about five miles SW of Nijmegen, at 0400 hrs on 22nd September.

Tragically, during the night drive, a 'C' Company DUKW amphibious vehicle had overturned, killing seven passengers, including Lt. Aubrey Barker, and six other men, with many others injured.

After the war, a special CRGS prize for Spanish was named in honour of Aubrey Barker, and his name included on the memorial window in the CRGS library. He is also commemorated in King's College Chapel and on the Poole Roll of Honour.

The gravestone of Lieutenant Aubrey Arthur Barker, pictured below, carries the inscription:

In loving memory of my only son. Mum.
How bright their glorious spirits shine

Terence Jack Priddle

Age:	22
Died:	5th November 1944
Service Number:	1610620
Rank:	Flight Sergeant
Service/Regt:	RAF Volunteer Reserve
Ship/Unit:	15 (XV) Squadron
Grave/Memorial:	Rheinberg War Cemetery
Plot/Panel:	Grave 8, Plot 6, Row 2

Terence Jack Priddle was born on 20th February 1922, the son of Walter Priddle, a labourer, and his wife Annie (née Edwards). Terence, who had a brother and sister, received his early education at Canterbury Road Council School, Colchester, before being admitted to CRGS, as a day-scholar in Form Upper IIIA, on 19th September 1933.

Terence Jack Priddle

Terence achieved some academic success while at the school, with *The Colcestrian* reporting on his winning two prizes in the 1935 Diocesan Scripture Examination, and a Form Prize in 1937.

He left the school on 27th July 1938, and entered employment as an office worker, later working with the General Post Office (GPO) for two years as a telegraphist and sorter. In April 1942, Terence joined the RAF, and was sent to train in Canada as an Air Bomber (or Bomb Aimer).

On his return to the UK, Terence would have been sent to an Operational Training Unit (OTU), where RAF personnel were formed into bomber crews, and began their heavy bomber training on aircraft such as the twin-engine Vickers Wellington.

The Cato crew, including Terence, was then sent to 31 Base at RAF Stradishall, in Suffolk, to complete their training at 1657 Heavy

Conversion Unit (HCU), where they learned to fly four-engine aircraft, such as the Short Stirling.

On 28th July 1944, having completed their training, the Cato crew arrived at 15 (XV) Squadron, at RAF Mildenhall, with the pilot (and captain) Hugh Cato being promoted to Flying Officer.

Over the next three months, the crew carried out eighteen missions over enemy territory, many in support of the Allied advance following the D-Day landings which launched the invasion of Europe. However, the crew also flew on missions to attack targets in Germany, including Duisburg, Bonn, Stuttgart, Essen, Leverkusen and Frankfurt.

NF916 'Z-Zebra', the Lancaster B.1 aircraft flown by the Cato crew, took off from RAF Mildenhall at 0955 hrs on 5th November 1944, to take part in a daylight raid by 173 Allied aircraft on Solingen, 20 miles to the north of Cologne in Germany.

The raid was led by aircraft equipped with the 'Gee-H' radio navigation system, so although the city was completely covered by cloud, crews were able to bomb successfully on the markers laid down by earlier aircraft.

The attack was a complete success, with German sources reporting that 1,300 houses and eighteen industrial buildings had been destroyed, with a further 1,600 buildings seriously damaged. It is estimated that some 1,500 people died in the attack.

The only Allied aircraft to be lost on the raid was NF916, the 15 (XV) Squadron Lancaster with Terence Priddle on board. Other crews reported seeing the aircraft being hit by a bomb dropped by another aircraft over the target, and disintegrating in mid-air. No parachutes were seen to open, and the aircraft crashed at Halfeshof in Kreis Solingen, Germany, killing all of the crew.

The crew were originally buried in the Krahenhöhe Catholic Cemetery in Solingen but were re-interred in the Rheinberg War Cemetery after the war, and lie in adjacent graves.

Edwin Alfred Borley

Age:	21
Died:	11th November 1944
Service Number:	1396469
Rank:	Flight Sergeant
Service/Regt:	RAF Volunteer Reserve
Ship/Unit:	224 Squadron
Grave/Memorial:	The Runnymede Memorial
Plot/Panel:	Panel 215

Edwin Alfred Borley

Edwin Alfred Borley was born on 9th January 1923, the only child of Edward William Harold Borley and his wife, Doris Kate (née Amos) of Cromwell Road, in Colchester. Edwin was educated at St. John's Green School in Colchester, before he entered Form Upper IIIC of CRGS on 18th September 1934, as a day-scholar and member of Parr House.

In addition to playing rugby for Parrs, the December 1935 issue of *The Colcestrian* refers to Edwin's academic abilities in a report noting the award of a certificate for Mathematics.

After passing the Cambridge School Certificate examination, Edwin left the school on 29th July 1939, and went to work in the Traffic Department of the Colchester Co-operative Society, while residing at the family home, which was now in Winsley Road.

Edwin joined the RAF in March 1942 and, after his initial intake course, spent twelve months in America undergoing flying training. In December 1943, *The Colcestrian* reported that Edwin had been awarded his 'wings', having qualified as a Sergeant Pilot. Returning to the UK, Edwin was posted for further training at No. 6 (Pilot) Advanced Flying Unit, at RAF Little Rissington in Gloucestershire (known to all as 'Little Rissi').

On 13th June 1944, Edwin arrived at his first operational posting, with 224 Squadron, based at RAF St Eval in north Cornwall. As a strategic part of Coastal Command, the squadron operated US-built, four-engine Consolidated Liberator aircraft providing anti-submarine and anti-shipping patrols off the south-west coast of the UK, as well as undertaking photographic reconnaissance and air-sea rescue missions.

Starting on 11th July, Edwin flew regular sorties as 2nd pilot on the crew led by Lieutenant RW Thorpe of the USAAF. Each flight, by day or night, would typically last ten to twelve hours, flying at about 1200 feet above the English Channel, while using radar to search for enemy U-boats and shipping. According to the 224 Squadron Operational Record Books (ORBs), in addition to test flights and training sorties, Edwin and the rest of the crew flew some twelve missions from St Eval between July and early September.

On 8th September 1944, the squadron ORB notes Edwin's promotion to Flight Sergeant with effect from 11th May 1944 and, at the end of the month, Lieutenant Thorpe's departure from the squadron, having completed his tour of duty.

By September, the success of the Allied D-Day landings in northern France, and the capture of French ports on the Atlantic coast, had drastically reduced the threat from German U-boats, and 224 Squadron was redeployed to RAF Milltown, on the Moray Firth, near Elgin in Scotland, in an effort to counter the continuing U-boat threat from Scandinavia.

After two weeks spent completing the move, and familiarisation with the local situation in Scotland, the squadron resumed operational flying in late September. On 8th November 1944, Edwin returned to active flight duties, flying as the second pilot with a very experienced crew, led by Flight Lieutenant Phillip Hill.

Three days later. Edwin flew a second mission as part of the crew, taking off from RAF Milltown in Liberator GR.VI EW312/XB-D at 1125 hrs, to carry out an anti-submarine patrol between Shetland and the Norwegian coast. However, the mission ended in tragedy, when contact with the aircraft was lost, and it failed to return to base. Available records appear to indicate that the aircraft was attacked by German fighters 30km west of Bergen, and crashed into the sea, with the loss of the lives of all on board.

The full crew of Liberator EW312 on that fateful day was as follows:

131895	Flight Lieutenant Philip Michael HILL	Captain & Pilot
1396469	Flight Sergeant Edwin Alfred BORLEY	2nd Pilot
1223050	Warrant Officer Kenneth Russell SAYWELL	1st Navigator
A/427280	Flight Sergeant William Vernon JOHNSTONE	Navigator/Bomber
NZ411578	Warrant Officer Hugh SMOLENSKI	Wireless Operator/Air Gunner
415574	Warrant Officer Richard William BECK	Wireless Operator/Air Gunner
1317278	Flight Sergeant Thomas Richard FRAYNE	Wireless Operator/Air Gunner
NZ421291	Warrant Officer Alex James PHILLIPS	Wireless Operator/Air Gunner
NZ1827174	Sergeant William IRVINE	Air Gunner
1812891	Flight Sergeant Frank ASHWORTH	Flight Engineer

As well as being named on the war memorial at St Mary Magdalene Church in Colchester, Edwin Borley's sacrifice is also remembered on Panel 215 of the Runnymede Memorial.

Linocut from The Colcestrian, December 1940

Edward Charles Gilders

Age:	33
Died:	22nd November 1944
Service Number:	207331
Rank:	Captain
Service/Regt:	112th Field Regt, Royal Artillery (The West Somerset Yeomanry)
Ship/Unit:	6th Battalion
Grave/Memorial:	Brunssum War Cemetery
Plot/Panel:	Grave VI. 322

Edward Charles Gilders was the third and youngest child of Hoskins Henry Gilders, a Licensed Victualler and former mariner, and his Belgian wife Marceline Marianne (née Brontin). Edward was born in Brightlingsea, on 20th March 1911, and had an older brother, Jack, and a sister Marceline Jane.

Edward Charles Gilders

Edward's father died in Burlington Road Nursing Home, Ipswich on 24th June 1923, age 51, following which his mother returned to Belgium, where she died during 1944.

Edward received his early education at the Wesleyan School in Brightlingsea, before he entered Colchester Royal Grammar School on 15th September 1922, as a day-scholar in 'The Remove', and member of Parr House. The school records also note that Edward spent the summer of 1925 studying at a school in Belgium.

From reports in *The Colcestrian*, it is evident that Edward was academically gifted, consistently winning Form Prizes as the top of his class. He was also good at languages, particularly Spanish and French.

Appointed as a School Prefect in the preceding December, Edward left CRGS on 27th July 1928, having passed his Cambridge School Certificate with Honours. He went on to train as a teacher, and in the 1939 Register, he was listed as a schoolmaster, living at 29 Kemps Lane, Beccles.

On 20th September 1941, Edward Gilders was commissioned as a 2nd Lieutenant in the Royal Regiment of Artillery, becoming a Field Artillery Officer in 112th (Wessex) Field Regiment. As part of 21st Army Group, the regiment started to prepare for D-Day, and the invasion of Europe, with a tough training regime in the south of England.

In early 1942, Edward married Anne Mona Gilders (née Taylor) of Nayland and set up home back in Brightlingsea.

After the Allies invaded France on 6th June 1944, the 112th Field Regiment was sent to Normandy as part of the 43rd (Wessex) Division, as reinforcements for the British Second Army. Leaving from the docks at Tilbury in Essex, and due to land on D-Day+6, the regiment got caught up in the worst Channel storm for 40 years. Since it was impossible to get ashore, the landing craft had to ride out the storm, a mile from the beaches, while being bombed and strafed by the Luftwaffe, and at risk from enemy mines.

Eventually the storm abated, and they were able to land on 'Juno' beach in the early hours of the morning of 24th June, going straight into the reserve for 'Operation Epsom' (First Battle of the Odon), fought on the outskirts of Caen between 26th to 30th June. On 10th July, the Division was involved in an unsuccessful attack on Hill 112 ('Operation Jupiter'), although it inflicted very heavy casualties on the defending German 9th SS Panzer Division.

After Caen had been captured, 43rd (Wessex) came under the command of General Brian Horrocks' 30th Corps, and the 112th Field Regiment started to head south through the difficult Normandy 'bocage' country, assisting in the capture of the vital hill range of Mont Pinçon, before fighting through to the Falaise Gap.

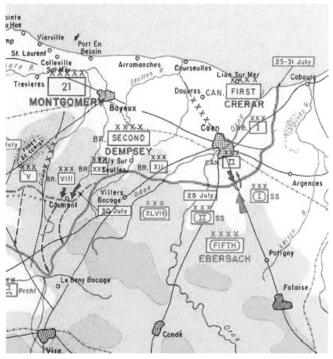

Force dispositions following the capture of Caen

In the first few days of August the German 7th and 15th Armies were caught in a pincer movement between British troops, in the north, and American forces in the south, which resulted in the two German armies being virtually eliminated by Allied artillery fire and air attack.

By the middle of August the Battle of Normandy had been won, and the 43rd (Wessex) was ordered to the town of Vernon, where it mounted an assault crossing of the River Seine against stiff opposition from the 49th German Infantry Division. Two bridges were built, at the cost of the lives of 80 Royal Engineers, and the 43rd Division was the first British formation to cross the River Seine, and thrust across northern France into Belgium, where Brussels and Antwerp were liberated on 4th September 1944.

The Division was immediately ordered forward, to take part in 'Operation Market Garden', with the objective of thrusting deep into enemy territory to gain a foothold over the River Rhine, and creating an Allied invasion route into northern Germany. The plan required the capture of nine bridges by airborne forces ('Operation Market'), with land forces swiftly supporting them ('Operation Garden') by advancing over the bridges.

The Allied forces successfully liberated the Dutch cities of Eindhoven and Nijmegen, as well as many other towns along the route, greatly limiting the opportunities for German V2 rockets to be launched against England. However, the Allies were unable to secure a foothold across the Rhine and were force to dig in on the south bank of the river.

Even after the Allies had been forced to withdraw south of the river at Arnhem, they continued to occupy an area known as 'The Island'. This low-lying polder land, between Nijmegen and Arnhem, and bounded by the Rhine and Lower Rhine, formed the 'Nijmegen Bridgehead'.

The Germans considered that the bridgehead posed a severe threat, as a base for the Allies to launch new offensives northwards, and they therefore tried to oust the Allied troops from the area. At the beginning of October, the Germans launched a major offensive, involving several armoured divisions under the command of the 2nd SS Panzer Corps, against positions held by the 43rd Wessex, around the village of Elst.

The German attacks on the 'Island' lasted for about a week. The fighting was hard, but the British defence held firm. As *The Colcestrian* later reported, it was during this period that Captain Edward Gilders distinguished himself:

> 'while acting as a forward observation officer, he was continuously engaged for several days in efforts to smash dangerous German counter-attacks, and was able bring the fire of the British 25-pounder guns to bear so accurately that the Germans were eventually routed.'

The 112th Field Regiment, with the rest of the 43rd Division, then moved south, to take part in 'Operation Clipper', a joint American and British attack, to capture the area around Geilenkirchen, on the Siegfried Line. The US 84th Division began the assault, and crossed the frontline, advancing north-east to take the high ground east of Geilenkirchen.

The British 43rd (Wessex) Division then moved forward to capture the high ground in the area of Bauchem and Tripsrath, to the west and north of Geilenkirchen. With the town thus virtually encircled, the US 84th Division was able to move in and occupy Geilenkirchen and its north-eastern suburbs. Despite adverse weather, which turned the field into a mudbath, both divisions then attempted to advance further north-east, along the banks of the River Wurm.

It was during this phase of 'Operation Clipper' that Captain Edward Charles Gilders was killed, on 22nd November 1944. His body was originally buried at Nuth, halfway between Geilenkirchen and Maastricht, in Holland. After the war, however, the Commonwealth Graves Commission re-interred his remains in Brunssum Cemetery on 3rd July 1946 (picture below).

The posthumous award of a Military Cross, for 'gallant and distinguished services in North West Europe' was published in *The London Gazette* on 27th February 1945.

Brian Edward Wright

Age:	22
Died:	17th December 1944
Service Number:	153605
Rank:	Flying Officer
Service/Regt:	RAF Volunteer Reserve
Ship/Unit:	57 Squadron
Grave/Memorial:	Runnymede Memorial
Plot/Panel:	Panel 210, Column 2

Brian Edward Wright

Brian Edward Wright was born on 18th January 1922, the elder son of William Wright, a carpenter, and his wife Edith Blanche (née Durrant) of Lexden, Colchester. Brian had a twin sister, Beryl Edith, and a younger brother, Peter Ernest, born in 1928. The family lived at 44 London Road, Lexden, later moving to 106 London Road.

Brian entered CRGS on 19th September 1933 from Lexden Council School, and was clearly a bright student, since he received a full scholarship from Essex County Council. Little is known of Brian during his time at the school, but it would seem that, after he left on 27th July 1938, he found employment in a bank, and continued to live at home.

From the information that is available, it would seem likely that Brian volunteered to join the RAF sometime during 1942. After completing his basic training, and having passed selection as an aircrew candidate, it is likely that Brian was sent, with the rank of Leading Aircraftman (1472381), to the US, or Canada, for flight crew training. On 1st October 1943, having successfully completed his flying training as an Air Bomber (or 'Bomb Aimer'), Brian was commissioned as a Pilot Officer in the RAF.

On his return to the UK, Brian would have been posted to an Operational Training Unit (OTU), for assignment as part of a crew. There, he would have met Alf Donkin and the rest of the men with whom he would fly on operations, and been formed into a crew. Many weeks of intensive training followed, as they learned to fly together, usually on reserve bomber aircraft such as the Wellington or Whitley.

Finally, they would have been sent to a Heavy Conversion Unit (HCU), where they would have been joined by a flight engineer, and taught to fly the four-engine Avro Lancaster, then in use by many operational squadrons. Having completed the HCU course, the Donkin crew was then ready for active duty, and were posted to 106 Squadron, where they arrived at the end of July 1944.

By the time Brian Wright arrived at RAF Metheringham, the home of 106 Squadron, he held the rank of Flying Officer, having been promoted on 1st April 1944. Once Alf Donkin had flown a mission as 2nd pilot, with an experienced crew, Alf and his crew were ready to fly their first operational sortie, on 14th August 1944, to Le Quesnay in France. During the next month Brian Wright, and the rest of the crew, flew a further seven missions with 106 Squadron, attacking enemy positions in Germany, Poland and Holland.

During September 1944, the RAF decided that 106 Squadron should become 'a nursery' for Pathfinder (PFF) crews. Along with several other crews, the Donkin crew decided not to volunteer for Pathfinder duties. They were therefore posted to 57 Squadron, also part of 5 Group, Bomber Command, and arrived at RAF East Kirkby on 15th September 1944.

The crew flew their first mission, bombing the Handorf airfield in Munster, Germany, on 23rd September 1944. Over the next three months they became an experienced crew, flying a further seventeen missions with 57 Squadron, against targets all over Europe.

Henry Medrington, the navigator, wrote pen portraits of most of his fellow crew members, in which he described Brian Wright in the following words:

'Brian:

Flying Officer Brian Wright. Bomb Aimer extraordinaire. Holds record for Group, we believe, for high-level bombing but has had no more experience than I have as Navigator. Tried for pilot in first place but was ploughed without knowing why. Very quiet. You would imagine his silence indicated deep thought. It doesn't. Very good-hearted type with capacity for beer equal to Tony's. Thickset, 5ft 10in, ruddy complexion, Public-School accent. Has a reputation, during leg pulling, of being asleep standing up or walking along snoring. A Londoner with few notable hobbies. Reads amazingly quickly and in bursts but doesn't seem to be interested in the content. Magnificent value when repleat *(sic)* but never gets tight. Age 21, worked in a bank but never regrets it.'

On 17th December 1944, when Lancaster III LM626 (DX-M) took off from RAF East Kirkby at about 1600 hrs, captained by Flying Officer Alfred Donkin, there was an eight-man crew on board, with New Zealander Flying Officer Noel Culpan flying as 'second dickie', to gain experience before captaining his own aircraft on operational sorties.

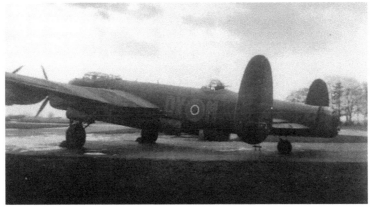

57 Squadron Lancaster III LM626 'DX-M'. Fred Cole Part 4, WW2 People's War

The Donkin crew, including Flying Officer Brian Edward Wright, were on their 26th mission together, as they took their place among a force of 280 Lancasters, dispatched from airfields across Lincolnshire and South Yorkshire, to attack Munich, as just one component of a much larger force of 1313 RAF aircraft, sent to bomb industrial Germany that night.

It is still uncertain as to what happened to LM626 that night, but it seems likely that while both aircraft were on the outbound leg of their journey, sometime just south of Rouen, not long after crossing the Channel into France, LM626 collided with a 463 Squadron Lancaster, LL487, piloted by FO Bennett RAAF. However, there remains the possibility that the aircraft were downed as a result of 'friendly' fire from British forces on the ground.

LL487, based at RAF Waddington, exploded on landing when it crashed near Le Gros-Theil, about 25km SW of Rouen. The bodies of the eight-man crew were buried in a collective grave at the local cemetery, by people from the nearby village.

Meanwhile, LM626, with Brian Wright among the crew, exploded in mid-air, and came down near the village of Bourgtheroulde-Infreville, about six kilometres south-west of Rouen.

The villagers who went to the scene, found the nose section of the aircraft largely intact, near a railway embankment, while the rest of the wreckage had fallen as small pieces of debris, covering a field beyond the railway line. The bodies of the two pilots, and one of the gunners were buried locally, in the St Sever cemetery, in Rouen. The remains of the rest of LM626's crew were never found.

During this single operation, on December 17th 1944, the RAF had lost nine aircraft, resulting in the deaths of nearly 70 crew, with a further twelve aircraft having returned to base, but damaged beyond repair. These losses were considered to be light.

The sacrifice made by the crew of Lancaster LM626 is commemorated on a plaque in the Mairie of the village of Grand Bourgtheroulde, in France. Flying Officer Brian Edward Wright is also remembered on the war memorial at St. Leonard's Church, Lexden, at the RAF Memorial at Runnymede, and on the stained-glass window in the CRGS library.

Sir Bertram Home Ramsay

Age:	61
Died:	2nd January 1945
Rank:	Admiral, Allied Naval Commander-in-Chief
Service/Regt.	Royal Navy
Grave/Memorial:	St. Germain-en-Laye
	New Communal Cemetery, France
Plot/Panel:	Ref. Grave 9

Bertram Home Ramsay was born on January 22nd 1883, son of Brigadier-General William Alexander Ramsay, an officer in the 4th Hussars, and Susan (née Michener), who hailed from Clontarf, near Dublin. 'Bertie', as he was known, was born at Hampton Court Palace, where his father was then stationed. The family moved regularly around the country's garrison towns and while his father was stationed in Colchester, Bertie attended CRGS for a year from September 1891 until July 1892. His elder brother, Alexander Fitzgerald Ramsay was also a pupil at the school. When his

Admiral Sir Bertram Home Ramsay

father was sent to Aldershot, Bertie left CRGS for Foster's Preparatory School at Stubbington in Hampshire. Winston Churchill, who joined the 4th Hussars in 1895 and served under William Ramsay's command, later recalled often having seen the young Bertie on the barrack square at Aldershot.

As he came from a family of soldiers, it may seem surprising that Ramsay was packed off to sea. However, as the youngest son he had the misfortune that much of the family's money had been spent educating his brothers and getting them into good regiments. Therefore, rather than continuing his education at a Public School, he enlisted into the Navy as a cadet just before his fifteenth birthday, joining HMS *Britannia*, on 15th January 1898. Upon passing out in May 1899, he joined HMS *Crescent* as a Midshipman.

HMS *Crescent* was the flagship of Vice-Admiral Sir Frederick Bedford KCB, who was the Commander-in-Chief of the North America and West Indies station, so this posting took Ramsay all around the Atlantic. He was a happy and active member of the gunroom, and his log book is marked by exquisite drawings of parts of the ship and the way that they function. These are interspersed with brilliant sketches of other ships. He flourished under the watchful eyes of the *Crescent*'s officers, and his second Captain, Henry Campbell, described him as 'a very promising young officer'. Ramsay often attributed the success he later enjoyed to the fact that he had served in the gunroom of such an outstanding ship.

Ramsay then spent his first commission as a Sub-Lieutenant on board HMS *Hyancinth* where he became involved in the Somaliland campaign of 1903-04. On 21st April 1904 he experienced his first combined operation (involving both the Navy and Army) at the Battle of Illig. He performed well and was rewarded for his services by being mentioned in despatches and promoted to Lieutenant.

Following a subsequent tour of duty in command of a turret on HMS *Dreadnought*, Ramsay chose to specialise in signals, despite this being a period when gunnery officers were those most likely to end up with flag rank. By his own admission, he disliked being closely involved with the material side of a ship and 'didn't like to get his hands dirty'. He preferred to see the bigger picture, the manoeuvrings of fleets and large-scale operations. Nevertheless, he proved himself to be a very able signals officer, who, according to the Captain Superintendent of Signal Schools, conducted himself with 'sobriety, zeal and to my entire satisfaction'. Ramsay then moved on to serve on the staff of Rear-Admiral Sir Colin

Keppel and then Rear-Admiral Sir Douglas Gamble and by 1913 was a well-regarded young officer.

Ramsay began WW1 back on *Dreadnought*, having been promoted to Lieutenant Commander. In his diary he recorded the arrival of Sir John Jellicoe to command the Grand Fleet and the declaration of war with little or no excitement – he had been 'expecting it'. He left the *Dreadnought* in 1915 having turned down the post of Flag-Lieutenant to the Admiral. This would have involved commanding cruisers aboard HMS *Defence* and was a fortuitous decision, since *Defence* blew up at the Battle of Jutland in 1916 with the loss of all hands.

Ramsay moved swiftly on to his first command, a small monitor M25 as part of the Dover Patrol. He was then promoted to Commander of the destroyer HMS *Broke,* and mentioned in despatches a second time. His star rose further when he transported King George V to France, after the end of the war, to visit the troops, impressing the King so much that he was invested a Member of the Royal Victorian Order (MVO).

Ramsay's inter-war career was relatively uneventful, although his reputation amongst his superiors continued to grow. In 1919 Lord Jellicoe appointed him to his staff as Flag Commander on a tour of the Dominions, the aim of which was to consider the future of Imperial defence. He won high praise from Jellicoe and, after commanding two ships in the Mediterranean, was promoted to Captain in 1923, whereupon he was successful in senior officers' war and tactical courses. He then moved on to Captain HMS *Dance*, followed by a period as an instructor at the War College.

Finally, after two more commands and another brief stint as an instructor, he was promoted to Rear-Admiral in May 1935. It was upon this promotion that his career faltered, when he was invited by his old friend, Admiral Sir Roger Backhouse, the Commander-in-Chief, Home Fleet, to become his chief of staff. Backhouse and Ramsay held opposite opinions about how the navy should be run, with Ramsay a moderniser, while Backhouse was a traditionalist. Ramsay spent only four months in this post before he asked to be relieved of his duties in December 1935. This was followed by three years of what amounted to retirement, and in October 1938 he was finally placed on the Retired List. He had married

Helen Margaret Menzies in 1929 and was now able, at least, to spend more time with her and their two sons at the family home in Coldstream, Berwickshire.

However, with the likelihood of another war increasing, it became clear that many areas of naval operations needed to be reviewed - Dover Command, in particular, now became vital to holding the Channel in case of invasion. As a result, Backhouse, by now First Sea Lord, recommended Ramsay for the task and he was, somewhat unexpectedly, appointed Flag Officer in Charge at Dover and promoted to Vice-Admiral (although still technically on the retired list). He made his HQ in the thirteenth century military tunnels beneath Dover Castle, which had been enlarged and extended during the Napoleonic Wars.

When the British Expeditionary Force had landed in France, Ramsay, with his force of destroyers, attempted to protect their flank. However, this proved extremely difficult and on 15th May 1940 he was forced to order his ships to clear the Dutch and Belgian coast as the Germans swept through the Low Countries. The BEF had no option but to withdraw to the coast and hope for evacuation by sea.

In the days leading up to 'Operation Dynamo', as the 'Dunkirk miracle' was officially known, Ramsay's reports to the Admiralty convey a clear sense of despondency at the situation. Yet Dunkirk would show Ramsay at his best. The evacuation involved a huge number of small ships, and he allowed - with great success - his captains to use their own initiative in the operation. Many of them were recommended for awards in his report. The successful recovery of 338,266 soldiers earned Ramsay his knighthood and also established him as the country's leading naval commander.

From 1940 to 1944 Ramsay enjoyed more success. After three years of command at Dover, he was given the responsibility of organising the invasion of North Africa, 'Operation Torch', followed by the invasion of Sicily, 'Operation Husky', where he personally commanded the Easter Task Force. Following the success of both invasions Ramsay was promoted to acting Admiral in October 1943 (confirmed in March 1944 along with his reinstatement on the active list).

In January 1944 Ramsay moved to London to join the rest of the High Command to work on 'Operation Overlord', the invasion of Normandy, and was successful in persuading Admiral Cunningham, now the First Sea Lord, to give him more ships than even Cunningham himself felt necessary. Once again Ramsay managed to organise a massive fleet which successfully landed the largest invasion force ever assembled on the beaches of Normandy on 6th June 1944. In addition to this, his task force continued to supply and reinforce the Allied push through France and ultimately into Germany. Ramsay was the only voice to oppose Eisenhower's and Montgomery's attempt to finish the Germans off quickly in September/October 1944, and though unable to dissuade his colleagues, did his best to provide them with all the support he could in a venture which was, as he had feared, ultimately unsuccessful.

Bertram Home Ramsay died on 2nd January 1945 when his plane crashed on take-off at an airfield at Toussus-le-Noble, just to the south-west of Paris, as he was on his way to a meeting with Montgomery in Brussels. Because he died before the end of the war and never thrust himself into the limelight, unlike some of his fellow commanders, he remains, to some extent, a forgotten hero. Yet he was forward-thinking, constantly trying to modernise the Navy, delegated well and was detail-orientated while still retaining a clear strategic overview. He was decorated by all the main Allied nations , being appointed Grand Officier Légion d'Honneur (France), Commander Legion of Merit (USA) and Order of Ushakov (USSR). His contributions to the 'miracle' of Dunkirk, the invasions of North Africa and Sicily, and the D-Day landings themselves were all crucial to the ultimate success of the war effort.

Ramsay Memorial, Dover Castle

Eric James Tracey

Age:	29
Died:	26th March 1945
Rank:	Sub-Lieutenant (Air)
Service/Regt:	821 Squadron, Fleet Air Arm
Ship/Unit:	HMS *Puncher* (D79)
Grave/Memorial:	Lee-on-Solent Memorial
Plot/Panel:	Bay 6, Panel 5

Eric James Tracey

Eric James Tracey was born on 22nd June 1921, the son of William Arthur Robert Tracey and his wife, Louisa. William, who had been born in 1874, already had seven children, four sons and three daughters, by his first wife, Alice, who had died in 1919, aged 45. A year later he had married Louisa Elliott (née Coffee), the widow of Henry Elliott, who also had died in 1919, aged 28, leaving Louisa with a son, Henry C Elliott, then aged three.

In addition to Eric, William and Louisa also had a daughter, Doreen, born in 1925. Although William had been born in Colchester, he had set up as a fishmonger in Plumstead, in South London. This was where he had met and married both Alice and then Louisa, and where Eric had been born. At some point after Eric's birth, William decided to move his new family back to Colchester. The CRGS Admissions Register records his occupation as 'Shopkeeper', which the 1939 Register clarifies, by stating that he was a 'Fish-fryer with his own business', on Harwich Road, Colchester.

Eric attended East Ward School in Colchester, before entering CRGS on 16th September 1932, on a full scholarship from Essex LEA. There are few references to Eric in *The Colcestrian*, apart from his occasional academic successes, which included passing his Cambridge School Certificate, before leaving the school on 23rd July 1937. Headmaster, Harry Cape, later described him as: 'a pupil whom I esteemed most highly because of his high ideals and standards, and his complete trustworthiness.'

Having left CRGS, Eric worked for Siemens Cables, in London, returning to Plumstead, to live with his half-siblings, before later moving to Bexleyheath. He continued to study in his spare time, and won a scholarship to King's College, London. Old Colcestrian Society records indicate that Eric returned to live on Harwich Road, in Colchester, and that, with the country still in the grip of war, Eric volunteered for the Fleet Air Arm instead of taking up his place at university, intending to resume his studies after the war had been won.

From naval records, it would appear that Eric joined the Royal Navy in the summer of 1943 and, after basic training, was select to train as a navigator at HMS *Jackdaw*, a Fleet Air Arm base in Scotland, otherwise known as Royal Naval Air Station (RNAS) Crail, near Anstruther, in Fife.

Eric was commissioned as a Sub-Lieutenant (Air) on 14th February 1944, and shortly afterwards posted to 821 Squadron, which was reformed at RNAS Stretton (HMS *Blackcap*), near Warrington, on 1st May 1944, equipped with twelve Fairey Barracuda Mk II torpedo bombers.

In November 1944, after several months training with their new aircraft, the squadron embarked aboard the HMS *Puncher*, which had just completed maintenance in a Clyde dockyard in preparation for her new role as a Deck Landing Training Carrier.

On 26th November, having completed tests of the ship's catapult and arrestor systems, including modifications to allow her to operate torpedo bombers, twelve Barracudas of 821 Squadron took off from RNAS

Maydown, Northern Ireland, and landed on HMS *Puncher* while she was steaming in the Clyde.

A Fairey Barracuda Mk II of 821 Squadron

A period of deck landing practice and exercises began in the Irish Sea the next day, but operations were curtailed when the wind strengthened in the afternoon. While returning to the Clyde that evening, the ship suffered major engine problems, which resulted in the ship limping back to the Clyde.

At first light HMS *Puncher's* Barracudas flew ashore to RNAS Machrihanish, while the ship spent the next month being repaired, before eventually returning to active duty on 30th December 1944, and re-embarking 821 Squadron to resume their deck take-offs and landings, and exercising the crews in various carrier deck procedures.

HMS *Puncher* completed her exercise period on 29th January 1945, and left the Clyde at the beginning of February, accompanied by her escorts, HMS *Towey* and HMCS *Iroquois*, to commence her first offensive operations with the Home Fleet, based at Scapa Flow.

After a few days spent on further flying training, HMS *Puncher* took part in five days of operations off the Norwegian coast, although the carrier was tasked with providing fighter cover, and the Barracudas played no part in the operations.

On 17th February, HMS *Puncher* embarked on a further operation in Norwegian waters, providing support for a minesweeping run through German minefields, and an aerial minelaying sortie by carrier aircraft, including the Barracudas of 821 Squadron. Instead of crossing the coast over Utsire, the planes made landfall over the heavily-defended town of Stavanger. As a result of this navigation error the Barracudas and their fighter escort lost each other, and two Barracudas were shot down by German flak. The remaining seven Barracudas successfully laid their mines in the Karmøy Channel and, having completed its mission, the naval task force returned to its base on 23rd February.

In the last week of March, a further anti-shipping strike in Norwegian waters was undertaken by a naval task force comprised of four carriers, including HMS *Puncher*, two cruisers, and an escort of destroyers. Despite poor weather conditions an attack was launched against shipping off the coast between Trondheim Kristiansand. Fighter aircraft from the carriers engaged a number of Luftwaffe aircraft, shooting three down, and damaging two more.

Finding no suitable targets, the bombers jettisoned their payload, while a Barracuda from HMS *Puncher*, MD 837, failed to return from an anti-submarine patrol. It was later determined that the three-man crew of the aircraft, consisting of Pilot, Lieutenant GF Cornish; Navigator, Sub-Lieutenant EJ Tracey; and Telegraphist/Air Gunner (TAG), Petty Officer AG Sumner had all been killed. The task force returned to Scapa Flow on the 29th March.

"I Hope I Batted Usefully"

Sub-Lieut. (A.) Eric James Tracey, R.N.V.R., of Harwich Road, Colchester, who died on war service in March, 1945, left £242 14s. 10d. He left his property to his mother. His will concludes :— To all my very good friends—my very best wishes. Cheerio, folks—I hope that I batted doing something useful, and if I bat along with my pilot and my T.A.G. please write a letter of sympathy to their wives—they must be very nice people.

Excerpt from The Colcestrian, July 1947

The sacrifice made by Sub-Lieutenant Eric James Tracey is commemorated on the Fleet Air Arm memorial at Lee-on-Solent, and on the window in the CRGS library.

Edward Philip May

Age:	26
Died:	5th April 1945
Service Number:	112978
Rank:	Captain
Service/Regt:	London Rifle Brigade
Ship/Unit:	8th Battalion
Grave/Memorial:	Hannover War Cemetery, Germany
Plot/Panel:	Ref. 15.C.1

Philip May
(Photo credit:
8thriflebrigade.co.uk)

(Edward) Philip May was born on 5th October 1918, son of John Percy May and his wife, Ruth. They had three sons, all of whom attended CRGS. John May's occupation was given in the CRGS Admissions Register as 'IETD Superintendent' and the family lived at 'Halcyon', St Mary's Road, Frinton.

Philip attended the Pre before attending CRGS Senior School from September 1928 to December 1935. He played rugby for the 1st XV, passed his Cambridge School Certificate in December 1934 and was a Prefect. After leaving CRGS he was articled to a firm of auctioneers and estate agents, and passed their final examinations before enlisting in the army.

Philip joined the 8th Battalion, London Rifle Brigade, attaining the rank of captain. The battalion participated in the Normandy campaign where Philip was awarded the Military Cross. The citation stated:

> 'On August 18 1944 Capt. May was in command of the vanguard consisting of a section of carriers and a motor platoon of a company of the Rifle Brigade, supported by a troop of tanks. West of Lunay enemy opposition was met

and heavy fire from artillery was opened on the vanguard. Capt. May organised an attack on the village with infantry, supported by tanks. During the attack Capt. May saw that the supporting fire from the tanks was ineffective and immediately jumped onto the Troop Commander's tank to secure better supporting fire. All the time the tanks were under machine-gun fire and Capt. May was completely exposed.

Shortly after this, two riflemen were killed in a farmyard. Disregarding his own safety and in spite of enemy small arms and mortar fire, Capt. May went forward by himself to see whether the men were wounded or dead.

The infantry under Capt. May's command continued to attack and harass the enemy with great effect until ordered to withdraw by his Company Commander.

Heavy casualties were suffered by the vanguard in this action and Capt. May's gallantry and complete disregard of danger were an inspiration to the men under his command.'

Following this, the 11th Armoured Division, of which the 8th Battalion London Rifles were a part, spear-headed the advance into Germany, aiming to reach the Baltic and split the country in two. By 5th April 1945 the 8th had arrived at the River Weser at the small town of Stolzenau. The bridge there had already been blown, so they had to attempt to force a crossing under the cover of farm buildings on the opposite bank. Capt. Philip May's platoon was about to cross in boats when he was killed on the riverbank by a single shot from a sniper. He was initially buried in the village of Nendorf, six miles to the west of Stolzenau and eighteen miles north of Minden. His obituary in *The Colcestrian* refers to a school career of 'marked honour and distinction' describing him as being 'of high intellectual ability and promise', concluding that 'his kindness of heart and innate modesty endeared him to all who knew him.'

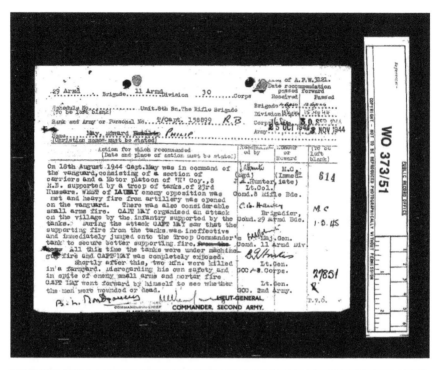

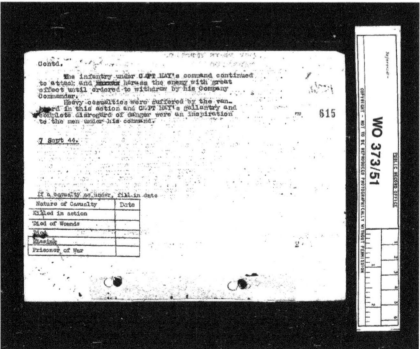

Citation for Military Cross (Photo credit: 8thriflebrigade.co.uk)

CAPTAIN E. P. MAY., M.C., THE RIFLE BRIGADE

It is with very deep regret that we record the death in action of Phillip May. He entered the School in September, 1928, just before his tenth birthday, and, as a very young boy, was placed in the lowest Form. His School career was of marked honour and distinction and he left school at Christmas, 1935, from the Upper Sixth. He was of very high intellectual ability and promise. More than this, his kindness of heart and his innate modesty endeared him to all who knew him. We heard with pride of the gallantry which earned for him his military distinction and, later, with deep sorrow that he had made the greatest sacrifice of all. Our sympathies go out to his parents and his brothers.

I am permitted to quote the letter which was sent to his father by Captain Willcox, the Medical Officer of the Battalion, and below it I quote the official citation which accompanied the award to him of the Military Cross.

> Captain J. M. Willcox,
> 8th Bn. The Rifle Brigade,
> B.L.A.,
> 22 *April*, 1945.

Dear Mr. May,

Thank you for your letter. It is quite in order for me to tell you where Phillip is buried and the Colonel has asked me to do so. The name of the village is Nendorf. This is a small village about six miles west of Stolzenau and about 18 miles north of Minden.

The action in which the battalion was involved at that time was at Stolzenau —on the Weser—and when we were relieved we went back for half a day to Nendorf. Phillip and five others of the battalion were brought back and buried there. Most of the officers of the battalion, some from the armoured regiment with which we work, some from brigade headquarters, and many men from the battalion were present at the service.

I shall be very pleased to come and see you when I get an opportunity and will write to you when this occurs.

> Yours sincerely,
> J. M. WILLCOX.

Letter to Philip's father from the Battalion's MO, published in The Colcestrian, July 1945

Ernest Alfred Last

Age:	38
Died:	15th December 1945
Service Number:	WX10084
Rank:	Private
Service/Regt:	Australian Imperial Forces
Ship/Unit:	Liaison Section
Grave/Memorial:	Yokohama War Cemetery, Japan
Plot/Panel:	Australian Section E.C.9

Ernest Alfred Last was born in Colchester on 25th November 1907, son of Henry James Last and his wife, Emma Sarah (née Wood). He had an older brother, also named Henry James, and a younger one, Arthur Charles. His father ran a bakers and confectionery business at 89 Crouch Street, Colchester. Ernest attended Colchester High School before coming to CRGS in July 1917 on a full scholarship. He was an academically able student who achieved his Cambridge School Certificate in 1924. He left the school in April 1925 to become articled to Colchester solicitors Sparling, Benham and Brough.

Ernest's elder brother, Henry, also attended CRGS and was prominent in the scouts. He left in 1916 to go into the family business, eventually taking it over from his father along with the third brother, Arthur. *The Colcestrian* records HJ Last as being the caterers for many school and OCS events, including OCS Dinners and AGMs. In addition to their Crouch Street premises, HJ Last also became the proprietors of a restaurant in Colchester High Street.

After qualifying as a solicitor, Ernest moved to London. He resided in Camden, Marylebone and Hampstead before deciding to emigrate to Australia. In 1938 he sailed from Southampton aboard RMS *Largs Bay*, arriving in Fremantle, Western Australia, on 10th May. In 1939 he married Leonora and they lived at 153 Palmerston Street, Perth, later moving to 22 Suburban Road, South Perth.

In December 1940 Ernest enlisted in the Australian Imperial Forces, joining up at Claremont, Perth. Strangely, given his professional status as a solicitor, his occupation is stated as 'cleaner at the YMCA' on his enlistment papers. After initial training, he sailed to Egypt, where he took part in the North Africa campaign. Wounded in action on 1st November 1942 during the 2nd Battle of El Alamein, the decisive battle which saw the defeat of the Axis powers in North Africa, he was hospitalised for three weeks with chest injuries, returning to Australia in February 1943.

Ernest was then involved in the war in the Pacific, sailing from Cairns, Queensland, in August 1943 to Milne Bay in New Guinea, the site of Allied airfields which were protected by an Australian garrison. The area was being developed into a major Allied base following the successful defeat of an attempted Japanese invasion at the Battle of Milne Bay in 1942.

Ernest was part of the Milne Bay garrison on New Guinea until July 1945, when he was sent to Morotai, a small island in the Dutch East Indies. This was another air base, vital to the Allies in the campaign to liberate the Philippines. Its facilities were expanded further in 1945 to support the Australian-led Borneo Campaign. For these reasons, the Japanese attempted to recapture the island, and there was intermittent fighting until August 1945 when the war in the East came to an end after atomic bombs were dropped on Hiroshima and Nagasaki.

On 29th August 1945 Ernest was transferred to Manila in the Philippines. Then in October he sailed to Yokohama, Japan, as part of the Australian Liaison Section at the General Headquarters of US General, Douglas MacArthur, Supreme Commander for the Allied Powers in Tokyo. The Liaison Section was to reconnoitre the areas of the country which were to be occupied by the British Commonwealth Occupying Force. The BCOF was also to oversee Japan's demilitarisation.

However, on 15th December 1945 Ernest suffered a fatal accident when he somehow fell from the Finance Building in Tokyo onto a concrete courtyard below. He died from multiple injuries, including a fractured skull. A Court of Inquiry into his death was held in January 1946 but found no evidence of negligence, carelessness or misconduct.

Peter Mark Ellis

Age:	24
Died:	3rd July 1946
Rank:	Lieutenant (A) (Fleet Air Arm)
Service/Regt:	Royal Navy Volunteer Reserve
Ship/Unit:	HMS *Colossus*
Grave/Memorial:	Colchester Cemetery
Plot/Panel:	Section E Division 6, Grave 64

Peter Mark Wooding Ellis was born on 9th February 1922, the second child, and only son, of William Mark Ellis (born 28th July 1891) and his wife Gwladys Amelia Kathleen (née Wooding), who had married in St Leonard's Church Colchester on 13th April 1914. By the time Peter's older sister, Joyce Gwladys, was born on 23rd June 1915, the Great War had started, with William seeing active service in the Royal Army Ordnance Corps.

Peter Ellis

After the war, William left the Army and worked as a printer. The family lived in Clacton for a few years, and Peter was born. In 1923, the family moved to Recreation Road, in Old Heath, Colchester, but three years later Peter's father passed away, from illness resulting from his service during the Great War.

On 19th September 1933, having received his early education at Canterbury Road Council School, Peter entered CRGS, as a day-scholar in Form Upper IIIA. During his time in the school, *The Colcestrian* carried a report of his performance as one of General Stanley's Daughters in the school production of 'The Pirates of Penzance' in April 1934, his winning of a school prize in December 1936, and appearances in the Junior Rugby XV.

The magazine also reported that, in the Science Society meeting on Monday, February 14th 1938, 'PMW Ellis of Form Vb gave a lecture on the development of the motor car.' After leaving CRGS, Peter joined the Old Colcestrian Society, living at the family home in Recreation Road, and working as a Civil Servant.

On his eighteenth birthday, Peter Ellis volunteered for service with the Fleet Air Arm and, after his initial training, was sent to HMS *Goshawk*, at the Royal Navy Air Station in Piarco, Trinidad, for his flying training. Over the next five months, he developed the various skills required for his role as an Observer, receiving his commission as a Sub-Lieutenant (Air) with effect from 2nd January 1943.

During the next three years, Peter Ellis saw service with the Air Sea Rescue Squadron in England, Burma, Ceylon, and other Far East bases, accumulating over 40 rescues to his credit. Lieutenant Ellis sailed back to England as part of the crew of the aircraft carrier HMS *Colossus*, which had left Simonstown in South Africa in May 1946 after a refit. On arrival in Portsmouth, the ship was paid off, and Peter returned home to Colchester on demobilisation leave.

Three weeks later, however, he fell ill and was admitted to the Chatham Naval Hospital for treatment. Despite the best efforts of the medical team, Lieutenant Peter MW Ellis RNVR died on 3rd July 1946, as a result of septicaemia, possibly as a result of a germ contracted in the tropics. He was 24 years of age.

In publishing his obituary, *The Colcestrian* reported that: 'much sympathy has been extended to his mother, and his sister, Mrs Joyce G. May.'

The inscription on his gravestone reads:

His life a beautiful memory. His death a silent grief.

THE CRGS WORLD WAR TWO MEMORIAL LIBRARY

Laurie Holmes

Those who use the library at CRGS are aware of the impressive stained-glass window on the north side commemorating the Old Colcestrians who died in World War Two. However, what they may not realise is that it is not just the window, but the library as a whole which constitutes the actual World War Two memorial.

Even before the end of hostilities the school was receiving enquiries and suggestions about what form the memorial might take. These included a memorial hall to be used as a theatre and concert venue, new squash courts, the creation of a small chapel for private prayer, or building a school library.

Initially the memorial hall was the preferred option. At a meeting in February 1946, Headmaster AW Fletcher stated that it had been approved by students, governors and the county, and he suggested that the Old Colcestrian Society should perhaps give their blessing to the scheme by agreeing to pay for a special part of the furniture and fittings, such as the seating and/or an organ. However, the Society appears not to have been convinced by this. It was agreed to defer the decision until a questionnaire had been sent to old boys and, especially, the parents of those old boys who had died. It would be for them to decide.

By February 1947 the concert hall plan had been abandoned in favour of a combination of the small chapel and library option. Presumably this was due to views expressed by Old Colcestrians and parents, though it may also have been significant that former Headmasters, Percy Shaw Jeffrey and Harry Cape, were both in favour. The names of the dead were to be recorded on a plaque, similar to the Great War plaque in the Hall – there was still no thought of a stained-glass window.

It should also be remembered that the school did not have a bespoke library at this time. The room which was to become the library was then used as the dining-room (prior to this it had always been used as a classroom). However, by 1947 CRGS had become a state grammar school, and it must have been clear that there would be a significant, and permanent, increase in pupil numbers. A properly equipped library was now a necessity - the problem was how to raise the money for such an ambitious project.

OLD BIG SCHOOL, NOW THE DINING HALL

By March 1950 little progress had been made, so an appeal was launched for the refurbishment and embellishment of the room which, by now, was being used as a makeshift library. The total cost, including the plaque, was estimated at £1,500. The plan now was to incorporate into the design two 1609 Jacobean fireplaces and their richly-carved oak overmantels, which had been purchased by the new Headmaster, Jack Elam, at the auction which followed the demolition of the Marks Hall mansion,

One of the Jacobean fireplaces in situ in Marks Halls prior to auction in 1951.

near Coggeshall. They were paid for by Percy Shaw Jeffrey, and work had already started on their installation at the east and west ends of the room.

By July 1950, the fund stood at just £354. All that could be done for now was the basic work of transforming the room into a proper library, so over the following eighteen months bookcases were all installed around the sides of the room, along with radiators for heating.

The creation of a library, with ornate fireplaces, meant that a large part of the plan had been accomplished, but there was still no chapel or plaque, even though the Old Colcestrian Society had been gathering, as best they could, the names of the Old Colcestrians who had died in the war. Once again it was the Shaw Jeffreys who came to the rescue. The chapel was quietly abandoned, and, instead of a plaque, the idea arose for a stained-glass window, to be in the name of Percy's wife, Alice, presumably since her husband had financed the fireplaces.

The window was installed just before Christmas 1951, with its unveiling taking place on Sunday 24th February 1952, the day after the Old Colcestrian Society dinner. With tragic irony Percy Shaw Jeffrey died just two days prior to this, on 22nd February, at the age of 89. The dedication ceremony was led by Canon Kenneth Riches Old Colcestrian, Principal of Cuddesdon College (now Ripon College Cuddesdon), a Church of England Theological College near Oxford. Old Colcestrian Society President, Tom Bloomfield unveiled the window after a short service held in the School Hall.

Former Headmaster (1900-1916) Percy Shaw Jeffrey, aged 88, with wife, Alice. Taken in 1950, at Bagdale Old Hall, Whitby – the home to which they retired.

The lower main lights of the window contain 71 names – not, in fact, a complete list of the Old Colcestrians who died in World War Two, as omissions have been discovered. Five additional names have already been engraved on a separate plaque in the library, see left (and at time of writing RJC Dobbie remains to be added). There are also three names, AB Grey, WW McMaster and J Sergeant, which seem to have been included erroneously on the window. There is one other name, F Pine, who attended CRGS but whose war service has proved impossible to trace.

316

The upper lights of the window (pictured below) contain heraldic arms and important dates in the history of CRGS:

1206 - then believed to be the earliest known mention of a town school in Colchester, along with the arms of the Bishop of London, tenant-in-chief of the property covering the school

1539 and 1584 – the Letters Patent of Foundation (of Henry VIII and Elizabeth I), illustrated by the Tudor rose and crown

1853 – the move from Culver Street to Lexden Road, accompanied by the Colchester Borough arms

1910 – the opening of the main buildings, with the Essex County arms.

The small tracery lights contain the shields of the four Houses of the school, flanked by the raven and wheat ear, symbols of St Helena, patron saint of Colchester, and Cunobelin (Cymbeline), pre-Roman king of Britain, respectively.

Beneath the heraldic arms is the Latin inscription:

In Piam Memoriam Huius Scholae Alumnorum Qui Terra
Mari Caelo Obierunt MCMXXXIX – MCMXLV Absentes
Adsunt Mortui Vivunt

'In faithful memory of the students of this school who
died on land, sea and air, 1939-1945. Though absent, they
are here; though dead, they live.'

A scroll at the bottom of the window has another Latin inscription:

Insigni Pietate Plena Manu Hanc Fenestram Dono Dedit
Alicia Shaw Jeffrey MCMLI

'With noteworthy devotion and generosity Alice Shaw
Jeffrey gave this window as a gift, 1951.'

WAR MEMORIAL: UNVEILING AND DEDICATION

Sunday 24th February 1952

Order of Service

PREFACE: The Headmaster

READING OF THE ROLL OF HONOUR: The School Captain
M. J. Southgate

HYMN: *I vow to Thee, my Country*

THE LESSON: *Wisdom III,* 1-9: Read by a member of the Staff.
R. N. Currey, Esq., M.A.

PRAYERS AND DEDICATION: The Rev. Canon Kenneth Riches, M.A.,
O.C., Principal of Cuddesdon College, Oxford

ANTHEM: THE SCHOOL CHOIR: Worship

PROCESSION TO THE MEMORIAL LIBRARY

REQUEST TO UNVEIL: The Chairman of the Governors,
Alderman H. H. Fisher, J.P.

THE UNVEILING OF THE WINDOW: The President of the
Old Colcestrian Society, T. W. Bloomfield, Esq.

PRAYER AND BENEDICTION: Canon Riches

God Save the Queen

POSTSCRIPT

'What you leave behind is not what is engraved on stone monuments, but what is woven into the lives of others.' (Pericles)

VE Day 75th Anniversary

Peter Rowbottom

Grabbing car keys and a small parcel, he checks a route on his mobile phone that will take him west out of his home city of Hannover. It's morning, about 9.30am and the traffic, whilst busy, has just begun to subside after the morning rush. It's not as busy as some months ago because these are different times - we are, after all, in the COVID-19 era of a pandemic sweeping the world into both frenzy and anxiety. But these concerns are beyond him at the moment. He pulls out along Schlosswender Strasse and points the car towards the A6 heading west. A soft blue sky welcomes him and the sun begins to illuminate the landscape, as he trickles out of the city's arteries into something approaching the countryside in its patchwork of green and flashes of sunflower yellow. On his black passenger seat rests the small parcel, a camera and some papers which he occasionally pushes back into the base of the seat to keep them from falling forward.

His route takes him over the Leine River brushing past Linden Nord a traditional working-class area of the city, an area he knows well since it is where his own father worked and he himself lived - roots of a sort. In fact, as he thinks about it, there is a connection between the small parcel and his father, but he decides to reach his destination before exposing it. Turning onto Heisterbergallee, he follows, in parallel, the tracks of the U-Bahn which runs west in the same direction as he travels. Here the land rises in a long incline, before falling away again into a slowly descending valley with a tablecloth of fields, fences and wooden buildings. It reminds him of old black-and-white photos of farmers, wheat and a different Germany.

A different Germany. He grins, catching the irony between those words and the purpose of his visit, but, before he can contemplate further, the gravel drive of a parking area opens itself before him and he drives towards it, braking more fiercely than expected to bring him to a stop. Clutching his camera and parcel, he gets out of his car and surveys his surroundings. It's a cemetery. This is the Hannover war cemetery. As cemeteries go, it's an attractive one, he thinks. At the entrance taut Cypress trees stand guard by a brick building, suitably barn-shaped to blend in with its surroundings - the Records Centre, he assumes.

Up ahead on a steepish slope stands the Cross of Remembrance - a brilliant white form etched into a blue background. In a line, running across the top of the slope, which includes the memorial cross, are more trees, framing the plot of the cemetery and giving it a natural symmetry. The mass ranks of pale-white sandstone gravestones stand erect in brutally correct rows, perfectly in line and distance from each other. He notes that there are, in fact, 2,407 of them. He seeks only one, however. Maintained by the Commonwealth War Graves Commission, the cemetery is the resting place of mainly Allied airmen and soldiers from the Second World War – a war in which his own father fought for Germany. He has come to place a small wooden cross on the grave of Captain Edward Philip May, known as Philip, a 26-year-old Englishman who died, one month before the war ended, in combat in the fields of North Germany, just 20km from this place. Philip May was brave. He won a Military Cross and, by the accounts of his school, was both kind and modest. He grips the small padded parcel more firmly, looks at the diagram of where the grave should be located and strides towards it, possessed of camera and purpose.

The above description, whilst imaginary, was in fact a real journey, made as I was writing this very article. I should know. I sent the remembrance cross to my longstanding German friend, Mr Udo Iwannek from Hannover. His father did indeed fight in the war, though in the meatgrinder of the Eastern Front against another dictator Stalin, but one who, due to circumstances, was more favoured than the German variety. Statistically speaking it is Udo's father who should have died in the war (80-90% of German losses were in the East) but fortune blessed him and he survived, shrapnel inside him to prove it. Had he met Philip May, I think he would have liked him, or at least respected him. Both would have known the adrenalin rush of fighting, the sadness of burying both men and emotions, and the residue of battle, both physical and psychological. Common experiences must shape personal outlooks without always duplicating them.

Born in October 1918 (one month before the armistice of the First World War), Philip attended Colchester Royal Grammar School, and was the last OC to be killed in combat in WW2, just a few weeks before VE Day. In fact, it is the school that is responsible for Udo's visit, since in the 75th anniversary year of the end of the Second World War it is attempting to place a remembrance cross on the grave of each of the former students who died in that conflict across the globe. Due to my links with the school (which my own son attended), I initially agreed to visit the grave of EP May - having achieved almost frequent flyer status to Hannover, the city of my friend!

Udo Iwannek at the grave of Philip May

Being unable to travel during the pandemic, I asked Udo to make the journey to Philip's grave. Somehow, we both felt it fitting that, as a symbol of our friendship over almost 30 years, we could combine to honour the memory of one soldier on the soil of another. It is familiar territory to us. In 2014 we jointly made a visit to the battlefields and memorials of the First World War. There we placed a wreath of flowers to the memories of those generations of young men on both sides, who gave up that youth optimistically in the hope of an end to war. History has disappointed them, though time has not quite done so yet. However, I wonder who will be visiting the graves of such men in another 100 years. It was the English war poet with the German name, Siegfried Sassoon, who presciently wrote in 'At the Cenotaph':

> Make them forget, O Lord, what this memorial means;
> their discredited ideas revive; Breed new belief that war
> is purgatorial...

We still live, 75 years on, in a time of wars - Yemen, Sudan, Syria, for example. Maybe war is endemic to humans but at least Europe has mostly been spared the annihilation of previous generations during that time. Visits to cemeteries, like that of Udo's, prick our synapses into remembering both the sacrifice and slaughter of the past, the individual and the collective, those who fought and died, like Philip, and those who survived, like Udo's father, and had sons to befriend Englishmen from the next generation. Our freedoms today were paid for and inscribed in those rows of marble and sandstone on solitary hillsides across Europe. Maybe that is still something worth remembering in an age of forgetfulness.

Perhaps the last words should appropriately be those of a German soldier's son visiting the grave of an English soldier.

> I felt deeply honoured to be asked to put that cross on Captain May's grave here in Hannover. 75 years ago, he and his comrades fought against the Nazi tyranny in Germany and he gave his life to that good cause. His sacrifice to the liberty of my country must never be forgotten.

Paul Woodward

Lightning Source UK Ltd.
Milton Keynes UK
UKHW021305201120
373702UK00003B/193